MEMOIRS OF
Nobody Special

MELANIE RIPPEY

Fulton Books, Inc.
Meadville, PA

Published by Fulton Books 2020

ISBN 978-1-64952-454-6 (paperback)
ISBN 978-1-64952-456-0 (digital)

Printed in the United States of America

LIFE LESSON #5942

*Just because you colored outside of the lines, it doesn't
mean you have to throw the picture away.*

I once was a kid.
 Yada. Yada.
 Hoda. Hoda.
 Now I'm not.
 I was born in the sixties and grew up in the seventies and eight-
ies, so...yeah. My mom was a hippie; my dad was not. They were
total opposites. How the two of them ever got married and had two
children is a mystery. I have an older brother named David. My parents divorced when I was around twelve. Not a shock. My father
eventually remarried. He's been married to my stepmother longer
than he was married to my mom. I gotta tell you that I was rude and
mean to her in the beginning. Ouch! Kids always feel that they have
to pick a side, and I picked my mom's. I love my stepmother now and
fully believe she is a better match for my dad than my mother ever
was. My mother, on the other hand, never remarried. In fact, I can't
remember her even dating. I would classify my mom as a "coaster."
She just kind of coasted through life. She didn't like confrontation,
wasn't the type to put herself out there, definitely not strict, and never
followed through with a threat. Mom was a "take it as it comes" kind
of person. I see myself in her a lot; however the older I get, the more
assertive I've become.
 My mom had a knack for showing up with all kinds of weird
animals when we were growing up. Dad was never thrilled with any
of them, but he wasn't home a lot. Probably because of all the weird
pets. We also had the regular cats and dogs too. I got a bunny for

my birthday one year. It was all white and super fluffy, so I named it Marshmallow. I used to let Marshmallow out of the cage all the time to play. It pooped everywhere! If he got out of sight, I could just follow the trail of poop pellets to find him. A little while after I got Marshmallow, Dad bought a new color console TV. Remember them? Weighed like seven thousand pounds and was the size of a mini Cooper? The beast took up one whole wall of the family room width wise but only about four feet high. The screen wasn't that big. It was the speakers and crap that took up most of the real estate inside that huge wooden box. Dad was so proud of that TV. We were the first ones in the neighborhood to get one. I would say it was maybe a week after the TV was delivered that I let Marshmallow out to play. I wasn't paying attention, as usual, and I couldn't find him. So I started following the trail of poop pellets, which was leading me right behind that big ol' TV. Marshmallow was tucked inside that wooden box, happily chewing through all the wires back there. Fucked that TV up good. Dad. Was. Pissed. The next day, after school, I went to check on Marshmallow, and he was gone! Mom told me that Marshmallow went to live at the zoo.

Mom came home with a baby alligator once. It was a little tiny thing, maybe four feet long. She thought my brother would think it was cool, which he did. I did not see the point. You couldn't play with it. I'm not really sure what she was thinking on that one. I guess it never occurred to her that those things grow. Like big and fast! So one day, Mom and Dave were cleaning the tank. They put the alligator in the bathtub, and my job was to keep an eye on it. The same tub I took a bath in now had an alligator swimming in it. I was not happy about any of it. I was thinking, *This grumpy, rough, ugly thing is giving me the eyeball and literally would eat my finger for a snack. And I have to watch it. By myself.* I stood on the toilet and started to scream. Top of my lungs screaming and crying. Mom came running in to check on things, I had to tell her the alligator scared me, and I didn't like it. The next day, after school, Mom told us the alligator went to live at the zoo.

Then there was Walter the water snake. Walter wasn't so bad. At least you could pick it up. Well, Walter went missing one day. We all just figured he just slithered away and found a better place to live or maybe died. It was about a year later that Dave and I had a babysitter watching us. Out of the blue, here comes Walter out from under the couch in the living room. Alive and well. Who would have guessed? Plus, Walter grew up some since he left. This was about the time we started having babysitter issues. Apparently, not all babysitters liked surprise appearances from five-foot snakes. About a week later, Walter went to live at the zoo.

Our strangest and most interesting pet was definitely George. George was a monkey. No clue where Mom got George, but we loved him. He wasn't that big and kind of greenish with a black face and huge adorable eyes. He spent the majority of his time in a huge cage, but Dave and I got to let him out to play sometimes. George *loved* Bazooka bubble gum. It was his special treat every once in a while. One day, my mom was hosting a Tupperware party. Dave and I thought it would be a brilliant idea to let George out to meet our guests. Guests who had no idea that we had a monkey. George starts hopping around the room, sneaking snacks off people's plates. At first, everyone was freaking out, but in a few minutes, things calmed down, and they seemed to be enjoying him. The thing was, though, George was distracting people from buying any Tupperware. Mom thought it would be best if we put George away. George had other plans. Mom started chasing George around the room with a piece of his favorite Bazooka bubble gum, and he was just hopping from one person to another thinking it was a game. Dave and I are having the best time at any Tupperware party *ever*! George landed on some lady's lap; she was wearing a really fancy blue-and-white dress. Mom went in for a quick grab at George, and he peed all over that pretty dress. Never saw a Tupperware party wrap up so quickly. But really? How many people get to tell a story that ends with getting peed on by a monkey? On a side note, Mom never hosted another one of those kinds of parties again.

Couple of months later, we had a new babysitter. She knew all about George, so things were good. Dave and I thought it would be fine to let George out to play for a while before going to bed. And it was fine…until it wasn't. Right before bed, we go to put George in his cage, and again, he had other plans. So again, chasing George around trying to bribe him with a piece of that damn bubble gum. To this day, I'm still not sure what happened. George ran into the upstairs closet, then Dave went into the closet, then George came out of the closet—but not Dave. Somehow the fire extinguisher went off and came flying out of the closet. The thing was spinning and spraying white foam everywhere. Including all over the brand-new hardwood floors my Dad had just finished installing a couple weeks before. You know what? About two days later, after school, Mom said George went to live at the zoo.

One Christmas, all I wanted was a hamster and a habit trail. I'm not sure if they still make them, but back in the day, that was the shizam! Ahhh, all the pieces, parts, and accessories were dreamy. You could snap them together to build shapes, tunnels, and whole cities. The ideas were endless. Add a cute hamster to that? I had to have one. I made all the appropriate empty promises all kids swear to when negotiating life-and-death deals with their parents.

I'll keep my room clean. I'll take care of the habit trail all by myself. I'll make sure they always have food and water. I would do it all. *I promise.* Now what my parents didn't know was that Dave and I had a secret deal for years. It became one of our traditions. On Christmas Eve, we would trade one secret gift each. So I knew I was getting the habit trail the next morning and all my dreams were coming true. I barely slept. Dave knew he was getting a dirt bike. I loved my habit trail. But…I needed more pieces. I spent weeks after Christmas throwing out more empty promises for more pieces. I'd take out the trash, put my laundry away, blah, blah, blah—I got more pieces. I spent hours pulling that thing apart, rearranging it, and starting all over. I practically built a city. The only thing I was missing? A friend for my hamster. He needed a buddy because he was lonely in his city. Mom was not having it at first. But kids can be relentless when they really want something, and I pushed and pushed hard. And Bingo was his name-o! The pet shop guy swore the new hamster was another boy. I don't know what minimum wage was back then, but he got paid too much. They started breeding imme-diately! A hamster bomb exploded in my habit trail city. Things got out of hand very quickly. That was right about the time a kid lost interest. Taking care of one hamster is a lot easier than cleaning up after twenty. I came from school one day dragging my feet because I knew I had to clean the city, trudging downstairs to the family room, and it was gone. All of it. Every piece, every exercise wheel, food, wood chips…everything. Gone. I ran upstairs to tell my mom, and she said they all went to live at the zoo. Hmmmm. The zoo story was just now beginning to come into focus.

LIFE LESSON #231

Sometimes a person's parents are a little iffy.

Not only did I have a lot of animals growing up, I had Christina.

We met in kindergarten. It was a show-and-tell day, and neither of us were prepared. Everyone was getting their stuff out, and the two of us were just standing there. She was a little girl with long blonde hair, and I was a geeky girl with mouse brown hair and wearing a god awful homemade plaid jumper. Somehow we realized neither of us had anything to show or tell. So I asked her if she wanted to be best friends for show-and-tell. The deal was sealed. We stood in front of the class, holding hands, and proclaimed our "best friend" status.

Kindergarten was different back then. You got snacks; you took naps and played. Everyone brought their own "nap towel." Mine had a mermaid on it with a slot at the top for a blow-up pillow. A blow-up pillow! Nobody else had a blow-up pillow. It made me feel special—for one whole day. My teacher blew that bright-blue plastic pillow up once. One time—total. I'm sure she had more important things to do. I get that now. Christina and I always got in trouble at nap time. We were way too busy talking and not napping. They tried to separate us; it didn't really work. That's how our moms met. The teacher called a meeting of the moms. That's how our moms became great friends.

Mom and Aunt T even became our brownie troop leaders. They took us camping; we baked brownies, had sing-a-longs. This is when I learned singing was not on my career options list. Our troop probably went down in brownie history for earning the least number of patches but having the most amount of fun. I'm sure I got some patches I didn't fully deserve, but Mom was one of the leaders and a pushover.

Christina lived about three suburban blocks from us. We were always at each other's house. I got mad at my mom one day, packed my bag, and proclaimed I was running away. Mom said, "Okay, you might want to put on some shoes first." I can be stubborn, so of course I don't need any shoes. I told my mom I would be at Christina's if she needed me as I stomped out the back door. Marching across the backyard with my bad attitude and little white suitcase, heading to my new, nicer family, and *bam!* I stepped smack dab in the middle of a fresh pile of warm dog shit. Keep in mind, I wasn't wearing any shoes because my mother was stupid, so it squished all up in between my toes. Disgusting. Which just made me angrier.

I marched back to my house to wash off my foot, and Mom said, "Told you to put shoes on."

"Whatever, Mom, shut up!" As soon as I was done, I told her I was still running away; I was still going to Christina's and to leave me alone. Back out the door I went, still not wearing any shoes out of spite. I win. Marching through the backyard with an even worse attitude and *bam!* Damned if I didn't step in the same exact pile of shit. I knew it was the same pile because I can see the footprint from the first hit right next to my new one. Defeated—by dog do. Mom never said a word during my second retreat to the bathroom. She just held the door open while I limped back to the tub, walking on my heel.

LIFE LESSON #116

Sometimes a mother's advice is simply said to help
you avoid a pile of shit in your future.

My brother and I shared a room for years when we were young. My dad eventually built my own bedroom over the garage. He made a dresser that was built into the wall. Christina and I realized that if you pulled out the bottom drawer all the way, there was a huge hidden room behind it. We would squeeze ourselves through there and spend hours in our secret fort. I often wonder what we left behind and how many other children found the secret and spent time back there.

We lived on top of a hill, and there was a small running creek at the bottom. One year, there was a big flood—well, not like a Katrina kind of flood but a flood that had the creek running way higher and faster than the norm. We were outside playing "Barbie and Ken." We had been out there for hours, doing almost every "Barbie and Ken" scenario you can imagine. Our original plan was to get in the *Guinness Book of World Records* for the longest Barbie game. Things were getting boring. Dave was out there too. He was trying to light his little green plastic army men on fire with a magnifying glass. Things weren't going any better for him. We could hear the water rushing in the creek and decided to take a break and check things out. Told Mom where we were going.

I would never have let my kids go do that at that age without adult supervision. But like I said, it was the seventies. There were no car seats or weight restrictions for the front seat. We drank out of the hose, we built totally unstable tree forts, and parents smoked and drank while pregnant. We're alive. Sorry.

Anyway, we headed down to the creek to walk around and check out the water. We came across this weird white thing floating in the water. We couldn't really tell what it was until we got a little closer. Turns out it was a dead dog. It must have fallen in the water during the flood and drowned. By now, a lot of the curly white fur was missing, and it was really puffy. I felt really bad. It was stuck in a pile of branches, bouncing up and down in the water. I grabbed a stick with the plan of just rolling it over. It didn't seem right that its head was still in the water and its legs were up in the air. It just looked so sad. So there I was, stick in hand, trying to roll it over. It only took a few tries. The thing popped! Like a death balloon. The smell and guts went everywhere! That was the moment I learned:

LIFE LESSON #96

Some actions have unwanted consequences.

Yeah, that lesson really sank in. Of course, parents try to teach their kids this from day one by taking away a toy or getting a time out. Sometimes it takes a long (but not quite long enough) stick and a dead dog for the concept to really take hold.

Dad liked the predictable. He always had an itinerary and a plan. Because of that, we vacationed every year in Cape Cod. We would camp in the same spot at the same campground, go to the same beach, went to the same boardwalk where Dad would buy the same sandals made from recycled tires. We always caught hermit crabs and put them in the same bucket. They never lived, but we did it every year, the same as we did the year before. We always took the same family picture by the same crooked tree. And we always had the same routine the day we were leaving. Mom and Dad packed up the camp; Dave and I picked up any trash we may have left behind. We got a penny for every piece of trash we picked up. Back then, they sold penny candy like a single Tootsie roll or a single piece of taffy. For us, it was a total score and worth the trash detail job. It took a couple of years until we realized that if we dropped more trash throughout our stay and had to pick them up when we were leaving, we got more pennies. Double the bubble, baby! The next year, same spot, same bucket filled with dead hermit crabs, we made an even bigger revelation: if we dropped more trash through our stay *and* then ripped that trash in half? Triple digit penny time! I swear I could already feel the sugar rushing thru my veins, rotting my teeth. Bliss in the eyes of a child. However, our dreams of dancing through the penny candy isle were squashed. We got busted. Our parents caught us red handed tearing paper in half. Bummer. As a punishment for cheating, we still had to pick up double the trash but didn't get any pennies for it at all.

To add insult to injury, that was the summer a bird shit on my head. Flew over me and got a direct hit right on the top of my head, dripping down my forehead. Crying, I looked to my mom for help and she's got this huge grin on her face, clapping. What the hell? Mom? A little help here. Mom dropped to her knees and start babbling on and on about how I must be the luckiest little girl on the planet. Ummmm…okay? She proceeded to explain to me how that bird had the whole world to poop on but it chose me! My dumb ass actually fell for it. Seriously? I am now the happiest little girl because a bird had shit on my head.

For the most part, Christina is in the majority of my memories from childhood. She was always there. Some of my favorite memories are sleepovers at Christina's. We would spend an hour or so before bedtime, collecting fireflies in jars. Then right before bed, we would close the door to her room, turn off all the lights, and let the fireflies go. It was magical to watch them fly around the room in random patterns of blinking lights. We fell asleep to the lights. Sometimes we would pinch off their butts and spread on our eyes and lips as glow in the dark makeup. It was so cool talking to each other while our eyes and lips glowed. In hindsight, we just wiped dead bug guts all over our face, which is kind of gross.

It's weird how some childhood memories stick out more than others. I don't understand how the filing system of our brains work. How something or someone makes you feel is always on top of the list though. Whether in a good way or a bad way.

There's only a few things I know for sure.

One of them is that true friendship is to be cherished. Distance and time are only branches on a tree.

At some point after George went to live at the zoo and before hamster city went to live at the zoo, we moved. We went to live in Virginia.

My dad got a new job which came with a new zip code. Everything was different in Virginia. We went from a quiet little suburban home not far from Philadelphia to a huge house in a huge neighborhood in a huge town. Alexandria, Virginia was very different from little old Wyndmoor, Pennsylvania. Total culture shock. The worst part was how much I missed my best friend.

The night before moving into our new house, we were staying in a hotel. Mom said Dave and I could call home and say hi to our friends. As soon as those words left my mother's lips, a full on balls-to-the-walls race issued. Whichever one of us got to the phone first got to call first. I am not the athletic type, but I was pumping my skinny little legs as fast as I could. Just not quite fast enough. Dave got that a mere second before me. He got there with just enough time to lift the receiver up in victory; it was that moment I caught up to him. Just in time for that receiver to smack me in the face and break my front tooth in half. Broke that thing like a chisel on an ice cube. Never got to call Christina—hell, it hurt to breathe.

So we were in a new town—didn't know anyone, didn't have a doctor or a dentist. The movers would be showing up in several hours with all our stuff; we had to be there to let them in, and I was in excruciating pain. Mom found a dentist in the Yellow Pages. First one that could see us right then. Now remember, the Yellow Pages went in alphabetical order. Not by ratings. We got there, and the dentist was in a rundown office. He was old, fat, sweaty, had bad breath and an even worse attitude to a kid in pain. No wonder he had an opening in his schedule. He built me a new tooth that looked like a gigantic bright white Chicklette. But it didn't hurt to breathe, so I guess that was a bonus. Needless to say, he did not become our regular dentist.

Life was very different in Virginia. The people were different, the kids were different, the school was different, our house was different, the way we lived was different. Hell, we even got a maid! She came every Tuesday, so we spent every Monday cleaning. We never had a maid before, so I thought cleaning before they showed up was normal. Like cleaning before a guest would show up for dinner. The maid did do some odds and ends things, but mostly, she and my mom would sit in the breakfast nook (never had one of those before either) drinking tea, eating snacks, and talking. My mom would try to make some kind of a snack for them to nibble on; however, Mom was not really a very good cook. Once, Mom tried to make a pan of brownies—from a box, mind you—but when she went to cut them, the knife actually snapped in half. It was a big brown brick of disappointment. So Mom decided to hide them in the oven since there wasn't time to soak and clean the pan before the maid showed up. Out of sight, out of mind.

A few days went by, and Mom started heating up the oven for dinner, totally oblivious to the fact that she had hidden the already burnt pan of brownie brick in there. The oven turns into a brownie crematorium. Mom couldn't figure out what the smell was. The "ah ha" moment came when smoke started coming out of the oven. On the bright side, we learned all the smoke detectors in the new house worked just fine. On a side note, that maid is who taught me how to fold a fitted sheet. A technique I still use today.

Dave, my Chicklet tooth, and I eventually made some friends, did the normal kid crap. Kinda. We were used to making our own fun. We made forts, tried to light ants on fire, pushed each other down the hill in a wagon, praying we could reach the bottom before flying out. That was our old normal. These new kids were different. They had money; money bought big toys. Lots of toys. Now we wanted toys. Lots of toys. And we got them. We got dirt bikes, BB guns, the hamster city. I got a canopy bed like a princess. All kinds of crap. We used to have BB gun wars. I know that sounds stupid, but we did have rules. You could only pump your gun ten times or less and no shots above the chest. Last one standing won. Stupid. The ten-pump rule was so we didn't get hurt, but it still stung like hell.

We also got some new bikes. Our parents took us to the store to pick out the ones we wanted. After walking around for a bit, I finally found *the one*. I turned the corner and saw it. I swear there were stars shining around it, and it sang to me. It. Was. Perfect. It was a beautiful bright yellow 10 speed. Dave picked out a purple bike. When it came time to tell our parents which bikes we picked out, I took my dad around the corner to see the beautiful crown. Dad looked it over, stood there for what seemed like hours, and then said "It's too expensive." My heart was crushed. He went and picked out this girly red Schwinn with a big red *S* on the seat. I hated it. Dave took him over to the purple bike he liked. He was told it wasn't big enough. Somehow, we drove home with my new shitty Swchinn and Dave's new bright-yellow 10 speed.

LIFE LESSON #97

Want in one hand. Shit in another. See what hand
fills up faster. Or some stupid saying like that.

Thing is, I never got over that dumb bike. Dave didn't even like that
bike. It was "too expensive" for me but not for Dave? That was the
first time I ever felt less than. I know Dad didn't do it on purpose or
really even think about it. It just…was. But it hurt, and it stuck.

Later that year, my dad was invited to a business associate's house
for a pool party and BBQ. They had a table set out on the patio with
a huge spread. There was a bucket of Kentucky Fried Chicken with
all the fixings, various sweets, snacks, drinks, chips, the perfect BBQ
set up. After stuffing my face and waiting the obligatory thirty minutes before swimming, I jumped in the pool.

I was wearing a cute pink bikini with white polka dots all over it
and a ruffle around the waist. I remember that suit so vividly because
the business associate and owner of the house spent his afternoon
chasing me around in the pool, trying to put his hand down the
inside of my bikini bottom. I spent the afternoon trying to get away
from him. I kept trying to get out of the pool, but he would pull me
back in. It must have looked like an innocent game of water tag or
surely someone would have done something. But innocent it was
not.

We'll call him Mr. D. I didn't say anything because I didn't
know what to say. Or who to say it to. Or how to say anything. I was
just a kid. I hadn't even reached puberty yet. I didn't even know the
right words to use.

When we were getting ready to leave, he suddenly asked my
parents if I could sleep over. Something about his daughter not hav-

17

ing many friends because she was always training for ice skating or something. I was having a hard time tracking the conversation. In my head, I was screaming *no*! But my mouth didn't seem to want to work. Next thing that registered in my brain was the sound of my parents saying yes. Arrangements for a morning pickup were made, and I was still not saying anything. I need to say something. Anything. I don't. I should have.

I only have snapshots of that night. Like I was there but not. I remember being in a den where there was a big console TV on and a couple of kids sitting on the floor in front of it. Mr. D had me sitting on his lap in the background not far behind the other people with his hands down my pants. He was talking to me in my ear even though I have no idea what he was saying, only that I was expected to agree. Surely the kids in the room knew something was going on. Surely they could hear him talking. But they never turned around. Never even glanced over their shoulder.

The next "snip it" was in the daughter's room. The daughter was in the bed; Mr. D had me on the floor without the pajama bottoms that I had to borrow. I can hear his wife calling him and telling him it was time to come to bed. I could see Mr. D in the hall bathroom because the door was open and the light was on. He was washing his hands and other parts before shutting off the light and walking down the hall, past me, on his way to go to bed. With his wife. She knew what was happening. They all knew. They had to have. No one came to help me, though.

I can't remember actually meeting the daughter but I know I was in a girl's room. I can't remember what the wife looks like or how many kids there were. I can't remember if or where I slept that night. I can't remember what we had for breakfast or my Mom picking me up. I can't remember what Mr. D looks like. But I can remember how I felt. I felt dirty. I hurt. I felt scared, confused, and angry. I felt alone.

For several weeks after, Mr. D kept calling the house to try to arrange another sleepover with his daughter. Every time he called, I would freak out and start crying about how I didn't want to go. After about the third attempt and my reaction every time, my mom got concerned. She told me to get in the car; we were going to the library. We were driving around for a while, nowhere near the library. Neither of us were saying much, if anything. I knew something was up. She finally pulled into a random parking lot and parked away from everything. She turns the car off and started asking questions. "What is wrong?"

I wouldn't talk at first. I was a little kid. I didn't know how to start. I didn't even know the words to use or how to explain what had happened at that BBQ. Mom didn't give up. I finally told her in the way a child could. She read between the lines and figured it out. I'm not sure how long we stayed in that parking lot, quietly crying. Her because of what had happened to me. Me because I felt guilty. Guilty because I let it happen. Guilty because I didn't say anything. Guilty because I told the secret when I was told not to. Guilty and bad. And scared I was going to get in trouble for lying to my mom for all those times Mr. D called.

Thing was, that's as far as it went. It was never talked about again. As a child, I didn't know any better. As an adult and especially as a mother now, things were not handled correctly. As an adult, I rationalize that my parents simply didn't know any better. It was the seventies, and those things weren't really talked about. Or maybe my parents didn't want me to have to relive the events. I don't know. I found out years later that my father quit doing business with Mr. D because my mom told me. I don't know if Dad told him why. I never asked. I'm angry that Mr. D got away with what he did to me, and I'm saddened that because of my parents' choice not to do anything, other little girls were most likely abused. I'm saddened for Mr. D's wife and kids and what their life was like. Surely they all knew something was happening to me that night but chose to turn a blind eye. I was handed to a beast as a sacrificial lamb. Maybe they were happy it wasn't them for a change. I'll never know.

I was ten. I couldn't eat Kentucky Fried Chicken for over thirty years. Most importantly, secrets fester.

Something I Know for Sure

The abuse or molestation of a child changes who
they are and who they could have been.

Having said that, it has taken me over forty years to realize that it doesn't define me. I may not be who I was or who I could have been, but that also doesn't mean I'm not worthy. I'm just a different version of me.

The events that took place at the BBQ slowly started directing my life. For years my choices, actions and decisions were not in my best interest. Of course I didn't know that at the time.

Summer before eighth grade, a few neighbor kids and I had a brilliant idea. I'm not sure whose brilliant idea it was originally, but I was all in. We decided to make our own cigarettes by wrapping dried pine needles in toilet paper. We all made a few "pine cigarettes" and figured no one would catch us if we hid under the pine tree to smoke them. Sounds totally safe, right? We realized our poor choice of smoking location almost immediately. Who would have thought dried pine needles wrapped in toilet paper would catch fire so quickly? I'm not sure who panicked first and dropped their fire stick. At that point, it didn't really matter because all those dried pine needles under that pine tree started glowing like mini fuses on a stick of dynamite. Things were going in a free fall and fast. We all began stomping around in a total panic. No one noticed the smell of melting rubber from the soles of our Keds sneakers. Crisis averted, we made a pact to never talk about that again. We disbanded, retreated back to our homes like nothing ever happened. Maybe ten minutes later, I was having a snack with my mom in the breakfast nook. The windows looked directly out to the backyard where that big old pine tree proudly stood in the distance off to the right. In slow motion, without saying a word, Mom started to stand up. I followed her gaze, peanut butter and jelly sandwich in mid bite, only to see a fire blazing under that damn pine tree. Mom tore out the back door, grabbed a hose, and went all housewife firefighter on that tree. I, meanwhile, was frozen. My legs simply would not work. After putting out the fire, Mom came in the house all frazzled, sweaty, and chock full of questions. I was thinking, *No way, man.* We made a pact. I was not saying nothin' to nobody. My dumb act was going pretty well until she looked down. I should have changed my shoes.

Of course, the neighborhood moms had a powwow. We all got grounded. We all had to rake up the charred pine needles from under our tree and every other tree in the neighborhood as punishment.

LIFE LESSON #263

Don't overlook the little things.
They matter more than you know.

After the burning bush incident, I began stealing cigarettes from my mother. Then I started stealing money to buy my own. Back then, cigarettes were .65 cents a pack, and they would sell them to a baby wearing diapers if they could ask for them. We would walk the back way into town, cross the creek, and cut through the field. I would smoke a good three during the walk home. During one of those walks to town, we came out of the field, and our legs were alive. From our kneecaps down, our jeans were covered in creepy, crawly ticks. I can't stand ticks. They drink blood for survival. But I still made the trek into town for a pack of cigarettes. I thought I was so sneaky, secretly smoking. And that made it even better. I even got a little brazen and started smoking in my room. I would open the window, blow the smoke out through the screen, and light a stinky candle. Mom came in my room one day right after I just finished smoking. Of course, she was curious about the tiny black *x*'s all over my lips from pressing against the dirty screen. Screw it. I 'fessed up. She said she would rather I smoke in front of her than behind her back. So I did. We went to the mall; back then, you could smoke in the mall and on airplanes, restaurants, etc. Anyway, I thought I was so cool that I could smoke in front of my *mom* that I smoked a ton of cigarettes. One right after the other. I made myself sick. Maybe that was her plan all along. It didn't work. I started smoking full time the summer before eighth grade.

It became apparent around eighth grade that things in our house were not all *Better Homes and Garden*. My father had always been a workaholic; however, now he was *never* home. As well as the long work hours, there was always some kind of social event to attend on the weekend. In the beginning, he would always try to get Mom to go with him, but she rarely did. It wasn't her thing. Dad brought her home this super fancy dress once, thinking that would help her to want to go. I thought it was fantastic. It was black velvet on the top with long sleeves, white satin on the bottom that was ringed in rows of fluffy white ostrich feathers. I would have never taken that dress off. She hated it and didn't go. Needless to say, my father finally found someone to attend those functions with him. Mom checked out. Dave started smoking pot on the daily, and I was left to float.

My father never really knew how to connect with me because I was a girl, and I don't think the Mr. D. incident helped. My brother and Dad were really into the whole Boy Scout thing. Dad always made time to take Dave to meetings, hiking, camping, fishing, anything Boy Scout related. I was never invited. Mom and I were either left at home or treated as the "support" team. We would drop the guys off at one end of a hiking trail and sit in the car waiting for them to show up at the other end. I could have gone hiking with them. Mom could have gone hiking with them too. I assume we were just more useful waiting in the car.

So to recap: My parents are on the brink of divorce, my Mom checks out, my brother is stoned, and I'm forgotten. For real.

I got drunk for the first time in eighth grade. It was a busy year. A bunch of us went to the local community rec center one night. At some point, the plan morphed from hanging out *in* the rec center, playing air hockey and drinking lemonade, to hanging *behind* the rec center, smoking cigarettes and drinking Schlett's malt liquor. Really not that different. Well, except *in* the rec center, you don't puke. *Behind* the rec center, you do. My dad showed up to pick me up at our arranged time in his brand new little yellow sports car, and all I was thinking for the eight-minute ride home was, *Don't puke, don't puke. In through your nose, out through your mouth, don't puke.* When we got home, Dad went in through the garage, I went around the back to go in through the basement. I held that puke back for about nine minutes. Total. Made it to the basement door and no further. I thought I got away with it until my mom came down the steps. She said Dad didn't know what to do with me, so he sent her to check on me. She asked if I was okay, and it only took one word out of my mouth: "Fine." She could smell the puke and alcohol on my breath. Busted after all. Mom has a tantrum. Yada, yada, hoda, hoda, blah, blah, blah. Who gave a shit? We all knew Mom's threats were filled with empty air.

Dad moved out sometime during the end of my eighth grade year. At that time, it was just another strike against my father. I hated having to spend weekends at his new place. And he had a girlfriend that I didn't like. Another strike. She could have been the nicest lady in the world but I didn't care. It didn't matter; it was too soon. She had a kid. Strike 3. By now, I was smoking pot every day with my brother.

I remember the first time I got really stoned. My dad enrolled me into a finishing school for girls. It's where they teach girls how to walk, talk, sit, cross their legs at the ankles—in short, total bullshit. Is there a finishing school for boys? *No!* He also suggested I join the Daughters of the American Revolution group. It's some group that direct descendants of the American revolution for independence can join. My great-great-great-grandfather signed the Declaration of Independence, Oliver Wolcott, second to the bottom. Not going to happen. Anyway, it's one of the nights I was supposed to go to this stupid class. My brother and some of his friends were getting stoned in the basement shortly before I had to leave, and I went down to say hi. They passed me the pipe, so I took a hit. Then it came around again. And again. I guess it was super strong pot. On this particular night, we were seated in a room surrounded by mirrors, even the ceiling, so we could see how we were sitting, etc. Imagine being stoned out of your mind, looking at dozens of images of yourself from every angle. Paranoia set in faster than Quikrete on a hot summer day. I couldn't spend one more minute in that torture chamber. I had my mom come get me, and I never went back. Let's face it—that shit was never going to stick with me anyway.

The next weekend was a visit with my dad. His girlfriend and her kid were there too. He was not happy with me for quitting finishing school; I was not happy with him for breathing. Now that I was a pot-smoking professional, Dave and I set out on a diabolical mission to get rid of the girlfriend and her kid. We got that girl so stoned. In our defense, she was bragging about smoking pot all the time. Obviously, that was not the case. She puked everywhere. Dave and I got busted. Girlfriend and kid were pissed. We were really too stoned to comprehend the situation, and I'm not sure we really cared. Oddly, we never saw that girlfriend or the kid again. Not sure if it was all because of us or if that was just the cherry on the cake kinda deal. We shouldn't have done that, but kids do dumb stuff.

Dad and Dave were still very involved in the Boy Scouts. Always camping and doing activities. There was a big retreat one weekend that I had to go on with them. You would think that would be a girl's dream come true but no. I only went when I had to. For a girl? Boring! I couldn't participate in any of the activities. I wasn't allowed to do anything. Dad and Dave were off doing whatever, while I sat in the tent alone. At least Dave and I could sneak off at night to smoke a joint.

During one of their Boy Scout camping weekends where Mom and I were left behind, we were just hanging out, watching TV. I'm not sure all this came into play, but somehow, we ended up getting super stoned. I know the pot was mine, so I'm guessing I'm the one that brought the whole thing up. All of a sudden, we were shoving taco-flavored Dorritos in our mouths while sitting on the floor, laughing our ass off at the *Sonny and Cher* show. The good thing about getting stoned with your mom is that she cooks. She made grilled cheese sandwiches and canned tomato soup to dunk them in. Top that off with some mint chocolate-chip ice cream and another joint? Perfect Saturday night. We never did that again. I'm pretty sure Mom's "give a shit" meter was broken at that point.

Just to note that my brother did achieve his Eagle Scout status although stoned the entire time; I have no idea how that happened. It was a really big deal for my dad.

The summer before ninth grade, Mom, Dave and I packed our boxes and moved back to Pennsylvania. Guess what house we bought? It wasn't even really for sale at the time. But we talked them into selling. It was the perfect house for us, and it was right next door to Christina! Of course we had all stayed in touch during our hiatus in Virginia. Christina and I took turns flying back and forth several times to see each other and talked on the phone at least once a week. I couldn't be happier. I was home. We could literally open our bedroom windows and scream to each other.

LIFE LESSON #341

Home is not just where the heart is. It's also where
acceptance, understanding, and safety lives.

*****

We all had an open-door policy. I could go next door and make a
sandwich whether anyone was home or not. Christina's house was
way different from mine. Her house was a home. Kinda messy from
life, someone always milling around, food in the fridge, that kind of
thing. I loved being at her house. I could just be me.

Christina's dad was a total sixties throwback pot head artist.
I couldn't tell you how many times I would wander over there and
Uncle F would be standing on the front porch wearing cut-off shorts,
no shirt, no shoes, hair all messed up, taking a waz 'cause he just woke
up…at noon! He made 3D art. Usually out of vinyl. Gigantic lips,
vaginas, sometimes bionic penises—things like that were all over the
house. As a kid, it was normal, just another day. As an adult, I don't
know how Aunt T kept it all going. There were three kids, house
stuff, vehicle stuff, life. I'm sure F sold some pieces here and there but
not on a regular basis. Plus, there was me. I was always there.

I can tell you that if it wasn't for Aunt T, Dave and I would have
been in trouble. At my house, Mom had completely checked out.
She slept all day, survived on an occasional Snickers bar, lost a ton of
weight. She rarely went grocery shopping, didn't make family dinners, barely unpacked boxes, and didn't work. Didn't even look for a
job. I'm Dad was footing all the bills. It was like she was waiting for
him to come get her. He wasn't coming. My house was not a home.
Christina's house was home.

27

During my mom's mental vacation, Dave and I started smoking tons of weed and did our own thing. No one to check in with. That's around the time that I had sex, by choice, for the first time. I met this older guy; he was like twenty or twenty-one. We went out on a date—well, kind of a date. We got some fast food and went to a park to hang out, smoke pot, and have a few beers. He picked me up in a freaking station wagon. Green with fake wood paneling down the sides, lots of room in the back. We started making out and he wanted more; I was curious. Everyone talked about sex like it was an enjoyable thing; that's not my experience. I figured, *Why not? This time it will be different, right?* It really wasn't. It still hurt; it was very invasive and totally impersonal. It could have been anyone; I had no feelings for this guy whatsoever. It was like following some secret main procedure: Step 1, a little kissing; Step 2, remove clothes; Step 3, the Deed. Done. Over. I didn't feel special; I didn't feel loved. I pretty much didn't feel anything one way or the other. *But* I did it by choice. That was enough for me. Never saw him again. He tried, but I wasn't interested. Honestly, I could describe the stupid station wagon better than I could describe him.

I couldn't wait to get home and tell Christina all about it. She was not thrilled.

Now I don't have any proof of this, but I'm pretty sure Aunt T had enough of Mom's "vacation." I only think it was Aunt T because Mom wasn't a social butterfly and didn't really talk to anyone else. I don't know what was said; it doesn't really matter, but it needed to be said. To cut to the chase, Aunt T told Mom it was time to get off her ass. I'm grateful for her in more ways than she'll ever know.

Things slowly got better at home—kinda. Mom didn't sleep all day. She began unpacking, got a job, went grocery shopping on a regular basis—you know, Mom stuff. But sometimes when you cast out a line in the water and leave it unattended for long, it's just a knotted mess when you reel it back in. That's where we were.

School had started at this point; I was in the ninth grade. I feel like I got along with everyone, but of course I gravitated toward the stoners. Art was my favorite class. French was the worst. The teacher was old and mean as hell. I found her home phone number and would entertain myself by prank calling her house all hours of the day and night. Let me tell you, she was just as mean and cranky over the phone as she was in the classroom, but after about three or four prank calls in a row? Dude—epic levels of cranky! I thought it was so funny! I can still picture her face in my mind. I bet it was all crunched up red spit flying out of her mouth. Some people just don't get it; if she had been all sweet or kind the first time I called, I would have gotten bored and never called back. Not that my actions were her fault, but…kinda.

I tried to join some extracurricular activities. I went out for cheerleading but didn't make the team. In hindsight, that was a smart decision on their part. I was not then nor am I now the coordinated athletic type. I went out for band. I really wanted to be one of the rifle twirlers. I loved the way the fake white rifles sounded when it slapped in your hand. They assigned me to the "silks." Those are the big flags with the school colors. Learning how to twirl then was actually hard. I would say about two weeks in after practice started, a choice needed to be made: go to band practice or go to the woods to get high? What to do? What to do? I went to the woods to get high. No more band practice for me!

School was school. Weekends were for fun. Our house had a pool, so we spent a lot of time up there. The pool was up a hill in the backyard surrounded by bushes. The perfect place for what we called "bong-a-thons." Dave was two years older than me, so of course as a fourteen-year-old girl, his friends were super cool. One of those cool boys introduced me to these little blue pills. Speed. Now those were the ticket. I instantly loved them. Smoking pot was okay, but speed was fantastic! I wasn't tired or hungry. A little bit of pot and a little blue pill was the perfect combo pack.

During one of our weekend "bong-a-thon" parties, my brother had some of his friends over, and those friends brought some friends. That's when I met Michael. Michael and I quickly became a thing. He didn't go to my school, but we got together every chance we could. He had his own set of problems. His mom was a mean drunk. She made great cookies though. Anyway, he began spending more and more time at our house. Eventually, he never left. We had a sit-down with Mom. She went over the rules; the main one was that we had to sleep in separate bedrooms. That lasted about a week.

Because of that, Mom and Aunt T decided Christina and I needed to get on birth control pills. They made an appointment at Planned Parenthood for us. I don't know if they still do this, but back then, it was an all-day process. First, we had to sit through an hour-long movie about reproduction, then a talk about STDs, then a full gynecological exam. Men have it so easy. After the Planned Parenthood amusement park adventure, Michael and I shared a room without any problems. I was fourteen. Living with my boyfriend. Michael dropped out of high school when he moved in with us, so he was around all day, every day. He even stayed at the house during the occasional visits to my Dad's for the weekend. Dad was still living in Virginia, and Dave and I would take the Amtrak train to go visit. I think Mom liked having Michael around for several reasons. She didn't have to be alone when we were gone. There was someone else to do things around the house, and most importantly, there was someone to keep an eye on me. She didn't know Michael and I were both doing drugs. Not just me.

At some point, I realized that if you pulled the little blue capsules apart and snorted the powder inside rather than taking it like a pill, you got way higher way faster. This became a daily thing, which began to interfere with my high school career. It's hard to stay up all night and get to school in the morning. I began cutting classes, my grades were crap, and apparently, I had a "general bad attitude" according to the principal. Told me I would do nothing in life except basket weaving. By the end of tenth grade, it was suggested that I not return to a public school. I needed a school with more discipline.

Introducing Mount Saint Helen's Catholic School for Girls. Seriously? We're not even Catholic. It was all girls, they wore hideous uniforms, and actual nuns taught the classes. No dope, no pot, no smoking, and I lived with my boyfriend. In sin. I would fit right in. Of course, I found the only teeny, tiny group just like me—well, except living with their boyfriend. But we even had a pregnant one in the group. She was allowed to continue going to school as long as she could have uniforms that fit. I guess they figured no one would notice? I liked her. She stood proud and tall and would not let them win. That was that. I was told I made history at that school for being the first one to cut school in, like, twenty years. Really? Not one person had ever cut? It was a conundrum. They didn't know what to do with me. They didn't have a detention class after school. No one ever even got detention? They came up with a plan that I had to spend every free second sitting on the bench outside the dean's office. Stupid!

I'm not going to go into day-to-day high school stuff because really, no one wants to relive that shit. But I'll give you some stand-out highlights. Probably not in chronological order—there was a lot of pot smoking going on!

My aunt and uncle shipped my cousin out to my mom for a while. They thought a change of scenery would do him some good and help straighten him out. That may have been true but not the scenery at our house. Mom picked him up at the bus depot, and he got to our house with a special box in his luggage. It was full of LSD. Lions, tigers, and bears. Oh my!

First time I dropped some acid was in the winter. There were a bunch of us over at Christina's house. I remember being in the powder room with Christina and someone else. We were all sitting on the floor laughing and passing around a Dixie cup full of water, simply amazed that it never ran out of water. Eventually, we all ended up sitting on the floor in front of the fireplace, tripping out of our minds, staring into the flames. Every so often, collectively, we would move back a few feet from the fire then return to the conversation. This happened a good two or three times over a twenty-to-thirty-minute period. I'm not certain of the time frame because we were all hallucinating, but I do know we were all as far away from the fire as we could get and the house was beginning to fill with smoke. It wasn't until the smoke alarm went off that we realized the chimney was on fire. We hatched a plan. One of the guys was going to climb the tree that was pretty close to the chimney and dump a stew pot filled with water down the chimney. By the time he got to the top of the tree, there was maybe a few cups of water left in the stew pot, which did absolutely no good. Thank God a neighbor had seen the flames shooting out of the top of the chimney and had already called the fire department. I can't describe the look on those firefighters' faces when they pulled up, lights and sirens, in full gear, to find some dumbass clinging to the top of a tree, holding an empty stew pot. Priceless. So they got the fire out, everyone survived, house was clearing out from the smoke, acid hadn't quite worn off yet. And hello, Grandma! Christina's grandma was staying with them at the time. She came storming out of her room wearing a white fluffy nightgown; hair was a mess and she was *pissed*. Sheed started screaming at us that we were just going to leave her there to die. No one came to get her. We are all horrible children. Yes, we all felt guilty, but as I said, the LSD hadn't worn off yet, so Grandma's rant was kinda funny. Laughing at a mad Grandma is not the proper thing to do, which leads us directly into the next level of *pissed*. I seriously thought I was about to get my ass kicked by a little old lady wearing a fluffy white nightgown and hot pink slippers.

We had a pool table in our garage and always seemed to have kids over on the weekends. Hanging out, smoking pot, drinking beer, doing speed, whatever. It was a known joke in our circle of friends that during a garage party, we occasionally had to call a "quiet time" to listen for my mom snoring. She was an epic snorer. If we could hear her, the party went on.

By the way, I was down to about 95 lb. from all the speed I was doing that I didn't drink very much. One beer could really mess me up.

Mom bought this fantastic old VW camper bus. The top could pop up, and there was a hammock-like bed up there. I loved that thing. It sounds funny, but it had its own special smell—not a bad smell, I call it the VW smell. My brother and his friends liked to go hang out in the bus sometimes, shut it all up tight, and smoke loads of pot. I went to check on them once and opened up the sliding side door; a huge cloud of pot smoke came pouring out. I don't know how they could even see each other in there.

Somehow we all got into the *Rocky Horror Picture Show*. It played every Saturday night at this wonky theater in Center City. *Rocky Horror* is an interactive cult classic movie. Just about every Saturday night, the whole group of us—Christina, Aunt T, Michael,

Cuz, whoever wanted to go—would pile into the VW bus and head to the city. We all had our own bag of props. At certain times during the movie, the audience threw certain props at the screen. There was TP, toast, newspaper, all kinds of stuff. We all knew all the lines by heart; we knew the dance steps and would get up and dance in the aisle when it was time with the rest of the theater. Sometimes we dressed up as one of the characters. We loved it. I tried to have my kids watch it, and they thought it was so stupid. Cracks me up now.

I always got ripped off as the second child, especially the second child who was a girl. My brother had this huge party for his sixteenth birthday. My parents didn't buy him a car or anything, but he still got tons of stuff. So my sixteenth rolled around, and I was expecting the same kind of thing. Big party, lots of stuff. Nope. At some point, we had gotten a huge fish tank with baby piranhas. Odd choice, I know. Not mine. Anyway, they were tiny at first, but they grew. We had to feed them live goldfish. They were called "feeder" fish. It was gross. One time we put the feeder fish in, and a piranha bit the whole back half of the fish off. The front half had been eating at the time, so the food it just swallowed went straight through. Disgusting. The piranha eventually went to live at the zoo. No one ever wanted to clean the tank. Well, no shit! I wanted to keep all my fingers, thank you very much. For my sixteenth birthday, I got to pick out fish for the now empty but clean fish tank and a new pack of "mood" underwear. Remember mood rings? They changed color depending on your mood? Anyway, the underwear had the days of the week on them and a little heart shaped patch to tell you your mood. Not only were my birthday presents totally disappointing but also massively frustrating. The days on the underwear *never* matched the day of the week it really was and the mood patch was always the same color. A crotch wrapped in cotton surrounded by denim jeans is always going to be a little warm.

Christmas at Christina's was a huge event. They had this enormous wooden chest filled with ornaments. No two were the same. Being involved in the decorating of the tree was an honor and a privilege. At my house, it was a "bota-boom-bota-bing" kind of thing. Always white lights (I'm still an all-white-light Christmas kinda girl).

But at Christina's? Things were different. First, we had dinner, then the opening of the chest. It was as if the Christmas spirit himself had been released to shine a light from above, directly into the chest. Angels were singing, hundreds of ornaments. All different shapes and colors. Some glass, some homemade; some had feathers, some old, some new. Aunt T was the director; we were her subjects. She would stand back, squint her eyes, and tell us where the holes were. And you had to make sure some were tucked in deep, not just on the edges of the branches. It took hours to decorate their tree, but the end results were beautiful. They always had the best tree, none of that theme bullshit either.

Talking about Christmas trees, one year we ended up with two by accident. My brother and his friends went out and cut down a tree from somewhere in the neighborhood. That same night, Michael went out and did the same thing. Oopsy poopsy. Dave had to ditch the extra tree somewhere. I don't think we were the best neighbors.

Every once in a while, Christina and I would take the train into the city to spend the day at the Philadelphia Museum of Art. Yup, that's the one where Rocky ran up the steps and did the jig. We saw some amazing exhibits. Those days were so calm. Like your brain got to take a deep breath it didn't even know it needed. We'd walk through the exhibits then get a soft pretzel and a Coke from a street vendor, sit on the grass, and just chill. The grass was so green and soft and perfect. Regular people can't possibly have grass that perfect at their house. If you took off your shoes and squished it between your toes, it was like running puppy ears through your fingers. If you didn't know any better, you would think it was fake. That's how perfect it was.

Oh my gosh! Going to a Neil Diamond concert really sticks out. Christina and I could have cared less; he wasn't our thing. We were into Led Zeppelin, Kiss, Queen, Reo Speedwagon, the Stones, which I think we've gone to all those concerts except maybe the Stones. I think. But the moms wanted to go. So we went with them. We got to our seats, and there were four nuns about three or four rows directly behind us. Like *nun* nuns. Wearing the full-on black-and-white nun habits. I'm thinking, *Well, shit, this is a wasted evening.* And it was, just not the way I was originally thinking. Aunt T, Christina and I shoved ourselves in a single stall in the ladies' room to smoke a big, fat joint. Now we had a wasted evening! I gotta say, the concert was amazing. The man never quit. He just kept going and going. Every time he turned around and wiggled his ass in those tight gray polyester pants he was wearing, the women went crazy! It was so very entertaining. But when he sang "Cherry, Cherry"? Holy Mother of God! The women went nuts. Crazy nuts. Including the nuns! Those habits they wear give them serious mobility. They were probably sweaty as hell (pun intended). First time I realized nuns are human too. The song "Cherry, Cherry" gives me great joy to this day.

LIFE LESSON #301

Never judge a person solely on the clothes they wear.

I worked every Sunday at K-Mart. Only on Sundays. Back then, Sundays were time and a half regardless of how many hours you worked during the week. I saved enough money to buy my first car. I bought a 1973 two-door green Chevy Impala from my aunt, my mom's sister. Mom's parents died when I was really young, so I don't remember them. Mom's brother is Cuz's dad. I like him. But her sister was a Jehovah Witness and lived really far away. To each their own on the religious thing, but they don't celebrate holidays or birthdays, which are the times when a lot of families that live apart try to get together. She was never there and never really made attempts to visit any other time except for a handful of times. Anyway, I bought the car from her, and it was a freaking tank. I would charge Dave and his friends to drive them around for gas money. Michael and Dave are the ones who taught me to drive. I failed my first go at the driving test. I called the instructor a bad name after he kept yelling at me to put both my hands on the wheel. I guess calling the driving instructor a dick is frowned upon and gets you an instant big, fat F. Who knew? Right after I got my license, on one of my first solo trips at night, there was this annoying breeze coming in the tank around my feet. I got totally distracted trying to figure out where it was coming from. Next thing I know, there was this big bump and a weird continuous high pitch squeal. It was the noise, not the bump, that brought my attention back to the fact that I was actively driving a car at the moment. Well, not actively anymore. At the moment, I was a giant green lawn ornament. It seems the bump was me jumping the curb, and the squealing noise were my tires digging into the wet grass

36

of someone's front yard. Oopsy! I slammed the tank in reverse and hightailed it out of there. I went back the next day to check out the damage. I made a mess of their yard. Of course, I didn't knock on their door, 'fess up, and pay for the damage but I still felt bad.

At some point, Michael and I got into a huge fight, and I slammed the driver's side door shut with the window halfway down; it shattered. I couldn't afford to fix it, so for the rest of the time I owned that Impala, I had to keep a big piece of wood in the trunk to shove in the open hole when I was parked. But there was nothing I could do when I was driving. The worst was when it was raining or snowing. Imagine driving while leaning as far to the right as you could while still being able to see the road. It sucked. Plus, I didn't win the argument, and the whole window thing just made me even madder.

I got arrested for the first time in high school. Our house was built on the front lawn of a once enormous estate that had been pieced out through the years. The Stotesbury Mansion was built in the late 1800s, early 1900s on over three hundred acres. Our house was on a big circle with a large statue in the center that used to be a fountain. The mansion was only a short walk away. Of course, by the seventies, it was a dilapidated mess and a total magnet for teens looking for a place to party. We would spend hours wandering the grounds, the countless outbuildings and the inside of the mansion. The bones of what it used to be were still there. It must have been magnificent once upon a time. All the walkways through the gardens and some statues still stood, covered in weeds and vines but still beautiful. The inside was huge. There was a gigantic set of stairs leading up to the second floor. They were curved and barely clinging to the wall. I only went up once because you had to walk right next to the wall where the stairs were kinda, sorta but not really secure. Totally unsafe. Heights are not my thing. But the second floor was just room after room after room. How many rooms does someone need? Then there were the basements. The bottom one was completely flooded, but the upper two were OK. I only went down to the first basement. My "creep-o-meter" was seriously screaming on high alert. Pitch black, stinky and you could hear but not see things moving around in there. Apparently, creepy basements aren't my thing either. And that, my friends, is why I got arrested.

A couple of the guys decided to go over to Stotesbury at night. I have no idea why they wanted to go, and I have no idea why I agreed to go with them. But I did. We grabbed a couple of flashlights and started walking our happy asses that way. If you think a crumbling, dilapidated, dead mansion is creepy at high noon, go at night. The shifting beams of the flashlights made the climbing ivy and weeds look alive. It was so dark beyond the beam of light that anything could have been out there, just hiding and waiting in the dark. Not to mention the noises of scurrying little rat feet. Annnnd, of course, they wanted to go in the basement. I definitely wasn't going down there. Instead, I opted to wait up top by the door. So there I was, all by myself, waiting, without a flashlight, terrified, and about to pee my pants. It probably hadn't even been ten minutes before I was starting to hear the sound of chainsaws buzzing in my head; my breath was coming out in quick pants and I was slightly dizzy. Out of nowhere, I saw this tiny single dot of light bobbing around behind me. Coming. Right. At. Me. And it was getting bigger. I immediately went into full blown ECS mode, emergency crisis situation mode. I screamed and kept on screaming. The light was now bobbing toward me at a much faster speed. Not helpful. Now I was screaming for the boys to come get me and come get me *now*! It never crossed my mind to hide. It also never crossed my mind that we were technically breaking the law. That realization finally came to me when the arm holding that beam of light was neatly wrapped up in a police uniform. We all got hauled to the police station, arrested for trespassing, fined fifty dollars each, and worst of all, had to call Mom to come get us.

LIFE LESSON #243

Calling a parent to come pick you up from jail, no matter
the charge, is an epic failure along one's journey.

Christina's grandma owned a big o' house at the Jersey shore. I got to
spend a lot of time over the summers at the beach. For letting me stay,
my job was to empty all the ashtrays every day and Windex all the
pictures every Sunday. This was a big house, where everyone smoked.
There were always tons of people coming and going. Christina had
lots of aunts, uncles, and cousins plus all their friends. And there
were pictures of all of them—everywhere. One big, happy family.
It was totally worth whatever chores they would have given me. We
spent the days sunbathing and the nights partying. One night, I got
so drunk on Southern Comfort that to this day, even the smell of it
makes me sick. We were walking around, just goofing off one night,
and got this brilliant idea to break into Lucy to hang out. Lucy is a
gigantic elephant that is a historic roadside attraction at the Jersey
shore. I mean big enough that you could go inside her and walk
around. She even has a window to look out of her butt. Back then,
she was kind of a mess, so technically, it wasn't breaking and entering.
It was really just entering. The door was all hanging crooked and not
shut all the way. We just wanted a place to smoke a joint out of the
wind. Of course, some Good Samaritan called the cops. This time, I
didn't scream. I ran! We all ran. Running in sand is tough. Running
in sand when you're stoned is nearly impossible. But it turns out that
being chased by the police is a huge motivational aide! I lost a flip-
flop along the way, but it needed to be sacrificed for the greater good.
The greater good being not getting arrested and, more importantly,

no phone call to my Mom. On a side note, I saw somewhere that they finally did repair Lucy and she's a museum or something now.

A bunch of us decided to go camping one weekend. It was Christina and her bf, Michael, me, Cuz, Dave, and his gf. Totally unrelated to this story, but Dave's gf at the time is the reason I never got to take drivers education classes. My brother got caught in the act of having sex with his gf, who just so happened to be the driver's education instructor's daughter. He saw my name and kicked me out. Just like that. No insurance discounts for me! Anyway, we headed to a National Forest campground not too far from home. We had good intentions, but when we got there, the designated camping sites were super close to one another and the place was packed. Families everywhere, little kids riding bikes, babies crying. Not the idea we all had in mind, so we packed our crap and started hiking deeper in the woods. We found a beautiful spot by a river with a big enough flat area for the tents and a fire pit, totally secluded from any other spots and the road. Perfect. We set up camp, gathered wood, built a fire, and roasted some hotdogs. Then we dropped some acid. Everything was fun and games for a while. Then the hallucinations really kicked in, and all the girls started hearing loud noises coming from deep in the woods. We retreated to one of the tents and started thinking it was a moose the size of a two-story building. I have no clue who came up with that, but we ran with it. We ended up being huddled together for the rest of the night, too afraid to turn off the flashlights, convinced we were on the verge of getting trampled to death by a gigantic zombie moose with a taste for blood. I have no idea if there are even moose in that area; it didn't matter. I also have no idea what all the boys spent their night doing. That was not a fun trip, and I couldn't wait for the first sign of light. Plus, our flashlights died one by one through the night, and that didn't help the bad hallucinations. Morning finally came, and it was safe to leave the tent. With just a residual of the high left, we all gathered by the river to soak our feet in the cool water. Michael simply bent over and caught a fish. With his bare hands! It was so weird, like that shit happened every day. We're all standing in the river by the bank, whooping and hollering with amazement, congratulating Michael on his catch of the day. He was holding the fish up in the air, a perfect scene for the forest service to walk up on. He was *not* happy. Said he had been looking for us since the day before. Saw our cars parked but no campsite filled. At that point, he propped his leg up on a rock and started to pick burrs out of his socks. The picking of the burrs was in sync with each word he is yelling at us. About how we were in a National Forest, camping beyond designated areas which was prohibited, fishing without a license (that one shouldn't count since he caught it with his hands), destroying government property by building a fire, littering… I tuned out at some point in the tirade. But he was pissed. He started yelling at us to put the fish down, pick up the TP, put out the fire, destroy the fire ring of rocks, pack our crap, and get out. He'd wait, so we had to make it fast. We were instructed to follow him back to our cars. When we got to the cars, he started on how lucky we were that he was not going to give us any tickets—we needed to learn respect, yada, yada. We kept our mouths shut, got in our cars, and drove home in silence. I'm pretty sure it was shortly after that trip that Cuz forgot to put away his special box of acid, and Mom found it in the morning. He was on a bus the next day heading home. Bye, Cuz!

Even though I didn't really fit in, I wanted to go to prom. For junior prom, I wore a black dress that ended right below the knee that I borrowed from Aunt T. To complete the look, I wore fishnet stockings and a black birdcage veil. Michael wore a black tux. We looked like we were going to a fancy funeral. Everyone else was wearing bright-colored long gowns with big hairdos. But their dresses didn't have matching black purses stuffed with lip gloss and a bottle of vodka. The nuns were the chaperones and spent their time patrolling the dance floor, separating couples who were dancing too close. When the nun came up to us to push us further apart, we started cracking up. Got a big stink eye for laughing, but it wasn't out of disrespect that we were laughing; it was out of the ridiculousness of it. We had been living together for years by that point. We had a lot of fun that night, though, so when senior prom came around, I wanted to go to that too. That year, I went rebel. I couldn't see spending money on a dress I would never wear again, so Michael and I rented matching white tuxedos with tails and matching red cummerbunds. I wore hooker-red high heels to top things off. When we showed up, we got the biggest "poo-poo" looks from the nuns because I was in pants. The travesty. I didn't care what anyone thought. I felt sexy, I was comfortable, and the tux pants had pockets. A pocket that was the perfect place to keep my cocaine. We had even more fun at that prom.

By the grace of God, I graduated high school. Me. I graduated from an all-girls, uniform-wearing, nun-toting Catholic high school. Say what now?! People that know me and learn that later always give me a double take when they find that out. It's funny. I did leave with one of my classic smartass moments though. At a Catholic gradua-tion ceremony, there's a mass involved. Since I'm not Catholic, I've always politely declined the "blood and body of Christ" portion of the mass. At graduation, I couldn't help myself and responded with a "No thank you, I'm driving" instead. The priest's face was very amusing to me.

I spent the summer after graduation job hopping and partying with Michael. First, I got a job at a local Roy Rogers fast-food joint. I hated that job and only made it about a week. It was the uniforms. Girls had to wear these stupid short western skirts and a fake cowboy hat. You're bending over all day in those stupid skirts. What were they thinking? I can guarantee a man designed that. Then I got a job at a 7-Eleven. I didn't really like that job either because I didn't like working the night shift by myself. The final straw, though, was when I had to take a lie detector test. They had a safe there for the cashiers to drop deposits in throughout the night. The safe had this hopper like thing that you dropped the wrapped cash in, then you had to turn the crank on the side for it to drop in the actual safe. Apparently, a bunch of cash went missing. Regular employees didn't have access to the safe. Only the manager did, and they had been off for two days before the missing money went noticed. That was a lot of shifts with a lot of employees, so we all needed to be tested. PS: The drug addict (me) didn't do it. Surprise! Even though I knew I didn't take the money, being hooked up to a lie detector machine is very nerve wracking. I had no idea what to expect and I knew I had eaten a candy bar or two without paying for them. Turns out, they didn't care about the candy; they cared about the cash. And they found out who did it. I heard one of the employees at the end of their shift banded their cash, dropped it in the hopper but forgot to turn the crank, and went home. Replacement employee relieved them, noticed the wad of cash, and figured the other guy would get the blame. Turns out, I didn't even work that day. I quit anyway.

Then I got a job at an authentic Jewish deli as a cashier. I loved that job. There were always people coming and going. The cashier stand was in the center of all the action. There was a deli on the left where you could get your kosher meats sliced—gefilte fish, lox, all the traditional Jewish fare. On the right was a restaurant. I loved taking care of the old Jewish women. They were so cute! I'm not saying that in a disrespectful way, and of course I got an occasional cranky person. They gave me advice if I asked for it or not. In general, they were very opinionated and stern but in a kind and warm way. When they spoke, I listened. When they were splitting the restaurant bill up, they would come and get 5 pennies for a nickel because they owed their friend $5.32. And $5.32 is what you would get. Not $5.30. That wouldn't have been fair. They made me wish I had a Jewish grandma to spend time with and learn from. I guess any kind of warm, loving grandma would have done.

My mom's parents were gone, but my dad's parents were still alive. We didn't spend much time with them, but when we did, it wasn't a warm and fuzzy visit. My dad's dad was sick with emphysema ever since I could remember. Every time Dave and I would go visit their house, we had to wait outside to be sprayed down with Lysol, front and back, before we were allowed to go inside. I guess kids are germ pits because Dad didn't have to get sprayed. Not exactly the happy "Hi, how are you?" Grandma was a very stoic person. She loved us, and she tried but it didn't come easy for her. I remember visiting her once, and she was so excited about this new hotdog cooker she bought just for us. It had about four or five metal cone-shaped things on both sides. You shoved each end of the hotdog on a cone thing and plugged it in. Electricity ran from one of the cone things, through the hotdog, to the other cone. I've never tasted a more disgusting hotdog. They tasted like electrocuted hotdog. But she tried. The best part about visiting them was the golf cart! They lived in a gated retirement community where all the curbs were set at an angle instead of straight up and down. Dave and I would take turns driving the cart up and down the street and up and down the curbs.

Thinking about my grandmother helps me understand my father a bit better. Dad grew up in a very stern environment with a brother who was ill. He had severe diabetes and needed and got more attention than Dad. My Uncle T was the obvious favorite. Because of the way he was raised, Dad never really learned how to communicate feelings and emotions, which didn't help in the raising of a daughter. Especially a daughter who experienced sexual abuse.

That went off the rails there for a little bit, but now you understand why I would have loved to have had an old Jewish grandma to meet me at the door with a warm, squishy hug and a plate of freshly made baklava.

That summer is when Michael introduced me to meth, beginning my ten-year love affair. Understand though, back then when you snorted a line of meth, you stayed up all night organizing your kitchen drawers. Nowadays, if you do meth, you want to eat your neighbor's face. I have no idea what kind of chemicals they put in it now but it's different. Pot too, has changed. Back then, you could get good pot or bad pot. It all just made you laugh, then hungry, then paranoid, then fall asleep. Now there's pot to calm you down, pot that amps you up, pot to make you eat, pot that helps with pain, and on and on. Pot these days has specific jobs. So many choices.

I sold my 1973 Impala that summer too. I bought a little green convertible MG Midget. I named her Gidget. Gidget was a stick shift; I didn't know how to drive a stick shift. Michael tried to teach me, but it was a bit sketchy there for a while. I pity the fool who found themselves behind me. I am especially throwing out an open apology to any fool that found themselves behind me on the upside of a hill. I'm sure the terror you may have experienced watching a green MG Midget roll toward you in reverse has passed by now but just in case it hasn't, I'm so sorry. I used to have theme parties with

44

Gidget. Like Gidget goes to the movies, Gidget goes to Hawaii (I taped big plastic flowers on her), Gidget goes to a party. Things like that. If you have ever had a convertible, you quickly learn people aren't always nice. I've gotten back to the car when someone had thrown trash in her. Once someone flicked a lit cigarette on her seat, a full soda—not nice.

At one of the parties I went to with Gidget and Michael, I got a tattoo for the first time. It was a small, simple flower on my chest. Thing is, Mom hated tattoos and forbade (that doesn't really work for me) us kids to get one. Every once in a while, Mom needed to come in the bathroom while I was in the shower. I was always conveniently washing my chest with my back turned, just in case. Somehow, Mom found out. I wrote her a letter of apology that went something like this:

> I know you know. And I know you know I know
> you know. So let's pretend you don't know. And
> let's pretend I know you don't know. To sum it
> up, you don't know what you think you know. I
> don't know what I think I know about what you
> may, or may not know. So sorry.

All was forgiven. She never brought it up. I never brought it up. Occasionally the infamous "I know you know" letter came up in conversation.

LIFE LESSON #512

A mother's heart is filled with quiet forgiveness.

After graduation, Christine and I both applied to the Philadelphia College of Art and got in. We stayed in the dorms our first year. We didn't get to stay in the same room, but we were close enough. The dorm rooms had two bedrooms each, one on each side, a small living room, kitchen and bathroom in the center. Each bedroom had one set of bunk beds, so four girls to a dorm. You didn't get to pick your dorm mates. I'm not sure how they came up with who got assigned to each room, but talk about complete opposites! The two girls in the right-side room were kinda uptight and prissy. One of them was a vegetarian but ate fried chitlins once a week for protein. No offense, people, but chitlins are gross. Even the smell of them frying grosses me out. And why chitlins? Isn't there anything else she could have chosen for her weekly protein? Really, anything else? Plus, she only wore huge white cotton underwear that got handwashed once a week and put on a rack to dry. Seriously? I didn't want to be surrounded by big-ass granny panties when I was trying to take a shower. My bunk mate and I were a much better match. She wasn't lost like I was, but we still got along. No one was as lost as I was.

Things started out really well. I was majoring in graphic design, keeping up with my classes and homework. Soon though, things started to deteriorate, and I hated my teacher. One of our assignments was to create a "dream green." WTF? WE were instructed to mask off a one-inch square on this big piece of paper that I had to pay for, total waste so I'm already aggravated, and to come up with a new color of "dream green." When I brought up the fact that "dream green" was subjective—my "dream green" may not be anywhere

46

close to your "dream green"—he snapped at me that the assignment "wasn't as complex as corn-studded shit" again, WTF? I'm going into debt for this? I shut my mouth, painted my square and showed it to him. He said it was close to "dream green" but not quite there. So I sat back down, didn't do shit for about thirty minutes, and went back up to show him the exact same square of green. He said I was getting closer but not perfect yet. Say what? I changed my major.

I took the train home every weekend to work and see Michael. I'm not sure what he was up to during the week when I was in the city at college, but I don't think it was good things. I say that because during one of my weekend visits home, Michael shot me up with meth for the first time. The rush was amazing. Your body gets all warm from the inside out. Then you puke. I know that sounds horrible, but if you didn't puke, you didn't do enough. Like I said though, meth was different back then because I still went back to the city for school on Mondays, and since I couldn't shoot myself up, I went back to snorting it. Of course I found a guy in the city to get speed from. He would come hang out in our dorm room every once in a while. The living room window was on the street side of the building, so every so often, someone would throw up a pebble or give out a shout looking for drugs. He would always bring this little bucket he had tied to a rope. He would lower the bucket; they would put their money in, bring it up, and then lower their drugs. Dealers were so much more trustworthy back then. Nowadays, the bucket with your money would be raised up to never come back down again. How times have changed.

But I limped through my first year of college snorting meth all week and shooting it up all weekend. Summer went the same. We did some gross stuff out of stupidity. We shared needles; we sharpened needles on the strike strip on the back of a book of matches, shot up in the car while someone was driving. Gross stuff drug addicts consider normal. I shot up a mix of cocaine and meth once. Only one time on that little combo. I thought I was going to die. It was like being propelled through a tunnel of darkness while your heart was pumping out of your chest. Hated it. I took PCP, which was also a one and doner. PCP makes you feel invincible; anything is possible

47

and you don't feel any pain. Not a good combination. We were down at a creek somewhere, trying to cross over by jumping from rock to rock. There I am, hopping along, doing pretty good until I got to a jump that was impossibly far. An Olympic gold medal long jumper could have probably made it, not me. But on PCP, you think you can do anything. Shit, I could fly, so I went for it. Needless to say, I didn't make it, not even a close call. I fell into the creek, put a huge gash in my leg, blood everywhere. I should have gone to the hospital for stitches, but I didn't feel a thing. In my mind, it was a "no harm, no foul" moment.

The next day was a different story. The PCP wore off, and my leg was killing me. We never even cleaned it out. It sealed up with dirt and tiny rocks stuck in it. I couldn't tell Mom at that point because there would be questions. Scrubbing that clean just about made me pee my pants. I stuck to what I knew after that: meth and pot. What a responsible drug addict I had become.

Christina and I decided we didn't want to stay in the dorms again so, we found ourselves a little row home to rent a few blocks away from college. First floor was a small living room, kitchen combo. Second floor was an okay-sized bedroom and a bathroom. Third floor had two bedrooms. Plus there was an unfinished base-ment. Pretty skinny and sandwiched in the middle of row homes on both sides.

We got two more housemates. We decided that the person who got the second-floor bedroom would pay the highest rent since it was the biggest and next to the bathroom, the two top bedrooms would pay equal rent, and the basement would pay the least since it wasn't finished but really not that bad. We found a guy for that room. He didn't care. I took the second floor because my dad was going to pay my rent and it was just another way for me to secretly stick it to him. Christina and S took the third floor.

Move-in day was very interesting. All the row homes on our block were built a long time ago, and I'm guessing people were hella short back then. The stairs were very narrow, curved almost in a "V" shape with a low ceiling. Moving things that couldn't bend like box springs and dressers was impossible. Even my headboard couldn't make the turn. We ended up having to take the windows out on the second and third floor and rigging a rope and pulley kind of system to hoist things up through the windows. People on the street below were not safe, and they knew it. Watching them stop and stare at a mattress dangling in midair from a flimsy-ass rope was very entertaining and a little bit distracting. Most people crossed the street, a few risked walking under it, but all of them looked up with their heads tilted to the side, and a "What the fuck?" look in their eyes. Nothing makes you question mortality quite like walking under a dresser dangling two stories up on a string.

I liked that house. It was small in size but huge in character. I risked my life to hang as far out of my window as I could to nail a pink plastic lawn flamingo on the outside. It was the perfect touch of gaudy. We had an avocado-green fridge, the old, old kind with the tiny freezer inside the big door. The handle broke so we had to tie a butter knife to it so you could jimmy the door open. It was so funny watching visitors try to figure out the avocado secret. At least no one could rob our food supply.

I loved living in the city. There was a small mom and pop corner store down the block, people walking up and down the street, something always going on. I still took the train to the suburbs every weekend to work and see Michael. He wasn't always around, though. Then he crashed my MG Midget running from the cops. That should have been a clue of things to come. Because one weekend he was gone. Never heard from him. I did hear a rumor years later that he had been running guns and drugs and got arrested. He went to prison for a while. Not sure if that's true. Six years with him and not a single word. We practically grew up together. I was very sad, angry, and full of questions which of course centered around "What did I do wrong?" Plus, who the hell was going to shoot me up? Back to just snorting the stuff.

All in all, my second year in college was going okay. But I definitely wasn't as dedicated as I should have been. And eventually I started dating again. First, I dated a real guy with a real job but that wasn't meant to be. He needed a real girl with a real job. Not some meth head with no self-worth or any direction in life. Then I met a

49

guy I had actually been working with for a while, but we never really noticed each other before. He was dating someone, and they just broke up, and I, of course, had Michael. Ironically, his name was Michael too. He was such a gentleman. Something I wasn't used to. He was very grounded and humble with a soft, kind soul. He shared a house with his brother. I liked him a lot. And I liked his brother so going over to his house was nice. I can't remember why he and his ex-girlfriend broke up, but in my opinion, she was bat shit crazy. She was the thorn in our relationship. She would call his house over and over if she knew I was there. She always wanted him to go to her place for one reason or another. She ended up pulling the suicide card once or twice on the rare occasion when he wouldn't go. I would finally take the phone off the hook because she was relentless. I felt bad and he was always so torn about what to do but she just wanted attention. It used to piss me off! It really pissed me off when he went though. It was always something stupid that she wanted, like changing a lightbulb that was too high for her to reach. And if he didn't go that night, he always went the next day. Michael to the rescue. That's just the kind of guy he was though. I had to call him for a rescue once or twice myself.

I had him come to the city in the middle of the night to get me once. I should mention it was in the dead of winter in Philadelphia and he drove a motorcycle. It was a true emergency though. You see, when you live in old row homes, with houses connected on both sides, it doesn't matter how clean your house is if your neighbors are slobs. Our neighbors on the right were slobs. Slobs with a capital *S*. Roaches are disgusting creatures. I'm sure God had a reason, but that reason still eludes my comprehension. And they don't die! Did you know that a roach can survive a week without a head? Or that if a roach is pregnant when you kill it with pesticides, the babies will continue to grow, eating the body of their dead mother, becoming immune to that specific pesticide? Vile creatures! Not to mention that in Center City Philadelphia, they grow so big that you can see people on the street actually walk around them. When they fly—yes, fly—by your head, I swear they whisper your name. I *hate* roaches. Having said all that and that our neighbors were slobs, they

50

got infested with roaches, which means they squeezed their disgust-ing, disease-filled selves through the cracks in the walls, and we got infested with roaches. Our landlord was what is now called a "slum lord," so it took a while for him to get an exterminator to our house.

He finally showed up and was the stereotypical "don't give a shit" exterminator. I'm sure he was the absolute cheapest our land-lord could find—didn't get paid enough, hated his job, ass crack hanging out, fat, sweaty, just wanna have a beer kind of guy. So I was home; he showed up, smelling like onions, spraying all harry carry, no method to the madness. I watched him do the first floor and was thinking, *What the fuck? That shit is going everywhere!* He started heading up to the second floor where the bathroom and my bedroom was. The "I don't give a shit" sweeping of the spray continued in the bathroom. My room was next. I stood in front of my door and was like "Oh, hell no!" I had been working on a project for a good three weeks, and it was due in two days. It was all spread out on my floor waiting to be put together. I couldn't take the chance that he was going to be careful and not douse the thing with pesticide. I didn't have time to redo it; I couldn't afford not to turn it in. I told him to skip my room. He grunted, shrugged his shoulders, and moved on up to the third floor. Never said a word. That night, proud of myself for averting a huge catastrophe, I snuggled in and went to bed. Now I'm not a pest control specialist, don't know anything about being an exterminator, but I can tell you this: those roaches were looking for a safe house. That safe house was my room. I woke up in the middle of the night because I felt itchy. I threw my blankets off, and there were hundreds of roaches under my covers, on the floor, the walls, everywhere! So yes, I called Michael B, for an emergency evacuation.

It was so cold riding a motorcycle back to the suburbs. But so worth it. On our way to his house, we drove through a parking lot to cut time. It was covered in black ice, the kind that's there but you can't see it. Michael B started to slide on the ice, and we were going down sideways. It all happened so fast. I threw my foot out from reflex to try to catch myself, the bike slid out from under me, and I was left standing in the parking lot. That could never happen again. Like a Hollywood stunt that we had spent months practicing and preparing for. He continued on the slide but was okay and so was the bike. We stood there staring at each other for a few minutes trying to figure what the hell just happened. So weird.

Things were going really good for us, but that ex of his never went away. She was always on the sidelines somewhere, somehow, all needy and irritating. I was in the city during the week and she figured out my schedule. Things started to change. She showed up at the deli a few times over the next couple weekends. Michael B was looking nervous. I knew but didn't want to admit it to myself. Things were happening during the week when I was gone. Like I said, he had a kind soul and couldn't take the betrayal to me for very long. He told me they were going to try to work things out. Perfect. I was angry and told him she would be pregnant and then married in six months. I heard through the grapevine it was about three. I also heard a story about them getting into a fight, so she retaliated by hiding all of his shoes and car keys. He had to walk to a shoe store in socks to buy a pair of shoes to walk to the bus and get to work. Actually kinda funny and very inventive but mean. I quit my job at the deli shortly after he broke up with me; I didn't want to see his ugly face every weekend.

Back in the city full time, no job, no boyfriend, short on money, short on drugs. The semester was coming to an end, and summer was coming. I needed a plan. I don't know how all this happened, but someone came up with the idea to leave the city behind for a couple of months and head to Ocean City, Maryland, for the summer. The timing couldn't have been more perfect. I was all in. We got a little summer rental and jobs at the boardwalk carnival. We were now referred to as "barkers." I got stationed at one of the dart booths right on the boardwalk. All day, I yelled things like "You hit one, you win one" or "Three darts for a dollar." My voice was toast by the end of the second day; it came back just a little deeper. The object was to hit a tiny black cut out of a T-shirt stuck on a huge bright white board. There were probably fifty or so T-shirt cutouts. If you hit one, you got a tiny, cheap stuffed animal. The trick was to keep them playing because they could trade the tiny one in for a bigger one if they hit another T-shirt. Until they traded up to the biggest one, which was still cheap, and it rarely ever happened. Thing is, all those games are rigged. The black cutout T-shirts were an optical illusion. One side was skinnier with a smaller sleeve that tricked the eye. One of us worked the bottle stand. There were empty beer bottles laying on their side on a small board. The player was given a pole with a string tied to it with a small plastic ring at the end. The object was to get the small ring around the lip of the bottle and stand it up. She spent every morning polishing those boards with bowling alley wax until they came to a high shine. The boards were also mounted to the base at an ever so slight angle so the task was nearly impossible. But she could do it all day, every day, with both hands at the same time. Very impressive! She made it look so easy that people would always be at her booth, forking over dollar after dollar. I never really got the hang of the bottle thing but I could throw a dart! I got so good I could throw one under my arm backward and hit a t-shirt cut out. That's all we did all day, practice and play carnival games. When it was slow, we would wander around acting like customers at each other's booths, whooping and hollering like we were winning something just to get new players. Or dust off and walk around with one of the biggest stuffed animals to get people to play, thinking those were actually a possibility. We had the system down. Sometimes we would sit on the counter at the dart booth, spread our legs, and play chicken with the darts; that always brought in players. Being a carnie was a lot of work though. You always had to be in high energy mode no matter how shitty you might really feel. There was a French fry and burger stand directly across the boardwalk from my dart booth that was always busy. All day, people ordered fries and doused them with malt vinegar. That smell first thing in the morning with a hangover was rough. Top that with a hot summer day, the smell was absolute torture. We worked seven days a week. One week, you got an afternoon off but still had to work at night. The next week, you got a night off but still had to work the afternoon. Those kinds of hours at high energy required some assistance. We were summer help, but a lot of the carnies were full-time workers that followed the carnival around after the summer season was over. Some of those guys were a bit sketchy and had no teeth, but they had connections everywhere with good drugs. And everyone was doing them. Skeevy things happened behind the scenes in the carnie life. I would have lines of coke and meth all lined up and ready to go right under the counter. Families with little kids would be walking by, eating French fries and ice cream while I was bending over snorting lines. Sounds horrible now, just another day then. I'm not sure what all the teenage girls saw in some of the carnies, but they were like groupies at a rock concert. The dark corners of the haunted house were well used, if you get my drift.

There was a bar right down the ramp of the boardwalk called the Bearded Clam. They used to sell this drink they called the upside downer. You sat with your back to the bar, leaned your head way back, and they poured basically a big margarita straight out of the bottles into your mouth. Quick and convenient because every so often through the night, we would take turns running the ramp. Then it was always a go to right after work. That's where I met this delicious guy. Tall, tanned, built like a brick house with dark hair and the chiseled features of a Greek god. Plus he was from Australia, so he had that whole accent thing going on. Yummy to look at. Dumb as a box of rocks. Like seriously dumb. I still dated him for several weeks but had a tough time not rolling my eyes every time he opened his mouth. He had these perfect white teeth, which I found out later were fake because he dove off a diving board into an empty pool. He didn't notice there wasn't any water in it. How does that go unnoticed? Water is an integral part of a pool.

I called it off after having sex one night. The sex was good, amazing actually. Afterward, he rolled over to me and began stammering, "I...I...I..."

I was thinking, *God no! Don't do it. Do not say I love you. Don't do it!*

He finally spit out, "I've been to three proms." What the hell? Who gives a fat rat's ass? But whatever. That was the cherry on top of my stupidity cake. I couldn't take it anymore.

LIFE LESSON #601

All beauty and no brains is as useless as
an empty pool on a hot day.

Shortly after I sent tall, dark, and empty walking, I met someone else.
He was from Scotland. That accent was working for me too. B and
I had a lot of fun together, nothing too serious but fun. Not that it's
relevant, but he was my first and only uncircumcised penis. Takes a
little getting used to, just saying. We kept in touch for years writing
letters. I'm thinking about three years or so. He and a friend came to
the States for a holiday way down the line. That visit did not go so
well for me. I thought we had been friends only for years. I picked
them up from the airport and the plan, was for them to come stay
at my apartment for several days before going on to their next destination. I took time off work to show them around, which I couldn't
afford to do, but that's what you do for friends. But I had gained a
few pounds over the years. When we dated, I was stick skinny; when
he got back to the States, I wasn't. I wasn't huge, not that that should
matter between friends. I was just normal. I was still the same person,
just not a stick anymore. I could see the look of disappointment on
his face when he saw me. It hurt, but I buried it. I was really good
at that. I showed them around the city for a while, got some lunch,
and headed to my apartment. I had a small two-bedroom apartment
at the time in the suburbs that I shared with a roommate. It had one
couch in the living room that I figured the friend could sleep on,
and B could sleep with me. *Sleep* in the bed with me. I was dating
someone at the time. B and I hadn't seen each other in years. Sex
was not on the table just yet. I could see the horror on his face when
I told him the plan. Like I was so disgusting that the thought of

55

having to share a bed with me to sleep was terrifying. Little did he know that I had been disgusted with myself for years so I knew "the look." He slept in the bed that night. He was all squished up against the wall, like he could catch a few extra pounds if he got too close. I was almost falling off the bed on my side. I accidentally rolled over in my sleep and touched him. He jumped up and found a way to squish even closer to the wall. I guess he was afraid I was going to rip his clothes off and make him earn his keep. I saw "the look"; I'm not stupid.

The next morning, they quickly packed their shit, said something about their itinerary changing, and left. That hurt. I guess I really am disgusting. Never got another letter. I know I shouldn't, but sometimes I hope he's fat and bald now. And can't afford the dentures he so desperately needs.

Wow! Got off track there for a minute, but it happens.

Back to the beach. We worked hard, but we played hard too. We decided to host a girl party at our rental one night but began prepping a few days in advance by soaking fruit in grain alcohol. We had a blast and ended up making hats out of lampshades for the night. One of our roommates started dating this guy that ended up hanging out all the time. He was interesting. Didn't like to wipe his ass after taking a poop. Instead, he got in the shower. So depending on how…active…things were on any particular day, he was in the shower in the shower at least two or three times. It was odd.

Most nights were fun, some not so much. We went to a local party one night, where I bought some meth. In the bathroom, immediately after snorting a line, I had to poop. Uncontrollably poop. And kept uncontrollably pooping. The meth had been cut with laxatives. A lot of laxatives by how things were going. Fantastic. The poop train had left the station. I did the best I could to clean up but Daisy Duke shorts and a halter top can only do so much. I stole a beach towel to wrap around my waist and walked out like nothing happened. I felt bad about the mess left behind, but I figured they brought that shit on themselves! Get it? Shit? I started getting mad on the way home. I wasted money to buy the stuff, I didn't get high, and now I had a memory that needs to go on the top ten "most embarrassing" moments. When I got back to the rental and hopped in the shower, I began thinking our roommate's weird bathroom habits might not be so weird after all.

As summer started to come to an end, I started thinking about college. I wasn't sure if I wanted to go back. I only confided this to Michael B. I know he screwed me over, kicked me to the curb, and chose someone else, but we still talked once in a while. I would get a letter from him every now and again, and I would write back. He thought taking a year off was a bad idea. I didn't know if I should trust his opinion, given our history. But I couldn't let the thought go. I even considered joining the carnival when they close down for the summer and travel the country with them for a year. The thought of telling my Dad that and seeing the disappointment on his face shut that one down. Looking back now, I see that I was on a roll of self-destructive behavior and wasn't done yet. Not by a long shot.

After our stint at the beach, we returned to our little row home in the city dragging a new roommate with us. Over the summer, the guy in the basement (that sounds so creepy) moved out, so Fer moved in.

I can tell you we came home with a new roommate. We did not come home to a house with hot water though. Young people don't always think things through. In our defense, we were paying rent in Philly and at the beach, and hello? Meth doesn't grow on trees, so there wasn't much extra money to pay the heating bills when we weren't even using it. That's a harsh wakeup call that hits you about three seconds into your first shower. The whole lather, rinse, repeat thing happens at record speed. I never knew I could bend backward so well, for so long. The motivation being to rinse your hair without the freezing cold water touching any other part of your body at the moment. That is also when I decided that the whole "repeat" part of the "lather, rinse, repeat" instructions on the shampoo bottle is bullshit. The big manufacturers think the general American public is stupid. The repeat isn't necessary. It just makes you use your shampoo twice as fast so you need to buy more, more often. It took about three weeks or better to get caught up on the back bills and get the hot water back on. That's a lot of cold showers and some really hairy legs.

More important than returning to the city without hot water was that I decided to not return to college. It seriously impeded on my party time. When you don't get to sleep until 4:00 a.m., getting up at 7:00 for an 8:00 class is tough. I figured I would just get a job and get going with life.

I got a job at a bakery. They made delicious croissants stuffed with all kinds of fillings. My favorite was the pizza one. An hour before closing every night it turned into "twofer" time. Whatever was left was sold at two for the price of one. Then at closing, we bagged up whatever was left after that to give to the homeless shelters. I liked it there. I worked at the counter, not in the back cooking. I didn't like having to walk home at night though. Our uniforms were khaki pants and white long-sleeved button-down shirts. Sexy? Not even close. But every night, I got propositioned like a prostitute. Seriously? How many prostitutes wear ugly-ass white and tan uniforms? Oh! And don't forget the non-slip black shoes. That really put the pro in prostitute. Plus, the constant barrage of the homeless begging for change. I don't know how many times I can say "meth costs money"! I finally started walking home with about eight or ten bags filled with a leftover croissant in each. Now when the homeless begged for change, I had something to give them instead of just walking by.

Once, when I was walking home one night, someone began to follow me. The faster I walked, the faster they walked. I crossed the street; they crossed the street. The hairs on the back of my neck were standing up, and panic set in pretty quickly. There was a huge, tall black man standing alone on the corner waiting for the bus. I started to run to him with my arms spread wide, yelling, "Honey! I'm so sorry I'm late!" He got this classic WTF look on his face, but I went for it anyway. I threw my arms around him, whispered in his ear that someone was following me and I was terrified. It was like hugging a board. But he saved me. He fell right into the role. He ended up walking me the rest of the way home, missing his bus in the process. He was so kind and, I don't even know his name to say thank you.

After that I started walking home with a key sticking out between each of my fingers on my right hand and my bags of croissants in my left.

I liked that job, and I liked living in the city. My brother was going to Drexel University, so we got to spend a lot of time hanging out. I liked that too. All siblings go through their ups and downs, but the older we got, the closer Dave and I got. We spent a lot of time hitting the bars and partying as a team. We hung out as often as we could until he started dating this waitress at a local Irish pub. After that, he never wanted to go anywhere else. Ugh.

Living in the city has it all, the good, the bad, the ugly, and sometimes the super funny. Our row home was right off Pine Street, which is one of the bigger streets in the city. Since Philly is one of the oldest cities, the streets in the main city are really narrow and one way. Barely enough space for parking usually on one side or the other, depending on the direction of traffic, so we got a lot of people walking up and down the street. The girls and I found this bar on Pine Street and quickly became regulars. The beer was cheap; it was close to the house and I could always score some meth. It didn't take me long to find out it was the owners who were the real sellers. One guess as to whom I targeted as a new friend.

Anyway, walking home from the bar one night, Christina and I had to go by an alley opening. It was a full moon that night so just enough light to see all the way down the alley. We're walking and talking; passing by the alley opening, both of us must have thought we saw something at the same time because, without speaking a single word, we backtracked the four steps to get back to the opening of the alley to take another gander. Right there, just beyond the opening, was a guy wearing a tan trench coat, pants down around his ankles, whacking away at his wenis! We stood there, in complete silence, watching for maybe forty-five seconds before bursting out laughing and pointing before walking away. Like we hadn't seen a penis before? We laughed the rest of the way home, which I'm sure he could hear echoing down the alley. We may be responsible for destroying a flasher's future. I'm sure that wasn't the reaction that got him off. I also wonder if there is a "flasher uniform"? Do they require flashers to wear long trench coats? Or is that a comfort choice thing?

On another occasion, we obtained a slightly newer couch than the one we were using, so we moved the old couch out in front of the house until trash day when we could push it to the curb. That night, around 3:00 a.m., I was woken up by the sound of a large party that was right outside under my bedroom window. What the hell? I lean out my window, and three bums were sitting on our trash couch, trading a bottle of MD 20/20 back and forth, whooping and hollering, telling stories, smoking cigarettes, and having a curb party. I yelled down that they needed to shut up, get off the couch, and move on. They actually asked if I would at least let them take the cushions. I told them they could, but they had to go away. They were so happy to have the cushions. Each of them grabbed a cushion and started stumbling down the street. It kind of made me happy for them.

We never really cooked meals, but we did have a little countertop toaster oven to heat things up. Did you know there's a tray in the bottom that you are supposed to clean out every once in a while? I didn't. Well, not until that day. I was heating up some grub, chilling on our newer couch, watching some TV and started to smell something off. Not quite a burning food smell, more acidic than that. I peek in the kitchen, and that damn toaster oven was on fire! The white plastic was now tan and becoming distorted. The handle on the door looked like a sad clown face. This was an ECS, an Emergency Crisis Situation for sure. What the hell would I do? I was thinking, *It's gotta go. Go now!* I opened the front door, ran back to the kitchen, grabbed a hand towel, unplugged the very unhappy toaster oven, and ran. As I was running to the door, the edge of the hand towel was beginning to join the fire party. Really, it was only seconds before I got outside to dump it on the curb, but it felt like hours. The hand towel was now completely engulfed with the toaster oven. I was standing there, thankful our house isn't on fire, thankful my hands didn't get burned, thinking I should probably go get some water to put out the fire. There was a bum stumbling in my direction. I was thinking, *He's going to ask if everything is okay*, but instead, he pulls a cigarette out of his filthy pocket, leaned over, and lit it with the burning toaster oven. Never even looked at me, never said a word. Just stood back up and kept on stumbling down the street. What the what? Well, you don't see that every day. Watching how nonchalant he was calmed me right down. Everything was going to be all right. I'm also curious if this was one of the bums that got a couch cushion.

My job at the bakery was going pretty good. I even got promoted to shift manager. Mo' money, mo' money! Now I didn't have to choose between lunch and meth. I could eat my cake and snort it too. Even though technically, I didn't eat lunch because of the meth. But I could, though. As the saying goes, "All good things come to an end," as did the job I liked. The bakery needed a new general manager and hired this guy who was freshly graduated from college with a degree in restaurant management. It only took a couple of days for him to settle in. You all know the type: Disgusting, Insensitive, Careless, Know it all. Let's call him Dick for short. Come to find out, Dick came from a wealthy family, never actually worked a day in his life. How is that even possible? Picked restaurant management because, and I quote, "He liked to eat out a lot." Seriously? I just loved the fact that I got paid less to teach Dick how to do his job. Which was a waste of time anyway since he had everybody and anybody do it for him. All he did was walk around holding a clipboard and drinking coffee. Until he found his new favorite game to entertain himself. He would throw those little plastic creamer cups on the floor and step on them. I'm not sure what the best part for him was. Did he like being able to boss us around into cleaning them up or was it watching us girls have to bend over to clean up the mess? Maybe both. Didn't matter, it was still a dick move. And he did it every single shift, at least once, usually more.

I stopped at the neighborhood bar after one of my shifts with Dick and was bitching about how much I hated my boss. Drowning my sorrows with a cold beer, an opportunity was presented to me. The bar needed a daytime bartender. The job was mine if I wanted it. Yes. Yes, I did. I told Dick I quit that next morning, and yes, I squished a creamer on the floor on my way out. Told Dick that was his mess to clean up now. Ahhh, the look on his face gave me huge pleasure.

LIFE LESSON #631

Simple decisions can have hard consequences.

I started working at the bar the next day. The owners were the typical older South Philly Italian couple. S ran the bar; hubby B only came in once in a while. The pay wasn't great, but the drugs were pretty much free. So was an after-shift beer or two. Hard not to like a job with benefits. It was a pretty easy job. The day shift wasn't that busy but busy enough not to get bored. I liked it except for this one regular customer. He came in every day and drank all afternoon. He was quiet, never really tried to strike up a conversation, never looked me in the eye, never tipped, always left at 3:00 on the dot. It was odd. He was odd. I was asking another customer what his deal was, and they said that's how he's always been and that he left at 3:00 to go to work. Say what now? He drinks all day and then goes to work? What does he do? He drives a cab! Oh, hell no! He's going to kill someone. Not on my watch. I took matters into my own hands and began a secret campaign for him to find a new bar. I began putting Visine eye drops in his beers. You can't smell it, you can't taste it, and it doesn't make your beer flat. It does give you the shits though. I started out slowly, a beer here and there, but he kept coming in. I had to amp up the campaign. Every beer, every time, every day. It took about a week and a half before he stopped coming in regularly. When he would pop in every once in a while, I would dose him down with more Visine. He stopped coming in altogether. I was good with that.

Christina and I went over to S and B's house every so often to hang out. Those were good days. They always had huge amounts of drugs and didn't mind sharing. I had my own system of doing meth. I liked to do a medium-sized line to start with and then small bumps

62

here and there. Other people like to do one gigantic line. It's a personal preference thing. Plus, I always saved the straws that we used and the empty baggies the drugs were in. You know, just in case.

I went home every once in a while to see my mom and hang out in the suburbs with my brother. On one of those weekend visits, Dave and I went to the bar on Friday night and had a nice, calm evening. Got up Saturday, took a shower right after Dave, realized I forgot to grab an extra towel to wrap around my head, so I grabbed Dave's used towel. No biggie. Funny fact, unbeknownst to me, Dave had crabs. He never said anything the night before. I'm not sure how that would come up in conversation, but he could have at least said he was itchy or something. So now in my personal resume, I have to say that I caught crabs from my brother. Totally Jerry Springer. Dave went to the doctor to get some special shampoo; he used half of it and gave the rest to me. I used it; everything was taken care of. There was a little left in the bottle, so I wrapped it up in a small brown paper bag and shoved it in the back of one of my dresser drawers. Forgotten.

Everything was going good. Working hard, playing harder. Just doing my thing. Reebok came out with these new red high-top sneakers. I'm not usually the kind of girl that has to have the latest and greatest. But these? I had to have some. I simply could not survive another day without these shoes. One of the downfalls of being a bartender is that cash is hard to save. You can always make more tomorrow. So I took my last fifty dollars in cash and went out and bought me some of those beautiful red Reeboks. Talk about "run faster, jump higher" sneakers—these were the shit! I could fly! They made me feel so cool. That night, after buying my new Reebok's, I slept over at a friend's. We stayed up late drinking and doing a little bit of drugs. Nothing special. I had all my crap in a big brown paper bag with handles. Walked home in the morning and threw the bag on my bedroom floor. I had the day off and was planning on going back to sleep, deal with the dirty clothes in the bag later. The phone rang. It was B, S's husband. He was telling me that he and S had a huge fight the night before, the bar is a mess, and S was going to call me to come in and help her clean it up. He told me, "No matter what, *do not go in.*" Okay?

Sure as shit, next call was from S. She tells me a different version of the fight, and in her version, B got so mad he took an axe to the bar. She needed me to go help clean up. I explained that B had already called, told me about the fight and to *not* go in. I was telling her about how I didn't want to be in the middle of this one and I didn't know what to do. So now she was asking me to meet her at the curb to get her collectable crystal figurines because B was smashing them. I knew she collected that crap, so I agreed. About ten minutes later, there was a honk under my window. I leaned out to make sure it's her and she told me to bring a bag. I figured she has lots of crystal crap, and the first bag I saw was the bag I just came home with my dirty clothes in it. Running down the stairs, bag in hand, I grabbed a bag of chips. Out the door I went with a bag of chips in one hand and my brown bag of dirty clothes in the other. S was parked right out front of our little house, and she had a passenger I don't know. S was in a tizzy, going on about the fight, how B smashed her stuff at home and then moved on to the bar. I was barely tracking, had been up all night drinking and doing some meth. I just needed a nap. Anyway, she started loading the bag, which I was holding up to the window, with crystal salt and pepper shakers, some figurines—I lost interest. I was talking to the passenger about my new red Reeboks, shoving chips in my face. I wanted to show off my new sneakers, so I put the big brown bag down on the curb, walked around to the passenger side, and had my leg up in the air, showing off my shoes. I was standing in the middle of the street, with my leg up in the air and a mouth full of chips.

That's the exact moment I got arrested, for the second time. Cops came running from everywhere, pointing shiny pistols at our heads and screaming *"Freeze!"* Like leg up freeze? Or leg down freeze? And those once delicious sour cream and onion chips I was shoving in my mouth turned to sawdust in an instant. *Holy. Shit. What is happening here?* We all got handcuffed and marched back into my house. One by one, we were taken behind an opened closet door to be patted down by a female officer. Then we were told they got an anonymous tip that a huge drug buy was going down. They had been tailing S all morning. B must have called, and that's why he told me *not* to go in to work. It was supposed to be going down at the bar, but S made a pit stop at my house first. Shit. At least there wasn't a drug buy going on. Surely, all this would be cleared up any minute. Except now they wanted to search my house from top to bottom. Lucky for me, I spent my last fifty dollars in cash on the glorious red Reeboks. I am now wearing with handcuff accessories. Lucky because I didn't have any cash left to buy drugs the night before and spent some time scrapping all those leftover baggies and straws I had been collecting for a quick fix. I had nothing in my room but was concerned about my roommates.

There were cops everywhere, going through everything. About twenty minutes into the search, a cop yelled that he got something on the second floor. They asked whose room that was, and it was mine. They marched me, still handcuffed behind my back, up the teeny tiny stairs and right into my room. Well, shit. Did I forget something? Did I miss a bunch of extra drug baggies? The cop was standing next to my dresser, wearing a huge "gotcha" smug face, as he made a show of reaching into the back of my dresser drawer. He pulled out this small brick-shaped item, nicely wrapped in a small brown bag. Oh, no! He pulled out a prescription bottle of crab shampoo, prescribed to my brother. The "What the fuck?" look took over his smug face in an instant. Priceless.

My house is clean, but I was still getting loaded into the back of a cop car on my way to jail. Why? When we got to the jail, the cops uncuffed us individually and recuffed us together. S was on one end, I was in the middle, and the passenger was on the other end. So S had a free hand and the passenger had a free hand; I didn't have any free hands. The passenger was getting pissed and started yelling at S. Pretty soon, those two started duking it out. I was being thrown around like a rag doll. There was nothing I can do. Thankfully, it didn't last long, but my wrists were toast. They threw us in separate holding cells. Jail sucks. These were the cells where you waited to be booked. There were rows of cells, all bars, a small bench in each and a metal toilet. If you had to pee—or God forbid, poo—everyone could see you, including the guards. Jail sucks. Hours later, we were put in front of a judge. I was released on my own recognizance and scheduled to meet with a public defender days later. I don't know what happened to the other two. Meeting with the public defender is when I learned there were 3½ ounces of cocaine in the brown bag, along with three thousand dollars in cash and various crystal figurines. Fan-fucking-tastic. However, they wouldn't charge me if I agreed to testify against S and B. They thought there was no way I could have known what was in the bag because I was stupid (yes, the word they used) enough to place the bag on the curb and walk around to the other side of the car, leaving it unattended. I also learned that day that B was a low-level mob guy who was running some illegal gambling machines. I think they only wanted him so they could squeeze information from him to get higher. I don't know. And the IRS was interested in S, and they knew she was selling drugs through the bar. Reluctantly, I agreed. I didn't want to go to jail for something I didn't even know about. I didn't think there was much I could tell them, though.

I left that meeting feeling very uneasy. I started thinking I was being followed. Could have been drug paranoia. Maybe not. I swear there was a guy watching my house. Good guy? Bad guy? No idea, but I figured it was time for me and my red Reeboks to leave the city for a while. Hi, Mom, I'm home!

Back in the 'burbs. No job, no money, no car, no drugs. Life sucks.

I had to notify the local police about my situation in the city, so they were making extra rounds in front of my house. This did not help me score any drugs.

Eventually, I ran into Christina's old high school boyfriend, J. J was a meth head and could hook me up. We started hanging out a lot. As friends only. I'm not even sure we should classify it as "friends." We did drugs together. We didn't go to the movies. We didn't go to dinner. We didn't have in-depth conversations about life or feelings or the future. We got high together. And he was a good "doctor." So I was back to shooting up again. Yeah, me. I don't think he even worked—can't really remember—but he was still living in his childhood bedroom, doing drugs all day. He used to make himself eat ramen noodles with frozen veggies in it for vitamins. A healthy diet is important for someone who shoots up meth all day! Like a few frozen peas and carrots are really going to make any difference.

My life was at a total standstill. I looked like shit; the trial was coming up soon, I needed a job, and every day was exactly the same. Wake up, if I slept at all, do drugs, hang out, repeat.

Dave would come home from college here and there, which always cheered me up. My dad and his new wife came to visit me. I still had a chip on my shoulder when it came to my dad, but he was trying. Nancy, his new wife, was really sweet, kind, and patient. She was very supportive and respectful to my mom. She was nothing like my mom, which was probably the point for my dad. She never complained about the extra money Dad gave my mom or us, for that matter. I didn't like her. It wouldn't have mattered if my dad had married Princess Diana at that point. I wouldn't have liked her either. It is what it is. People change, though. They grow, they see things from different perspectives, they learn. She is all the things I said she was. The same exact reasons I hated her then is why I love her now. It just took some time.

Trial day came. My nerves were shot. It didn't help that I couldn't do a bump of speed because I didn't want to be all wiry in court. I couldn't smoke a joint and be all paranoid. It was all natural, and that was not my norm. Sitting up on that stand, everyone staring at me, including S, who by the way looked like shit, was a horrible moment in time. My mouth was so dry. I felt like I could throw up and pee my pants at the same time. They were throwing questions at me. Some irrelevant, some not so much.

Asking me how the bar operated on a day-to-day basis. "I don't know—I'm just a daytime bartender."

Asking about the books. "I don't know—I don't do the books."

"Where do they keep the books?"

"Which books?"

"There's two sets." A whole new barrage of questions. I should be trying to protect my own ass, but honestly, I'm a shitty liar. Always have been. Don't get me wrong, I still try sometimes, but I usually tell on myself. Do I sell drugs for S? No! I have handed specific people specific packs of open cigarettes. I never looked in them; I've never taken money for them. I don't know who lives upstairs or anything that goes on up there. I've never been there.

Questions about the day I was arrested started coming up. Then that damn big brown paper bag got brought out. The one I placed on the curb. It had been a good six months since I'd seen that bag. To verify that it was my bag, a very well-dressed man began pulling out items from the bag. In front of a room full of strangers, he pulled out a T-shirt. "Is this yours?"

"Yes."

"A pair of shorts?"

"Yes, mine."

"A pair of dirty, balled-up socks?"

"Mine."

And finally, a pair of dirty, unwashed, black lace panties that had been packed at the bottom of a brown paper bag for six months. He used a pencil to fish them out and hold up for the entire court-room to see. "Ah, yes. Mine."

I had found a new level of embarrassment. The rest of my time on the stand was a blur. All I could think about is that a group of strangers had just seen my dirty underwear hanging from the tip of a pencil, swinging back and forth to make sure everyone got a good look. The only positive point is that they were grown up undies and not my white cotton daily mood underwear from the past.

Now that the trial is over and I wasn't in jail or dead, it was time to get back on track. First things first, move my stuff out of the row house. Move-out day was just the same as move-in day, just in reverse. All the big stuff out the windows tied to ropes. It was much easier lowering stuff down instead of trying to hoist it up. And bonus, if it fell to the sidewalk and smashed to pieces, I didn't really care. All the big stuff was loaded, and Mom and I were now boxing up the rest, making trips up and down the narrow, crooked stairs out to the car. Several trips in and a very nice young man came pedaling up on his bike asking if we needed some help for a couple of bucks.

Hell, yeah. I could respect a kid trying to earn some cash and things would go way faster. The three of us head upstairs, we each packed a box and trudged back down to throw them in the VW parked on the curb. Second trip up went about the same. The kid finished packing his box before we did and headed back down. We were done a few minutes later and on down. The box of art supplies the kid packed was in the middle of the living room floor. What the hell? The kid was gone. And so were our wallets. Dammit! We were so stupid. He looked like such a nice kid. There went that judging someone by the clothes they wear thing. In our defense, thieves don't usually wear black T-shirts that read "Got wallets?" What really pissed me off was that my drugs were in there! The city and I definitely needed a break.

Dad helped me get a used car so I could get a job. Back in the days when I was working in the Jewish deli, we had a great manager named H. She was very kind and sweet. Turns out, she was now managing a new pasta restaurant not too far from where I lived. She got me a waitressing gig there. It was a good job, the place was busy, our stations were of good size, and there was money to be made. H treated me like a little sister. Remember how I mentioned dating a "real guy with a real job"? She's the one who hooked me up with him. I met him right after he was in a motorcycle accident where he lost his leg. The doctors tried to reattach it, but it didn't take. We dated right after they removed it. But like I said, I wasn't the right fit. He dumped me when I didn't want to go skiing. He met someone on the lift that weekend. Anyway, H could tell I was in a slump, so she invited me to go away with her and some friends one weekend for a beach getaway. Her friends were all super hot guys. Like, super hot. All beachy and tanned. They wanted to go water skiing. I'd never been water skiing, but I was game. H lent me this swimsuit that was really low cut in the front, high cut on the hips. Luckily, I was skinny as crap and had no boobs that could pop out.

We were in the boat; the guys were giving me a quick "how to." Sounded easy enough. I was in the water ten minutes later, got my life jacket on, got my skies on, tips up, waiting for the boat to take off. Things were going pretty good at first. I actually managed to get up. I was thinking, *I've got this!* Less than one minute later, I shifted backward and was being towed behind the boat feet front, hanging on to the rope with a death grip. That battle was soon lost. I was bobbing in the water like that dead dog from years ago, waiting for them to swing around to pick me up. I was wrong. When they plucked me out of the water, that low-cut swimsuit was all caddywompus, and both of my boobs were getting some sunshine. As an added bonus, the suit was shoved so far up my ass that Jesus himself could not have parted those waters. Not once during my quick "how to" lesson did anyone say "Let go of the rope if you fall." That would have been informative. I spent the rest of the weekend pissing sea water out of my ass. Water skiing is another activity on my to-don't list.

My brother graduated from Drexel with a degree in accounting. He was staying with us in the suburbs while he and his girlfriend looked for an apartment in the city. I loved having my brother around. We hung out all the time. What was nice about hanging with Dave was that there were no expectations. I could just be me, and he liked me anyway.

Dave, some of his friends, and I went to a club way out in the boondocks one night. I didn't know why we had to go to that specific club but whatever. I learned later he was trying to score some Quaaludes. We stayed for a while, had some drinks, Dave got his drugs, everyone was happy. Time to head home. I was driving since they were all stoned on Quaaludes. I felt like I had been driving way longer for the drive home than what it took to get there. Nothing looked familiar, but it was dark now. The boys were no help whatsoever for directions. I decided to pull over to find a payphone to call my mom for guidance. On the first call, some guy answered the phone, and I hung up. No man lived at our house; I must have dialed the wrong number. I called back, same guy. What the hell? Indignantly, I asked to speak to my mother. The guys were like, "I don't know your mother."

"Ummmmm, you're in my house. You better know her. Let me talk to her—*now!*"

He had the balls to hang up on me! I was going to try this one more time. I called back, and now the guy started asking me questions. "Who's your mom? Are you okay? Where does she live?"

I answered all his questions. On his last question, he informed me that he was in New Jersey. If I wanted to reach my mother, who lived in Pennsylvania, I needed to use an area code when I dialed her number. *Oh my god!* I was so lost that I had crossed state lines and didn't even know it! The boys, in their doped-up stupor, thought this whole situation was hilarious. I did not. It was about 3:00 a.m., and we were hours from home.

Things were going pretty well. I was making good money, staying at Mom's, no rent, plenty of extra dough for drugs, and even enough for a small stash of cash. I met another waitress at the pasta place, and we decided to get an apartment together. It was a cute little apartment. K was way more responsible with her money than I was. Plus she worked way harder than I did. She always took extra shifts and volunteered for the late lunch shift. That's the one waitress that stayed on after the main lunch rush, before the dinner servers came in. I quit waitressing and started hostessing full time. I was better at that, and it was better for me not to have cash on hand every day. K was super cute and smart with a bubbly personality. The perfect person for a waitress job. She met these guys who were in the oil business somehow. They made good money, tipped very well, and always had tons of drugs. She brought me into the fold of friendship. We would hit the bars as a group or sometimes go to their house to party. When they laid out lines of meth, they were huge lines. I couldn't do them like that. I went back to my old ways of stashing half of it in my cigarette cellophane for later. We had a lot of good times with those guys. They were married, but the wives rarely partied with us. We weren't involved in any kind of sexual relationships with the guys, but it still must have been odd for the wives.

I started dating one of my brother's old high school friends. S was a simple man with simple needs. He worked hard, drank a little beer, only did a little drugs, and cared for me. In general, I treated him horribly. When you believe you are nobody special, it's almost impossible to believe it when someone else thinks you are. Don't get me wrong, we had some really good days too. But when I was shitty, I was super shitty. Remember when I was talking about the guy from Scotland coming to visit? Well, my apartment with K is where I brought them, and S was the guy I was dating. S is the guy I told to stay away for several days while I visited with someone else. How rude was I? And he did it because he wanted to see me happy. I was mean.

S and I were doing good for a while, regardless of how mean I could be. He always wanted more than I was capable of giving. Then something big happened. I missed my period. They didn't have home pregnancy tests back then. You had to go to a doctor for a blood test. But I knew. I wasn't going to tell S until I was sure. I knew he would want to get married because that was the right thing to do. I made a doctor's appointment for a Tuesday. The Friday before that appointment, I was at work and not feeling so well. I went to the bathroom and passed a big bloody blob. And then began bleeding pretty good. I had a co-worker race me to the hospital, where I found out I was pregnant for the first time. Unfortunately, I had most likely passed the fetus and needed an emergency D&C. I was also told that I had O negative blood with the RH factor. Which meant if the baby's blood type didn't match my blood type, it usually ended with a miscarriage unless you got this special shot.

S made it to the hospital right after my D&C. He was crying over the loss of the baby, consoling me, and saying things about trying again. Thing was, I wasn't sad. I was relieved. God made the right decision that day. I was nowhere near capable of raising another human being, in any way. I'm not even sure if I could have made it through the pregnancy without doing drugs. Any child under my care during that time would have had a devastating future. I'm not saying that for everyone in that position; I can only speak for me. For me, all I can say is that sometimes God answers prayers that may not ever have been voiced.

But S was so sad. I couldn't take it. I felt so bad for him and yet happy for me. I had to walk away; we were in very different places in life. I hope he got to be a dad. I hope he was a good one.

Several weeks after my emergency D&C, the doctor I saw came into the restaurant. When I saw him come in, I was super embarrassed. All I could think was that this stranger had seen my vag! Hopefully, he wouldn't remember me. Thankfully, the hostess quickly showed him to a table. Unfortunately, he came walking back up to the hostess stand and tells me he doesn't like where he's been seated. Damn! I had to go move him to a new table. After I found something that makes him happy, he turned to me and said, "See, I take care of you, you take care of me." *Shit. He does remember me. And that, people, is why you never invite your gynecologist to a BBQ.*

Shortly after my miscarriage, my brother broke his leg pretty severely. He had a job at a big CPA firm in the city and an apartment with his girlfriend. He was playing in a company softball game trying to slide into base. His body slid; his leg did not. He had to have surgery to repair the damage. Two problems with his injury: He drove a stick shift car and couldn't work the clutch in a cast. So that one was an easy fix. We traded cars for a while. Funny thing though, I broke my right wrist shortly after the trade in a freak accident. I had to teach myself to cross body shift. The second problem with Dave's broken leg was way more serious. He was prescribed heavy pain pills after the surgery. He was instantly addicted. I know that even after his leg healed, he was always in a little bit of pain. The doctors kept refilling his prescriptions, but he never made it through the full thirty days before needing more. He was a functioning addict. Now we both had serious drug problems. Not a good family legacy.

I got the proud honor of getting K and me evicted to add to my personal resume. I'm sure she was secretly happy to be rid of me but not so happy with the inconvenience of how that went down. I wasn't the best roommate. Late on rent and bills, up all night, lots of visitors. I'm sure there's more than that. The eviction was technically but kinda, sorta not my fault. Our rent check did bounce. But I had to get new checks, which came in, and I started using them. One of which I used for the rent. What I didn't know was that the deposit slips were printed with one number off from my account. I never checked. Who does? Apparently, all my deposits were going into someone else's account, and my checks were coming out of my account which had no money in it.

The landlord came knocking on our door unannounced to see what was going on with the rent. When I opened the door, two cats came running to see who was there. K had a cat. I had a cat. We weren't supposed to have cats. The landlord was pissed. Two cats, no rent. I tried to say we were babysitting the cats for a friend, but I've always been a shitty liar. Poker is not my game. We got the eviction notice the following week. Back to Mom's with a cat. Hi, Mom, again. The bank did reimburse all my money eventually. They just had to mail it to a different address.

K and I had some really good times as roommates. We made a split decision to head to Florida for a long weekend once. It was dead of winter in Philly, and we needed a break from the cold. We stayed with a friend of hers. She had a couple snakes as pets that had the run of the apartment. Like seven-foot snakes. I was not privy to this information prior to our stay. I found out about the snakes the first morning I woke up on the couch with one of them slithering across me. That was a hell of a "Hi, how are you?" first thing in the morning. Not only did this friend of K's have gigantic surprise snakes as pets, but she also had a gigantic secret talent. We were driving around in the rental car and she had to pee. That girl managed to pee in an empty beer can without missing at all while K was driving, in a small rental car. That, my friend, takes talent. Or maybe just a lot of practice in which case, I don't want to know how things went in the beginning.

We also went to a Grateful Dead concert together. We each ate some magic mushrooms before the show. We were wandering around before the show started and ended up being asked if we wanted to go backstage. Why yes! Yes, we do! We walked through the buffet, danced on the stage, had an absolute blast! I was so high on the mushrooms. I kept thinking the people standing in front of me were openly having sex. K kept trying to tell me I was hallucinating, but I wouldn't listen. I had to go out for some fresh air. Problem was, I was too high to walk straight and couldn't find the car. I was playing bumper cars with my body. I even walked into a cop on a horse. Eventually, I found the car, but in my state at the time, I didn't think things through since I didn't have the keys. I don't know how long I sat on the bumper. Someone realized how screwed up I was and gave me some bread to eat to try to help absorb some of the magic mushrooms. I couldn't tell you if it helped or not. The next morning, my thighs had deep purple bruises on both legs right at the height of a car bumper. I heard some girl was super high at the concert, and at the end, she climbed the rail of the stadium, jumped off thinking she could fly, and died. Not sure if that is true. K was a good roommate, though. We had some good times while it lasted.

I didn't stay at Mom's for long. One of my old roommates and I found a beautiful apartment back in the city. It was a newly converted warehouse. Ground floor was a huge open space with a small galley kitchen. Gorgeous hardwood floors, brand-new fresh paint smell. Downstairs, two bedrooms and a bathroom. Rent wasn't bad either. I was still working at the pasta place in King of Prussia but still liked living in the city. The bonus with this apartment was the small parking lot around the back of the building. What we didn't realize when we signed the lease was how close the projects were. First time I got mugged was when I was coming home from work late one night. I parked my car in the convenient but dark parking lot, threw my purse over my head, cross body style, grabbed the rest of my crap, and headed toward the back door.

That night, at work, someone gave me a huge blow-up dinosaur balloon hanging from a string on a stick. I got across the parking lot and halfway up the steps to safety. He was such a good-looking young man. He politely told me to give him my purse. Of course I told him no. The next time he asked, he was not so polite. By the third or fourth go round of the "request and refusal" game, all manners had gone out the window. I was now being referred to as "bitch," and the request had turned into a demand. He was begging to grab at my purse, which hurts because it's on my neck. The whole time this push and pull thing was happening, that stupid dinosaur balloon was bouncing around like it was trying to grow wings and get the fuck out of there. That not-so-nice-anymore young man won. My purse strap broke. All that fuss over twenty dollars in cash, some tampons, and a small stash of drugs. I don't even know why I was fighting for it. The worst part is getting a new driver's license. MVD in any state is a pain in the ass.

The second time I got mugged was shortly after I got my license back. The old team got together for a girls' night out. A little drinking, a little drugging for me, a good time. My roommate and I caught a cab back to our apartment, and as soon as we got out of the cab, I was pushed down from behind. They grabbed my purse and kept running. It all happened so fast. This time I was pissed from the get go. I mean, I had just got my license back! I took off after him. I was not going to let this happen again. He was the rabbit, and I was the greyhound. Good thing I'm not a high heels kind of girl. I was doing pretty good keeping up with him until I realized I was smack dab in the middle of the projects. My feet skidded to a halt like a cartoon character on a dirt road. What the hell am I doing? What was the plan if I caught him? I didn't know where I was. I didn't know if he had friends. I was sure he was not just going to give my purse back and say he's sorry. It was time to throw the towel in on this one. Shit, another round at the MVD. We didn't renew our lease on that apartment. Back to Mom. Again.

Christina and I saw less and less of each other. She finished school. Got a good job. Got married. I was at the wedding, and eventually, she had a beautiful daughter. She moved on in life. I stayed stuck in stupid. Still doing drugs. Still making bad choices. Still not putting any value on myself, my life, or my future.

The one positive thing I can say is that I always went to work. No work, no money. No money, no drugs. An odd but effective motivator. I actually got promoted to a manager. More money, more drugs. Sometimes being a restaurant manager is not a glorious job.

H quit shortly before I got promoted. The manager was always the last to leave at night. We had the typical security system by the back door. Last one out punches in the security code on the keypad right next to the back door and has thirty seconds to get out before the alarm engages. H was the last one out one night. She punched in the code and pushed open the door to leave, but someone knew the routine. They waited outside by the door; when it was pushed open, they pushed her back in. Door shut. Alarm set. None the wiser. I've heard the stories about what happened that night, but those aren't mine to tell. I just know that she never stepped foot in that restaurant again, and I can't blame her. I also know, the next day, heavy-duty security lights were installed above the back door and parking lot. A peephole was put in the door, heavy-duty locks were installed on the inside of the office door and a panic alarm under the desk. I also know how horrible we all felt.

Most of my stories involve impossible customers. This was back in the day when people could smoke in the restaurant. The smoking section at the pasta place was near the front by the bar. Which I never really understood because the non-smokers had to either walk through or pass by the smoking section. But the whole restaurant was basically open with four-foot walls designating different areas. I had a secret rule: if a customer came in and was rude from the get go and a non-smoker, they got seated as close to the smoking section as possible. It was my way of giving someone the invisible finger!

Working with the general public is always interesting and sometimes not in a good way. One day, I was standing up front by the hostess desk. This little old man came in the front door doing a fast shuffle, holding his butt and making a beeline for the men's room. I was thinking, *He's got a shitty situation going on.* A little while later he walks out, never making eye contact. I better go check things out in the men's room, before I even get there, I see a pile of poop on the hallway floor right in front of the men's room door. Fantastic. I get a very unhappy dishwasher to mop up the poo and inspect the men's room. Happy to announce, the men's room is fine. I'm surprised. A few days go by, poop puddle forgotten. Then we start having some plumbing issues. We would plunge the toilets; things would get better then start all over again. The owners had to call in the professionals. Real plumbers with real tools. They started snaking the drains, and lo and behold, guess what they fish out? A pair of old man underwear! That little old man flushed his underwear down the toilet! Why couldn't he have put them in the trash? I mean, he already shit in the hallway; how much worse could it get?

Speaking of poop, I went into the ladies' room once, and a woman had pooped all over the walls in one of the stalls. How? She literally had to have been bent over, with pants down and turning in a circle. It wasn't smeared on there. It was squirted on every wall and the toilet. I don't get it. I understand people have accidents, but don't you at least aim for the toilet? I can't even describe the level of unhappy that dishwasher was.

We had a small kitchen fire one night, and the ventilation system failed. The restaurant started filling up with smoke—thick, choking smoke. People just sat there. The fire engines showed up to make sure all was well, and people just sat there, eating. Seriously? Is your dinner so good you're willing to die for it? There were fire engines parked out front, lights blaring, front doors propped open for fresh air, where smoke was still pouring out, and people were still coming in to eat. If it were me, I would have picked a different restaurant that night.

Another time, a customer unfortunately had a heart attack right in front of our hostess stand. One of our waitresses was performing CPR and mouth to mouth while waiting for the ambulance to arrive. People were actually getting irritated that they were taking so long to be seated. They had to walk by the woman on the floor. They could see there was an emergency happening, and they didn't seem to care. I found it shockingly coldhearted.

Oh! I got spit on once. A big family group came in for dinner. They ordered appetizers and drinks from the bar. They all ordered big entrees and enjoyed every last bite. The bill comes, and all of a sudden, there's a fly in their salad bowl. They demanded to see a manager and didn't want to pay for anything. I looked at the said fly. It was not covered in dressing, so it was never mixed in. It looked like it was placed on top. Front and center so it couldn't be missed. And they didn't want to pay for anything?! I didn't think so. I offered to take off the appetizers or get them some dessert on the house. But I would not comp the entire check. That did not go over well. Not well at all, in fact. Things escalated so fast. They started batting around the empty dishes like a two-year-old that didn't get a lollipop. In hindsight, I shouldn't have said that out loud. That's when the guy spit on me. Right in the face. How mature. I called the cops, didn't take anything off the check or give them dessert. I also told the cops to suggest that they leave the waitress a very nice tip since I wasn't pressing charges…yet.

Then we had a tragic day. We had a gal that worked a special area up front. It was the pasta station. We made fresh pasta almost daily. We made regular noodles and spinach noodles. The customers loved watching her make the pasta. Especially the kids. And she was really sweet, explaining the process, answering questions, engaging the kids. It was nice. The machine itself was very large and had a huge hopper up top that held all the semolina flour and other ingredients. There was a bar that ran through the center of the hopper that had intermittent spokes on it to mix all the ingredients together before being squeezed out in wide, flat sheets ready to be cut. When you lifted the clear lid of the hopper, the machine automatically shut off. On that day, she had made a batch of spinach noodles earlier and was working a batch of regular noodles. She saw a piece of spinach in the mix and didn't want to ruin the batch. She lifted the lid, reached in the hopper to grab the spinach, and somehow the machine malfunctioned and started up. A spoke poked through her arm and started twisting it around the center bar. I heard it made two and a half revolutions before quitting. I'll never forget that scream. Employees came running from every direction. Customers kept eating. She was a short gal and began to pass out from the pain which pulled on her arm. One of the cooks stood behind her, holding her up until 911 arrived. I remember her looking me in the eye and asking if she was going to be okay. It was probably the only time I got away with a lie. I told her yes even though I wasn't sure. The medics showed up and decided they couldn't risk giving her any pain medication and have her droop even further. They also decided they were not going to be able to get her arm free where they were. The helicopter took off with the gal and a big part of the pasta machine still attached to her arm. She lost her arm that day. They never could get her it detached. After the helicopter took off, people were coming in all excited from watching it take off. We couldn't reciprocate their enthusiasm. None of us were able to function properly. None of us really cared what they thought. The general public is a fickle bitch.

I started dating one of the dishwashers. We were just having fun at first. Very casual. It slowly became more. He came from a jacked-up family. Both of his parents were gone; he had a sister somewhere, but they didn't see each other much. My mom *hated* him. She thought he was a complete loser. I thought I could fix him. He didn't have a car and moved in with me to ride to work together. Mom was not thrilled with that at all.

One night, after I was done working but Rick wasn't, I drove another employee home and went in for a quick beer. I was sitting on the floor, drinking a beer, when their English sheepdog came into the room. I love dogs. Dogs usually love me. Not this dog. Out of the blue, the dog lunged at me and bit me in the face. Twice. The employee was freaking out, apologizing for his dog. He loaded me in my car and took me back to the restaurant to get Rick. I walked in the back door, and everything froze. I hadn't looked in the mirror, but I guessed it was bad. Plus, I had blood all over my shirt. All I knew was that I tasted blood in my mouth and I was having a hard time seeing out of one of my eyes. Rick raced me to the hospital where I underwent emergency plastic surgery to repair my eye and my lips, which were both ripped and shredded. I eventually sued and won a couple thousand dollars, which I used to pay off the medical bills. The extra went up my nose.

All my friends were getting married, and my brother got married, so when Rick bought a used ring from a pawnshop and asked me to marry him, I said yes. I'll never forget telling Mom the news. I called her and said, "Guess what."

She immediately said, "You broke up with Rick!"

I told her no, that we were actually getting married. Things went radio silence. "Hello?"

Mom finally responded with "Oh, God. Now I have to hug him." That should have been a sign for me.

I got married for the first time in a quickie courthouse ceremony wearing black pants, a white shirt, and a black jacket. Mom came; she did hug him, and she left quietly shaking her head.

I joke about the fact that at the wedding, I said, "I do," and Rick said, "I don't want to work anymore" because he didn't. I would have been okay with that if the house was clean, laundry done and dinner ready, but that was not the case. I'm not sure what the hell he did all day except wait for me to get home with the drugs and beer. I thought I could fix him. I thought if I loved him enough, he would become a better person. I thought he just couldn't find the right job. I thought he just needed some time and support and everything would work out. I understood he didn't want to be a dishwasher forever. I thought he was trying to better himself. Hehehehe!

We got an apartment for a while, but it was hard for me to keep up. It was tough to be the only one paying rent and bills and pay for all the drugs by myself. We managed, but there wasn't any extra for anything extra. Just to get out of the apartment one night, we decided to drive around and drink a few beers. One thing led to another. We were getting a little buzzed, a little frisky, and thought it would be a good idea to pull off the road into a cornfield to fool around. I had a small truck at the time. We started in the cab but quickly needed more space. Abandoning the cab, we got in the truck bed. It was such a beautiful night. The stars were shining, the moon was high, and we were going at it like two bunnies. All of a sudden, the beautiful night sky was filled with flashing red and blue lights.

I got arrested for the third time with my pants off and socks on, in the middle of a cornfield. How did they even find us? Did the high moon turn Rick's shiny white ass into a beacon of light? Turns out, there was a farmhouse a little deeper in the corn. They saw our lights enter the corn but never leave. Shit. Didn't think about that. The cop tells us to get dressed, but our clothes were in the cab of the truck. We only had our underwear in the bed with us. As embarrassing as it was to be standing in front of a cop only wearing a T-shirt and underwear, it was worth it. We had been drinking; we had open beers in the truck and should be getting a DUI. But for the fact that the keys were in Rick's jeans pocket and the jeans were not in our possession. I'll take that technicality standing in my underwear any day. We did get arrested for public indecency. How public is a cornfield? My truck got towed because neither of us were in a position to drive, and we were brought back to the apartment in separate police cars. I didn't know that the back seat of a police car is hard plastic, but I guess that makes them easier to wash.

Valentine's day rolls around, and I thought it would be really sweet if I got his name tattooed on my hip as a sign of my support and love. I got a rose with his name tattooed across it as a surprise. When I got home and showed him my gift, his response was, "Wow! You're the first person to ever get my name professionally tattooed on them." Seriously? I'm an idiot.

I started letting Rick drop me off at work and take the truck "to look for work." He wrecked the side of it one night. He said he was trying to avoid a deer. I believed him at first. Of course, that wasn't the truth. He was drunk. But I went with the deer story for insurance. After paying the deductible, I fell behind on the rent and bills. I couldn't do it all by myself. We had to move back to Mom's. That's when things started to go to shit.

He did absolutely nothing all day except hang out with friends, drink beer, and do drugs. We started fighting all the time. I worked fifty hours a week and he couldn't even make the bed? After he was so drunk the night before and pissed the bed? I would still have to come home and deal with that. He would get mad when I didn't split the drugs evenly. I always saved an extra bump for work the next day, and he didn't think that was fair. Really? When I was at work one night, he got a DUI. I told him not to go anywhere that night because we didn't have any money for him to be tooling around, goofing off. But I still got a phone call to bail him out. I caught a ride to my car and then headed over to the police station. After talking to the police, I decided to leave his ass in jail. That did not go over so well when he got home.

Then money started missing from the account. Little bits here and there at first. Then one day, he cleaned out the account. When I got home, he was drunk as shit, sitting with a friend who was also drunk, and there was a huge bag of meth on the table. I don't know what happened. I was so mad I literally saw red. I'm yelling about the money and the drugs while he was sitting there with this smirk on his face. He's trying to act like a big shot in front of his friend, and it was pissing me off. Then he had the balls to say, "Shut the fuck up, you stingy bitch."

I popped. Before I knew what I was doing, I reached out and slapped him. He popped. Instantly, I knew I had made a mistake. How dare I disrespect him in front of his friend? He got up, and I got to running. The only thing that saved me was the fact that he was only wearing socks and no shoes. We had hardwood floors, and he was having a hard time getting any traction. But he was right on my ass. Even got hold of the back of my shirt for a second. I reached the bedroom and locked the door with a mere second to spare. He was banging and kicking at the door, screaming how he was going to kick my ass. Mom was downstairs, screaming about calling the cops. I was terrified he was going to get through the door. His friend was trying to calm him down. It was a mess. He eventually calmed down and agreed to go have another beer with his friend. I slept with the door locked that night.

The next morning, he was all apologetic. He was drunk, I shouldn't have slapped him, yada, yada. I start thinking he's right. It was my fault. I should have handled things better. I deserved it. I would do better.

Mom took a vacation out to Arizona to see her brother. When she came home, she announced she was going to pack everything up, sell the house, and move to Arizona. Rick and I decided we were going too.

It took some time to get the house ready, go through everything, decide what to keep, sell, throw away. Moving was a pain in the ass, but we were finally ready. I gave the pasta place a one-month notice. They had been good to me. I figured two weeks to find someone and two weeks to train.

The plan was that we would pack all the big stuff in a U-Haul, Mom would drive that out to Arizona, and I would stay behind to finish out my notice. Then we would pack what we had to live on in my little truck and head out in a couple of weeks. But two days before the U-Haul was scheduled for, I was at work thinking about how shitty my relationship with Rick was and wondering what was going to be so different in Arizona. Nothing, nothing would change. Same people, different scenery. I hadn't fixed him at all, and I was tired of trying. In fact, he was making me worse. I got home from work and told him I was going; he was not. Shit hit the fan. Not only was he mad about not going with me, but he was also mad that his stuff was packed in with mine. My brother, his wife, Mom, and I spent the next day frantically going through all the boxes for his stuff. He was not being helpful. He was way too busy stomping around, acting like an idiot. But we got it done!

I had two weeks before leaving. The first week was spent at the house, but Rick kept showing up unannounced, begging me to change my mind. It was horrible. I spent the next week sofa surfing at friends' places. I had no idea where Rick was staying, and I didn't care.

He kept showing up wherever I was. It didn't matter if I was at a friend's or at a bar—there he was. I don't know how he knew where I was unless he was watching me, and it really started to scare me. I remember a story he told me when we first got together about his mother. She was at a bar doing a flaming shot. Someone bumped into her, and the flaming shot splashed on her chin and chest, burning her pretty badly. She thought the bar should pay for the medical bills. The bar didn't. Rick thought it was funny how that bar burned to the ground a couple weeks later. Wink, wink. I never met his mother, so I don't know if that's true, but nonetheless, I was still scared and my nerves were shot. The next time he showed up unannounced, I told him he needed to quit. I wasn't changing my mind. He leaned in to kiss me, but I turned my head. So he bit me on the neck. Hard enough to draw blood. I couldn't take it anymore; I called Mom.

Mom flew in two days later to drive with me to Arizona. She was there for moral support. She said she had just taken this drive and everything was going to be okay.

LIFE LESSON #1236

Mothers are full of shit sometimes. Everything was not okay.

Day 1. Mom got us so lost we took a tour of the entire state of Pennsylvania.

Day 2. Finally crossing the Ohio state line, I threw a picture of Rick and I out the window as a gesture of washing my hands of him. I call this my "starter" marriage. It only lasted a few years. Thank God we never had kids. I never have to see his face again.

Mom locked the keys in the truck at a rest stop with my cat in the back seat.

Day 3. A little lost again, Mom went to back up to turn around and slammed a pole, denting my bumper and tailgate.

Day 4. Final night of the journey, hopefully. Mom picks out a cheap hotel for the night. My cat was oddly obsessed with the mirror on the dresser that faced the two beds. The cat kept staring in the mirror and pawing at it. It was weird. The next morning, we were walking to the truck, and the door to the room next door to us on the side where the mirror was, was wide open. There was all this video equipment set up. What the hell? Was that a two-way mirror? Is that why my cat was acting so goofy? They must have been seriously disappointed when Mom and I checked in!

Day 5. Arizona!

*****

Arizona, here we are! It's a dry heat, they say. Bullshit! It's hot! My truck didn't have air-conditioning. Arizona is so different from Pennsylvania in so many ways. Everything in Pennsylvania is really green. The summers are humid, and the winters are really cold. Most of Arizona only has three seasons. Really hot, not as hot and hot. Everything in Arizona has spikes or thorns. Or both spikes and thorns. And there's so many rocks. Big rocks, small rocks, red rocks, round rocks, and even rocks stacked on rocks. Why is that? Even the clouds seem closer to the earth. Another interesting thing about Arizona is that you can see rain but not get rained on. It can be raining from one cloud that you can see, but everything around that cloud is dry and sunny. A person can drive into the rain and right back out ten minutes later. They are also much more casual. It's okay to go to church in shorts. Not that I went to church. I wouldn't want to risk everyone's life around me when I got struck by lightning. Mom and I went to the zoo, and there was a lady there walking around with curlers in her hair. What was she getting ready for? She was already out and doing something! People in Arizona wear their pajama bottoms and fuzzy slippers to the grocery store. That would never happen in Pennsylvania. They are way too uptight to allow that. And the first time I saw a man wearing a gun on his hip, I freaked out! I thought we were going to die right then and there. And the houses are different. Most of them are one level, with no basements. Or they have flat roofs. It's different.

Mom found us a three-bedroom house only a few blocks away from her brother and his family. Hello, Cuz! This was perfect because my stash of drugs was getting dangerously low. I needed to get my ducks in a row. First order of business: find a new supplier. Then unpack, learn my way around, and find a job. Cuz had gotten married, had a kid, and had a house right around the corner. I didn't know anyone in Phoenix and was totally relying on Cuz for an introduction to a new dealer. I'm sure he knew someone.

I started spending a lot of time over there. I would sit and shoot the shit with his wife, drink beer, and wait for Cuz. Luckily, I liked his wife. Spending time there was nice and peaceful. But Cuz was never there or he was busy or had friends over or was sleeping. I didn't know anyone else to get my drugs from, and weeks went by. I don't know if he was avoiding me on purpose or what, but that was the longest I had been without drugs since the day I started. Slowly, it became less and less important. Then one day, I didn't think about it at all. If Cuz had gotten me some drugs or introduced me to someone who could, I'm not sure where my life would be now. I probably would have never quit. Whether it was on purpose or not. Whether he knows it or not, Cuz saved my life, and I owe him a long overdue thank-you.

I started working one or two days a week with Steph, Cuz's wife, at a busy uniform store in the heart of Phoenix. I worked with her in the office. She was a bookkeeper, and I was helping her keep up with logging in uniform allowance balances. I hated it. I'm not a numbers person, I don't sit still well, and I'm a people person. A full-time sales position opened up out front, and I jumped on it. I knew zip about selling or fitting uniforms. But I was willing to learn, and I didn't have a problem asking questions. We sold uniforms to police, firefighters, postal workers, security companies, and more. If I didn't know something, I faked it. Eventually I got better. I listened and learned all about things like ballistic vests, pepper spray, fire boots. It was interesting. I was busy meeting new people, learning things, and I was doing it drug-free. It felt good. Life is so different when you're not living in the cycle of drug abuse. I could actually concentrate on the task at hand instead of always worrying about when and where I would get my next fix. Who knew?

Then I thought, *I quit meth, let's quit smoking.* That was tough. I threw out an open apology to all my co-workers before my quit date. I tried the gum, but it irritated my mouth. There weren't a lot of options back then, so I went cold turkey. One of the other sales-people I worked with was an older gentleman who was goofy and sweet. He became my target. If I became snippy—no, when I became snippy—he always became the brunt of it. He took it like a champ. I would snap at him, and he would come back with some encouraging words that would piss me off. That too, got easier. I quit doing meth and smoking right before my thirtieth birthday.

For me, it seems no good deed goes unpunished. Without the drugs and cigarettes, I started getting anxiety. Just a little at first. But it kept getting worse. More frequent, stronger, lasting longer. I began to learn my triggers and would avoid those things that I could. My world was getting smaller and smaller.

So I did what any normal person would do. I got a dog. A dalmatian puppy. Turns out, he was one of the dumbest dogs on the planet and partially deaf. Fun fact: dalmatians are born totally white and their spots don't start showing up until they are about three weeks old. One of his spots was right under one of his eyes, so if he was lying on the other side, you couldn't tell if his eyes were open or not. And he couldn't hear me calling him, so it was kind of frustrating. His first emergency vet visit was when he decided to eat rocks. I bought him all kinds of chew toys and playthings, but he opted for rocks. I didn't know he was eating them until he tried to poop them out. It wasn't going so well. He was in the backyard trying to poo and started yelping and whimpering. I raced him to the vet, where they took an x-ray and found a belly and intestines filled with rocks. They gave him some drugs to help him poop, and he needed to have a sleepover at the vet's so they could monitor him. The vet said I needed to spend the time he was gone clearing away any more rocks he could get to. Seriously? This was Arizona. There were fuck-ing rocks everywhere! I did the best I could. I had to cook and make him a special diet of rice, pumpkin, and chicken for a week. I didn't even cook for myself! I turned into a stalker on poop patrol. I think he started getting a complex because he started trying to hide when he had to poo.

Mom went back to Philly to visit Dave for a month, and that's when the dog really got busy since he had all day by himself to goof off. I never knew what I would come home to. He found a red sharpie to chew on one day. I came home and he looked like a three-year-old that got into Mommy's makeup—only Sharpie doesn't wash off. He wore that haphazard lipstick for a good week. Another time, I came home and gave him a kiss. The hair on the side of his face was all stiff and crunchy. What's up with that? Then I saw the chewed-up tube of super glue. I didn't even know I had any super glue. About a week later, he got something going on between his toes. They were all red and oozy. Back to the vet. Apparently, when he got into the super glue, he glued his toes together. I guess gluing his toes together wasn't as fun as he thought it would be, so he ripped them apart, tearing his skin and causing an infection. After a tough day at work, I couldn't wait to get home. Until I walked into a house scattered with white fluffy stuff. That damn dog entertained himself with the couch all afternoon. There was a very small hole in the center where he had fished all the stuffing out of the seat part and most of the back. I guess I ruined his party when I came home. It looked like a deflated air mattress.

Finally, Mom came home from Philly, and I thought his antics would stop, but it turned out, Mom was a horrible dog sitter. She was taking a nap on the new couch in the living room while the dog lay on the floor next to her, eating the carpet. This dog was driving me crazy and costing me way too much money. So I did what any normal person would do. I got another dog. I thought the new dog would keep him company, entertain him, and wear him out. Surprisingly, it didn't work. I eventually found him a new home through my work. One of the firefighters I waited on said he would take him. He had a stay-at-home wife and two older kids that could take the time to work with him. Thank you! Of course, now the dog I still had at home was lonely, so I went back to the pound to get him a buddy. These two were great. Calm, loving, and lazy. Perfect.

Meanwhile, my anxiety was becoming debilitating. I couldn't go through drive-throughs anymore. If there was already a car in front of me and then a car would pull up behind me, I was stuck. Instant panic attack. I had a tough time at the grocery store for the same reason when in the checkout line. In fact, any line, anywhere. I couldn't let anyone drive me anywhere because I couldn't trust them to stop when I needed them to. I hated going anywhere I wasn't familiar with. I wouldn't go anywhere that didn't have a public restroom I could hide in. Crowds were a no. Anybody standing directly behind me and not at an angle where I could see them out of the corner of my eye gave me panic attacks. Hell, even someone facing me but standing to close gave me panic attacks. I began having to psych myself up to go beyond the driveway. I couldn't even walk the dogs.

Something had to give. After all those years, I finally got myself into counseling. I went twice a week in the beginning. He prescribed me some anti-anxiety medication that I could take when I was having a panic attack. But I was afraid to take them given my history. We talked about everything. Some stupid stuff. Some really hard things. He taught me some techniques to use when I was having a panic attack. He taught me how to be nice to myself. My anxiety was backing off a bit, so I started going only once a week. It took a while to believe I didn't deserve what had happened to me all those years ago. The choices I had been making were a result of never dealing with that. They say to heal, you need to forgive. I forgive Mr. D's wife and kids for not helping me that night. I don't know what their lives were like. But honestly, I'm not sure if I forgive Mr. D fully. I want to believe I do, but I also don't want him to be able to go to the same heaven I go to. So? I don't know, do I? More importantly, I have forgiven myself. That was huge. I was carrying a lot of guilt about that night. I felt guilty for not saying no, for not stopping him, for not telling someone that day or the days after. I truly felt I deserved what had happened and it was my fault. I don't feel that way anymore. It's so easy to blame ourselves even when it's not warranted.

It took me two years to get my shit together. To get clean and confident, to quit smoking, work on my anxiety and the whys behind it all. I didn't date, and I didn't want to. Don't get me wrong, I still have anxiety issues. I still don't let too many people drive me anywhere. Crowds are a little sketchy, but they're not controlling my life like it used to be.

And my divorce was final. Of course, I had to pay for the whole thing because—wait for it—he didn't have a job. The minute I found out it was final, I ran to the store for supplies. I bought white shoe polish, white balloons and streamers. I decorated my truck, taping the balloons and streamers all over it. I wrote "Just Divorced" as big as I could across the back window in shoe polish. I got so many honks and thumbs up for the week I drove it like that.

I also got my wedding ring set resized to fit my middle finger. The snooty woman at the jewelry store was appalled when I explained what I wanted. I loved it. Sometimes it's the littlest things that give me the greatest joy.

Two years of being clean. One of the nice things about being clean and not spending all your extra money on drugs is that there is money to spend on other things. Like a brand-new car! I bought myself a brand-new, nobody-owned-it-before car. It was a sporty little stick shift Saturn. I loved it. It came with the new car smell and no stains on the upholstery. More importantly, it had air-conditioning. That is a major plus in Arizona. I originally thought I could go from my air-conditioned house to an air-conditioned job. Not the case. The "in between" was a major factor. Especially when you were stuck in traffic between the air-conditioned house and the air-conditioned job. I started to feel like a grown-up.

It was time to get back out there socially. I had been hanging out with one of my co-workers a lot and not so much with Steph anymore. Not that I didn't like her, but she was married with a kid and liked staying home. I was single, no kids, and wanted to do things. Go places. My co-worker was married too, but her husband worked the night shift. We went to jazzercise classes and went to the tanning salon. We went out for dinner and margaritas. We went places like Sedona to look in all the little shops. Sedona is beautiful with all the red rocks. We went to the Renaissance festival, which, come to find out, I am not a fan of. It's very crowded, and we all know how I feel about that. And it's expensive. I really don't want to walk around eating a turkey leg out of a paper basket. I really don't want to watch other people do it either. I'm not interested in any of the trinkets they sell or the music. I don't do rides. I think the costumes they wear are heavy and cumbersome. Plus, I always have to pee when the porta potties are on the complete opposite side from where I am. Some people really love the Renaissance festival and wait for it to come around every year. Not me. That's another thing on my "one and doner" list.

What's really weird is that during my two years of me time, no one even tried to ask me out. As soon as I was ready, guys started asking me out again. I went out on some dates here and there but wasn't quite ready for a real full-time relationship. My co-worker, T, set me up with a friend of hers. He was a really nice guy, super smart. Like nuclear engineer smart. He owned his own house that had a pool. It was nice. We went out on a few dates before I decided it was time to do the deed. Went to dinner, had a few drinks, and headed back to his house. We were starting to fool around, pants come off, and WTF is that? It was an inch-high private eye. Not joking. Okay, maybe two inches tops. I know it's not the baton, it's the conductor and all that, but he at least needs to have *a* baton! When I was thinking about getting back in the game, that was not my dream. Sorry. I didn't go out with him again. I heard a short while later that he got some chick pregnant and was planning on marrying her. Good for him, but all I could think was how far his little sperm had to swim to get that job done!

LIFE LESSON #601 (REVISITED)

All brains and no penis is as useless as
an empty pool on a hot day.

Then I met this slightly older man through my job. He was married.
Yes, I know it was wrong. He gave me the whole "my wife doesn't
understand me" routine. How his kid was almost eighteen and he
didn't want to get a divorce because he didn't want to pay child support. I'm sure I wasn't the first or the last. Regardless, I didn't care.
I wasn't married, and I wasn't asking him to leave his family. We
had a good time together. It was mostly based around sex. I secretly
nicknamed him "the lunker" because he was huge! This was exactly
what I needed at the time. Someone to do things with without any
expectations. And it stayed that way for some time until eventually, I
did want more but not from him. We had an understanding from the
beginning. Besides, if he did leave his family for me, how could I ever
trust him not to do the same to me later on down the road? Having a
long-term relationship that originated from an affair might work out
for a few people. Not me. I have enough trust issues.

I was at a tough age for dating, though. All the men I was meeting were either already married or older and didn't want to have any
more kids. Or worse, already had little kids. I didn't want to take
care of someone else's kids every other weekend. I wanted kids of
my own and didn't want a guy saying "I'm having another baby"
when it would be my first. Not to mention all that ex-baby mama
drama bullshit. Having said all that, my potential pool of possibilities
dropped by a good 75–80 percent.

Being in a relationship wasn't the top priority in life, but I was
always on the lookout. In walked this guy from a very small town in

western Arizona with a volunteer fire department in need of T-shirts. He was really tall, 6'6", totally up my alley. Very respectful, patient, and a no-nonsense kind of personality. I waited on him, placed the order with the screen printer, and told him it would be two weeks or so for the shirts to come back in. I'd never even heard of this town or met anyone from there.

But about a week later, another guy from this town walked in for a pair of fire boots. I waited on him too. Fire boots come with an option for a zipper up the front. If you want the zippers, it takes time and practice to lace them in. After the zippers are laced in, they need to be tightened and fitted to the individual's foot with a special tool. That's about thirty to forty minutes of conversation time. I started out with the usual "How's the weather?" bullshit before I started asking questions about the guy who ordered the T-shirts. I found out he wasn't married, never had been (Sweet! No baggage), no kids (no mama drama, check), not dating anyone (sold!). Boots guy said he'd tell T-shirt guy I was interested and asking questions. Good deal.

A week or so went by, and the T-shirt order came back from the screen printers. I called to tell him this, and he started telling me that boot guy was telling him that I was asking a bunch of questions about him. I told him that was true, and in a second of confidence, I asked if he wanted to go to lunch when he picked up his order and talk about it. He said, "Sure."

A week later, we went to lunch. I found out he lived in a very small, company-owned mining town. He worked at the mine for a living and had a passion for the volunteer fire department as a firefighter and EMT. I learned he had one younger brother and his parents had been married for a gazillion years. An all-around good guy.

We started seeing each other when we could, but he lived several hours away, worked rotating shifts, and volunteered at the fire department. We talked on the phone almost every day. He would come to Phoenix whenever he could, about every two or three weeks. We would head to the movies or out to dinner. He had a portable phone in his truck that I thought was really cool. It was the beginning of cell phones. This one was huge—it had a battery about the size of a bible, a full-size handset and keypad with a twelve-inch cord attached. I used it to call my mom once but there was a charge for every call made or received.

Mom went back to Philly to visit with Dave, so now I had an empty house. We hadn't been intimate yet but first things first. I had to tell the married man I had met someone I was interested in. Someone there might be a possible future with. He completely understood and didn't want to get in the way of my happiness. He still came in the store from time to time to say hi and see how things were going. But he was always respectful.

My conscience was clear. I've never been good at having two relationships at the same time. It's just too much work. I can't remember who I did what with or when. I've had a couple or even a few one-night stands in the same month but not relationships where real conversations happen. That's too much effort.

Will and I became an exclusive couple doing the long-distance thing. We tried to get together every weekend either in Phoenix or at his house. Will was not a fan of dogs, and I still had Ned and Buddy Stubs, so he liked it better when I went there.

The first time I went to his house for the weekend was a complete culture shock. Leaving Phoenix and heading to the mining town was all normal until I turned off the highway onto the road that cut over to the town. Don't blink because you'll miss the turn off! The road was about twelve miles long, very narrow, two lanes with a lot of hills, twists, and turns. Very little traffic except the occasional semi truck heading in or out of the mine. I came around one of the turns, and there were two cows in the middle of the road doing it. I literally had to come to a stop and wait for them to finish the dirty. That's not something you see every day. Back in drive, I went another couple miles and there was the biggest owl I had ever seen eating a dead snake in the middle of the road. That's not something you see every day either. Almost there, now in the middle of the road, was a rabbit that must have gotten run over. One ear was sticking up in the middle of a pile of guts like a birthday candle. What the hell? Where was I going, and did I really want to go there?

The town itself was tiny. There were two main streets. One went through the main part of town; the other turned off and led to the mine. The main street went by a small grocery store, post office, a small parts store, convenience store, and gas station. That's it. No traffic lights anywhere, only a stop sign. The rest of the streets went to housing, a few mom and pop shops, one bar, and a couple little places to eat. It was a company-owned town, meaning all the land, houses, and buildings belonged to the company. A person had to be a mine employee in order to rent a house. A few retirees owned their own mobile homes but not the land they sat on. And rent was cheap. A person couldn't drive through the mining town on the way to someplace else. You either aimed for it or you accidentally ended up in it. Very, very different from anything I was used to.

Everybody knew everybody and their kids. I was the new face in town and quickly became identified as Will's girlfriend from Phoenix. The more they saw my face, the less stares I would get. I was always afraid I had a piece of spinach between my teeth or a boogie hanging that I didn't know about. It was uncomfortable.

We spent some time doing things at the fire department, so people started getting to know me as me and not just Will's girlfriend. I wasn't there enough to make friends, but I knew people. Will wasn't a super social person, so it wasn't like he had a group of close friends to bring me into the fold.

After about two years of dating, we were on the phone talking one night, and I started asking where he thought our relationship was going, and he said he was happy with the way things were. I wasn't. Well, I mean, I was, but if this wasn't ever going to be more than what it was, I needed to move on. I was getting older, and I wanted a family in my future, and I wasn't willing to invest another two years if he didn't want those things too. We decided to get married. He picked out a beautiful engagement ring.

I got married for the second time, in January. We didn't have a huge church wedding. That's not my thing. I didn't buy an expensive wedding gown. That's also not my thing. I can't comprehend someone spending thousands of dollars on a dress you'd only wear one time for a few hours. The only thing I really cared about was that my dad got to walk with me.

I found a beautiful hotel in Prescott that had a gorgeous, curving staircase that led to a very large sitting room with a fireplace in the center. There was a bar off to the side that served beer and wine for anyone that wanted to buy some. I found a beautiful off-white gown at a high-end department store that was less than three hundred dollars. I kept the rest simple and cheap. Only one bridesmaid, I asked her to pick out whatever black dress she wanted that she thought she would wear again. Just a few red roses and baby's breath here and there for decorations and a 2:00 ceremony time. That way I didn't have to serve a big dinner, only finger foods and appetizers. And Will's aunt made the cake. For me, the goal was to get married, not pay for a huge, stressful party.

It was a nice wedding. My dad got to walk me down the stairs; my mom, my brother, and all my friends were there. And since it was huge, I got to visit and spend time with everyone. Some people got rooms at the hotel, and a bunch of us decided to go to a bar and listen to some country music. Dance a little bit, have a drink or two. It was fun.

I spent my wedding night with my head hung over the toilet in a very nice hotel suite. That was not fun. In my defense, I hadn't eaten for two days because I didn't want to look fat in the dress, and my brother gave me a valium right before the ceremony because I was so nervous about walking down the stairs and falling on my face in front of everyone. Will was not a happy camper. He wanted to make sure that was not going to be a regular kind of thing. It wasn't.

My first marriage, I tried to fix him. I thought with enough love and support, I could turn him into a decent man. That didn't go so well. This marriage, I was going to fix myself. I had a tendency to go overboard with things. Like that's not a blatantly obvious statement. Will is a rock. He is calm and steady. He is reliable and responsible. I was going to become those things. I was going to remain cool, calm, and collected. I was going to be normal. I was going to do normal things and have normal days. No more going overboard on anything.

I didn't move to the mining town on a full-time basis for about four months. Mom and I still had the house in Phoenix for the time being, so I worked three days a week at the uniform store. That gave us some time to pack up the house, find a place for Mom to live in Prescott, and figure out what to do with the dogs. As I said, Will is not a fan of dogs, but I didn't want to leave Ned behind. Mom said she would keep Buddy Stubs with her, and eventually, we found the perfect place. It was one half of a small duplex. Ground floor with a big side yard but it wasn't fenced. No biggie. The landlord gave us permission to put up a fence so Buddy could go out to pee without Mom having to walk him all the time. I convinced Will to let me bring Ned with me, but he was supposed to stay outside. We had to build a chain link run for him in the backyard. No biggie. We got a manual posthole digger, and I figured it would take me about two days to get all the holes dug while Will was at work. Will was like, "Good luck with that." I was thinking, *How hard could it be? I got this.* I got up in the morning, started pounding away with that posthole digger, sweating my ass off. I got about six tablespoons of dirt out in like three hours. The ground was so hard! Apparently, not only were there rocks above ground that you could see, but there were rocks below ground that you couldn't see as well. We ended up having to rent a gas-powered posthole digger to get the job done.

LIFE LESSON #1673

Some things sound so much easier than they really are.

Last step before the big move was the obligatory yard sale. It's amazing how much shit a person can collect in a relatively short period. Plus some stuff I felt the need to save is ridiculous. Why? What on earth was I thinking? I hate having yard sales. I never know what to price things at, and I feel bad asking for money for shit I don't want anymore. My co-worker friend brought some of her stuff over too. A lot of the stuff ended up becoming a yard trade instead of a yard sale between us.

Everything was finally buttoned up, got Mom to her new pad in Prescott, and I was living in the tiny mining town full time. Everything about living in a small town was new to me. For example, there is no mail delivery to your house. Everyone gets a post office box; mail is posted and in your box around 11:00 a.m. I would do my normal thing every morning. Shower, style my hair, full face makeup including lipliner and gloss, pick out an outfit for the day with matching shoes. Took about an hour of prep time to go get the mail at the post office. Big event of the day. It was a five-minute drive to the post office, park the car, three minutes to walk in and get the mail, five minutes home. Thirteen minutes top for one hour of prep time. Now I understand why people go to the grocery store in their pajamas and slippers.

There was a grocery/hardware/company store in town that was tiny. A person could buy a gallon of milk, get a key made, and buy shotgun shells all at the same time. But the groceries were disgusting. The store was independently run. They were overpriced, usually outdated, and expired food with very few choices. I never knew carrots could turn into complete mush if left in the bag too long. Basically, it was only good for an emergency gallon of milk and a loaf of bread. The real and closest grocery store was more than an hour away in Prescott. There really wasn't any "swinging by" the grocery store on the way home if you were missing something for dinner.

The first time Will and I drove all the way into Prescott, did all the grocery shopping and errands, and stopped by to see Mom, I was exhausted. I thought surely we were going to sleep over and go home in the morning. But no. All the way back to town, unload all the crap and put it away. I quickly learned to get more organized. I would come up with ten-day meal plans and shop accordingly.

That wasn't the only adjustment I had to make. There wasn't much to do, and I was used to getting up and going to work every day. I had a purpose and a schedule. I had friends and could go shopping; there were things to do. Now I didn't really have friends. Will worked thirteen-to-fourteen-hour shifts, and I was stuck at home, alone and bored. A tiny bit of depression started to seep in. I could remember sitting in the recliner one day and thinking to myself, *I bet I could will myself to simply quit breathing*. And I tried. It's actually a lot harder than you would think.

Will would finally get home from work, and I would run to greet him at the door. I was so happy to see him and have someone to talk to. Keep in mind, he's never lived with anyone before, was in his thirties, and very used to doing things on his own time. He didn't like me bombarding him the second he walked in the door. Remember how I said he didn't have any baggage? He also had no training. I'm not saying that in a mean way, but people learn things through relationships that didn't work out. It just is the way it is. He needed ten minutes to decompress when he got home before I could talk to him. I complied, but it secretly hurt my feelings. Plus, I have a tendency to jump to the negative side of things and thought he wasn't as happy to see me as I was to see him.

I needed to get out of the house and quit spending all my time watching TV and cleaning. I decided to do some landscaping. Get some fresh air, some exercise. I should tell you that I do not have a green thumb. But I try. I figured I just haven't found the plants that you can't kill yet. Power of positive thinking and all that shit! I was outside, soaking up some vitamin D, raking the yard, and feeling pretty good. Productive. I ran inside to grab a quick glass of water and right back out to get back to work. *Wham!* Someone punched me in the mouth! Why? But wait, there was no one there. Someone threw something at me for no reason! Except there was nothing on the ground in front of me. There was the rake, though. That's when it dawned on me. My dumb ass stepped on the rake and punched my own self in the mouth. And I did a really good job, considering the amount of blood pouring down my chin and all over my shirt. Turns out, my teeth went through my upper lip. There was a small clinic in this tiny town, but I had no clue if they do stitches, what the hours were, if they took walk-ins—I knew nothing. I eventually got it to quit leaking blood and seal up. I couldn't really eat solid food for a week because of the cut on my lip and the fact that my front teeth were a little loose.

There was a lot to learn about living in the desert. I had the front door open one day with the screen door shut. There was about a one-inch gap at the bottom of the screen door. Out of the corner of my eye, I saw something moving under the gap in the door. I take a closer look and it's a huge freaking tarantula slowly making its way into my house! Oh no, it wasn't! I grabbed the broom to shoo it away. Tapped it lightly one time. Hundreds of baby tarantulas went scurrying in every direction. Whaaaa! What was happening? I'd never seen anything like it. I never knew baby tarantulas rode on the backs of their mothers. I was freaking out! I was swinging the broom like a crazy lady, hopping from foot to foot because they were everywhere! And they were quick little bastards. So glad there wasn't anything like YouTube back then because I'm sure I looked and sounded like a complete idiot!

Not only do all the plants in Arizona have spikes and thorns and things that hurt you, but the creatures that live among those plants can hurt you too. Ned only stayed in his kennel out back for a couple weeks. He howled all night long from loneliness, and then we got a thunderstorm. Very rare in Arizona. He was terrified. I couldn't leave him out there. He was my fur baby. Will and I came to an arrangement for him to live in the house. I kept him tied up out front a lot of the day with the door open so he was still a part of the family, and let him come in at night. No furniture!

So he was tied up out front and started barking excessively one afternoon; I went out to see what all the hoopla was. There was a big, fat red-and-black lizard slowly walking down the driveway. I went in to tell Will what he was doing and he instructs me not to touch it! Well, I wasn't planning on it but why? He told me it was a Gila monster and went to grab a broom and a bucket. "What the hell is that? And what are you doing?" He starts explaining that Gila Monsters are a venomous lizard and if they bite you, they don't let go right away. They like to bite and then kind of chew on you for a minute to get more venom in. It won't kill you, but it sure hurts like hell. Nice. "So what's up with the broom and the bucket?" Will says he was going to catch it in the bucket and take it back out to the desert where it belonged, away from town. Never heard of a Gila monster before.

We spent a lot of time hanging out in the desert, just driving around in the hills on the dirt roads and enjoying the scenery. I learned that I needed to be much more aware of my surroundings when we were out there. I learned that when I almost peed on a rattlesnake. I was squatting behind a bush going to pee. I heard a noise but didn't make the connection. Will did. He was yelling at me to move but move slowly. I was like, "What the hell? I'm midstream peeing!" It doesn't work that way.

He was like, "Rattlesnake!"

I was looking all around; I didn't see anything. What was the emergency? Turns out, it was behind me and not so happy about my big white ass interfering with its personal space.

We decided to spend a weekend at the lake camping and fishing. Fishing's not my thing. I find it kind of boring. You just sit there and wait. It takes patience. Being patient is not in my wheelhouse of skills. Hell, I had to google how to even spell *patient*. But I do like being out there and camping. At this particular lake, there were wild donkeys wandering around. They look so cute, but looks can be deceiving. While Will was sitting down by the lake fishing, Ned and

I went exploring. We were walking up the trail, heading toward the parking lot, when I spotted a donkey kind of pacing us about forty feet away. How cute! It started coming a little bit closer, and I was getting a little warm and fuzzy, thinking it must like me and wanted to be my friend. I was wrong. That fucking donkey locked eyes with my dog, my dog started barking, and it started coming straight at us. And not with little heart bubbles in its eyes. It was pissed. I guess it didn't like my dog; it couldn't possibly be me, I'm not sure. But it was not slowing down, and now it was making all kinds of weird donkey noises. This had quickly turned into a classic ECS. I spotted a bright blue box of safety. The race was on! Even my dog, at this point, was sensing danger and had decided to zip it and run right along with me. We reached the porta potty in the nick of time. Luckily, it was a handicapped porta potty, which is bigger because my dog is a big boy. What are the chances of that? First, finding a porta potty in the middle of nowhere and the fact that it was a handicapped one? Score for us!

But that donkey was a sore loser. I could hear it out there, clomping around back and forth and still making noise. I started getting nervous that it was going to start kicking at the box and that would not end well for me. I don't want my obituary to read, "Stomped to death by pissed-off donkey. Body contaminated with human waste. No open casket available." We hid out in the porta potty for a good thirty minutes. Do you have any idea how hot and stinky a bright blue plastic box gets in the middle of summer in Arizona? Really hot. Almost hot enough to wish I had been stomped to death! The donkey finally threw in the towel and gave up. After a quick check, Ned and I went tearing out of the death box and ran back down the trail to Will, who had no idea of the ordeal we just lived through.

Later that night, thinking all the donkey drama was behind me, I started hearing all this noise right outside the tent. I peeked out and now there was a herd of those damn donkeys. Surrounding our tent, eating off the tree branches. That fucker had found me and brought his gang! This time, I knew I was going down. Will was trying to calm me down but he didn't understand that I had to pee now. "I can't go out there to pee!" And the more I knew I couldn't pee, the more I had to pee. Damn donkeys. Once again, I was hiding out, waiting for the donkeys to go away.

One time, and only one time, Will and I were out in the hills, driving around and goofing off, just enjoying the sunshine. I had a brilliant idea. I decided to take off my shirt. I thought I could soak up some vitamin D, get a little color on my boobs, and turn on my husband. I'm a multitasker for sure! About ten minutes into my "Girls Gone Wild: Boobs Out" episode, I caught a glimpse of myself in the side view mirror. Not good. I thought I had a pretty good body. But shit was wiggling and jiggling and not in a good way. Then we hit a rock in the road. Holy hell, things that were already wiggling and jiggling took on a life of their own. I was honestly mesmerized by the grotesqueness of it all. This was the total opposite of sexy. This was nexy. *Not* sexy. Shirt back on pronto! Another thing to add to my "one and done" list. Needless to say, I did not get laid that night, and I can't blame him.

One of the other things we liked to do was ride motorcycles. Well, I rode on the back of Will's. He had been riding for years, and I loved riding on the back. The freedom of being on a motorcycle, out in the open, wind in your hair, but none of the responsibility of having to pay attention. That's right up my alley. We went to this motorcycle rally every year that was held in Laughlin, Nevada. It was so much fun. I'm a people watcher. I am happier standing on the sidelines, watching, than be in the middle of all the action. And yes, sometimes I am secretly judging people's choices. There were always motorcycle shows where people would display their custom bikes. Beautiful bikes. Paint jobs that were artwork, chrome everywhere, custom-shaped gas tanks, lots of money behind some of those bikes. Problem was, some of the guys sitting on those expensive choppers only had one tooth! Personally, I would have scaled back on some of the custom work for a while and spent the money on some choppers I could eat with. Just my opinion. Sometimes you would see a beautiful gal being led around by a dog collar and leash. Why? Or wearing a bikini top with thongs and leather chaps so their ass cheeks were hanging out. I saw a gal sporting that outfit once, and she had some sort of rash on her ass. It was all over, bright red and bumpy. Looked uncomfortable. It was like a car accident; you didn't want to look but you couldn't stop yourself. All I kept thinking was that maybe that wasn't the day for that outfit, and why didn't any of her friends tell her that? Nudity wasn't allowed at the rally, so the women did a workaround by putting round Band-Aids over their nipples. This might sound interesting, but when those band aides are just about even with the belly button? Not so much. Half of my brain wanted to commend them for their positive body image, but the other half was screaming, "*Why?*"

And all that was going on during the day. At night, things got really crazy. Bikers cruising back and forth on the main strip, the drinking, the crowds. I loved standing on the sidewalk watching all the action. But as they say, all good things must come to an end. After years of going to the rally without any real incidents, a couple of rival biker gangs had a tiff and turned the lobby of one of the casinos into the OK Corral. Several people died, lots of injuries. Just a mess. Things changed after that. Lots of police presence, understandably, but they curtailed most of the weirdos the following year, and that was one of my favorite things. Luckily, that following year, I graduated from riding on the back of a bike to riding my own motorcycle.

I was a bad-ass bitch. Or so I thought. Will bought me a Honda Shadow 1100. I didn't want a smaller bike that I thought I would grow out of in a short time. Since I had no idea how to ride a motorcycle, I might as well learn on a big boy from the start. The bike was used, had straight pipes, so she was loud and a custom paint job of sherbet and dusty rose. Basically, pink and pinker. Will started me out with the basics on some of the empty side streets. Slow and easy. Turning was more of a problem than the shifting. Then I took a weekend course at the local community college. That helped a lot. But they had these itty-bitty loaner bikes to practice on and I was used to a way bigger and heavier bike, so it was a little squirrely in the beginning. If you passed the test at the end of the weekend, you got a certificate for MVD to get your motorcycle endorsement without having to go through their testing process. I passed.

With my newly endorsed license in my wallet, we decided to head up north for our first ride. I was slightly nervous but confident.

I was loving how cool I felt as a woman on a big-ass motorcycle. I feel strong and independent. I've got this. Wind in my hair and all that bullshit, even though I always wore a helmet. Arizona had a no-helmet law, but I always wore mine. Gotta keep my dome safe. Besides, I bought one that matched my bike, so yeah. We had to stop for gas and pulled into a small little gas station that was off the beaten path. There was a girl working in the station, and since my bike was so loud, she couldn't miss us. We finished pumping our gas, and the gal came out to tell me how much she liked my bike. *That's right, I am a bad-ass bitch.* I thank her. We're just getting ready to take off and I decided I needed a piece of gum from my backpack. I leaned the bike to the side to get into my pack, resting it on the kickstand. Tiny problem. Since we were just getting ready to leave, my kickstand was already in the up position, unbeknownst to me. In slow motion, I leaned the bike to the side to the point of no return. It was too heavy to stop it from going over. I smashed my head into the side up the gas pump and gently laid my bike on the ground. Bad-ass bitch right there! More like a dumb-ass bitch. I was trying to be so cool and failed miserably. I deserved it. I know I'm not that cool. What added insult to injury was the smirk I saw on her face when she was walking back into the station.

Our second day trip did not reflect my new badass title either. We decided to head into town to do some goofing off for the day, get some lunch, do a little light shopping. Can't carry too much on a motorcycle. "Town" is about sixty-five miles from our tiny mining town. The road is narrow and curvy. Lots of switchbacks. Perfect ride for motorcycle enthusiasts. There are no stop lights or stop signs even, until you get to the very edge of town. I was doing pretty good. Going slow but keeping up through all the twists and turns. We finally got to the first light, Will went through, but by the time I got there, it was turning yellow. I cranked on the brake and began to skid sideways through the intersection. I could hear Will yelling: "Honey! Honey! Honey!" I could see the faces of the people in their cars watching my demise in utter shock. Another slow-motion Hollywood moment. Miraculously, I made it through the intersection in one piece and still upright. I straightened the bike out, threw my arm in the air, and yelled "I'm okay!" like that was a planned stunt on my part. Maybe I am a badass? People don't need to know I peed myself a little bit.

I did get better with more time and practice. We spent a lot of our free time riding throughout Arizona. We saw some beautiful places, the red rocks in Sedona, the pines in Mormon Lake, Four Corners. That was cool, being able to stand in four states all at the same time. I hear you can't really do that anymore. They put a barricade up so you can see it but not actually stand on it. Not sure.

Life was good. Really good. But something was missing. I wanted kids.

*****

I knew making a baby wasn't going to be easy. I had that O negative thing going on, plus I had quit taking birth control way back when, when I was working on my personal overhaul. There was no point then and then after I stepped back into the arena, I really wasn't extremely sexually active, so I never got around to getting back on. But I was active and hadn't gotten pregnant, so?

Will wasn't in a hurry, but I was getting nothing but older. The older you get, the more difficult it gets. I went to our local gynecologist, gave him my history, did an exam, and all that crap. He prescribed me a medication that helped stimulate the ovaries so they would produce and drop more eggs at ovulation. That crap was expensive! Something like fifty dollars for five pills back then was pricey. The way the pill worked was that you had to chart your cycle, then you took the pills on certain days, then after you took the pills, you had sex on specific days. It was fun for the first several months. Practice makes perfect! The next several months, it started to become a chore. Something on the "to do" list. The last month, I took it was my final straw. I had already paid for and taken the pills, then I got super sick for the "sex" days. There is nothing worse than having to have sex when you feel like utter shit. I had to suck it up or I had wasted all that money and another month of trying. I cried after. Not because of the sex. More because I felt like my choice had been taken away. All that and no results.

All that time as a teenager spent worrying that I would get pregnant had quickly flipped to all my time as an adult worrying that I would not get pregnant. Odd how time can change everything. Back to the gyno. He wants to do an "antibodies test," whatever the hell that is. Then I found out I had to have sex with my husband and get to the doctor's office with my legs in the air within a specific amount of time. Seriously? How mortifying. I don't know about other people, but for me, going to the gynecologist is a huge anxiety flag. I feel like I am never far enough down on the table, so they always tell me to scoot down more so then I'm afraid I'm going to fart in the doctor's face from the effort of scooting. My butt gets all sweaty from nerves that it sticks to the stupid paper on the table, and then that scoots down attached to my ass. Then I start thinking about the rare possibility of having an unknown piece of toilet paper stuck to my ass. Then I wonder if my hoo-ha looks like everyone else's, which goes on to a whole new rant of anxiety in my head. It's awful. I follow every unwritten pre-gyno visit rule ever written. Always shower as close to the appointment as possible, shave then, legs too, no sex the night before, socks on during the exam, Immodium and Xanex on board, just in case. And may I ask, why would anyone choose to stare into hoo-has all day? Not all hoo-has are pretty. What about the seriously infected hoo-ha? Or how about the hoo-ha of the person who only showers once a week and they're at the gyno at the end of that week, not the beginning? The doctor's face is right up in there. But now the doctor wants me to poke right before going to the appointment? Me? But I did it. The test sucked, and the results sucked even more. My body was positive for the antibody properties. Which means that my body viewed semen as a germ and attacked and killed it before it can get to an egg. Nature's birth control. Fan-fucking-tastic. I asked him how I had already gotten pregnant once years ago, and he had no idea. He referred me to an IVF clinic that might be able to help.

IVF is expensive and, at the time, not covered by insurance. It was still considered "experimental" even though it had been being used to create families for more than twenty years. I had a very long and involved conversation with the insurance company and find it very interesting that they would pay to end a pregnancy but not create one. I also find it interesting that they cover the surgery for a man to have a penis pump installed because "it's a man's right to have an erection," but it's not a woman's right to have a baby? They started using penis pumps around the same time IVF started being used, but that's not still considered "experimental." Pisses me off. Obviously, insurance rules are written by men. But I did it.

The closest IVF clinic to our tiny town was three hours away. First consultation, legs up, a total vaginal maintenance check, slightly tilted uterus, everything else looks normal (no shit), hoo-ha smear, blood tests. Will needs to have his boys checked.

That was interesting. We found a lab closer to our tiny town but not close enough to get it there in time. The sample needs to be kept at body temperature and delivered to the lab as soon as possible. We decided to get a hotel room as close to the lab as possible. I waited in the truck with the engine running. We raced to the lab with the special cargo safely tucked down my shirt, between my boobs. We got to the lab, which was packed with old people waiting to get blood tests or what not. I was number 2 in line to check in, waiting with a jar of sperm secretly shoved in my bra. Finally, it was my turn. I leaned over the counter and whispered, "I have a sperm sample to turn in."

The gal behind the counter said "What?"

I looked around and said slightly louder, "I have a sperm sample to turn in."

She's like "What?" *Dammit!* I got the lab tech that's hard of hearing on the one and only day I ever have to turn in a sperm sample. Well, shit. So I said it again in my normal voice; everyone turned to stare at me while I was pulling the container of fresh sperm out of the safety of my boobs.

She was asking all kinds of questions. "When was the sample collected?" "Was it kept at room temperature?" etc. It seemed that all this information was extremely interesting to every single person in the waiting room. How embarrassing. I couldn't make eye contact with anyone on my way out. Turned out, his boys were fine; all issues were mine. Sometimes I think I must have really pissed off God somehow and he was just not in the mood to throw me a bone.

We started the IVF process as soon as possible. Everyone's IVF treatment is different depending on their personal issues. For me, growing my eggs was the easy part. I started giving myself two shots a day when I was instructed to. No big deal—they were small needles, so they didn't hurt at all. The real pain in the ass part was the six-hour round trip drive to the office for all the tests and exams to see how the eggs were progressing. They need to be a certain size before they can be retrieved. They do a vaginal ultrasound to figure that out. My first one of those was quite a shock. Again, on the table with legs up, the doctor was holding this two-foot-long tube-like thing. I have no idea what that is. He starts rolling this gigantic looking condom thing on it and lubing it up. What the hell is that thing? And where the hell is it going? Cause that is not going to fit in my hoo-ha! I mean, I know I dated "the lunker" years ago, but even he bows in submission to this thing. I didn't look. I didn't want to. I do not want to know how far that thing is in there. Nope. I got used to that ultrasound device from hell because I had to make that drive and get tested every other day for about a week. Finally, my Easter basket was ready! The doctor sent me home with a special onetime last-minute shot. Retrieval was scheduled for three days from then.

Both parties needed to be present at retrieval. I got home from the doctor that day and told Will what day he needed to take off work and how he was going to need to drive home because I would be put under a light sedation to keep me calm and still during the procedure. Both Will's mom and my mom were visiting at the time. Will's mom started insisting that she would drive me so Will didn't need to take time off from work. Huh? I tried to explain, without really going into detail, how he needed to be there. She was not understanding. I told her he needed to be there because we needed his half of the baby-making juju. She just wasn't catching on. Then she started in on how we were going to drive home since we were both having surgery. Huh? Will wasn't having surgery. He needed, like, ten minutes in the oval office with a magazine or two! He might need a nap but definitely not a ride home! I was baffled how she had raised two boys and didn't know how things worked. All I knew was, I was not the one who was about to explain the birds and the bees to her. Not under my job description!

Extraction day came, and I had to say, thank God for valium. While Will was busy in the oval office, I was getting prepped on the table. After getting undressed, I was put on a table that had not just stirrups but also these ski boot-looking things attached. I sat on the edge of the bed, and they strapped my feet into these boot things, then I was laid back while the bed is lifted and tilted slightly back. A small window opened up directly across the foot of the bed. My legs were separated and locked in place. The person in the window had a perfect, unobstructed view of my vagina! And there was more than one person back there. Did anyone else want to see my vagina? Now was the time! I was thinking, I should start to sell tickets to the show. In fact, I was starting to get pissed off. That's right about the time the valium kicked in. Perfect timing. I couldn't care less, at that point, who saw inside my vagina. I can't really remember much after that until about halfway home. I guess I dressed myself. Can't remember. I guess I got in the car. Can't remember.

We ended up with three viable and inseminated eggs. Time to cook. If I remember right, the embryos took three to five days to become strong and big enough for transfer. Those were some long, weird days. But back in the boot bed, vag open for viewing, things happening in reverse order. So clinical. Not the way a girl dreams of making a baby. But it is what it is. Now we wait. This is when things got really rough for me. Now I had to take steroids, these disgusting vaginal suppositories, and a huge shot in my ass every day. That shot hurt like hell. And I couldn't give it to myself. But it would all be worth it. Right?

I got pregnant! We were having a baby...or babies! We transferred all three embryos. Not sure how many took. Don't care. That would get determined later from another date with the dildo ultrasound machine. I must say, I was getting a tiny bit more comfortable with the open hoo-ha policy thing. Besides, all that mattered was my baby. Turns out, only one of the three embryos took. I was okay with that. I was more than okay with it.

What I was not okay with were all the hormone shots and steroids. The steroids were making me super hungry and cranky, and the hormones were making me super emotional. I had made some friends at this point and even got a part-time job at the tiny little gift store to meet more people. Being a hangry bitch does not help someone make friends. I would snap at random people for no reason and then have to spend time apologizing, which would piss me off all over again. Or I would cry from a McDonald's commercial, while shoveling macaroni and cheese down my throat. I'm sure I was a joy to be around. Hell, I couldn't even stand being with myself.

I got released from the IVF clinic]s care and sent back to my regular gynecologist as a normal pregnant lady with some special conditions. I needed to continue the shots and steroids through my first trimester, and my gyno could regulate those for me. My ass was a mass of different colored bruises in no time. But it was all worth it. I was gaining weight from the steroids so fast that I figured I would just wear the few maternity outfits I bought instead of buying bigger pants.

Life was good. My brother and his wife, back in Pennsylvania, decided they too were ready to start a family. How perfect! They had an easy go of it, though. I think it only took them a couple of months to get pregnant. I was so happy for all of us. Dave was doing really good at a top-notch CPA firm in the city; they bought a cute little row home, and his wife was going to school to be a shrink or something along those lines. It was such good timing.

I went to the gyno for a regular checkup and to get my first regular ultrasound. The lady came in the room, squirted some goop on my belly, and started moving the thing all around, stopping occasionally to mark some areas. Other than the fact that I had to pee, it felt pretty good. All warm and squishy. She was a young thing, not saying much. She left the room, said she was going to get the doctor and would be right back. I've never met her before, but I was thinking she doesn't have much of a personality. A few minutes later, the doctor came in. He went through pretty much the same routine she just did. But he was taking a bit longer than she did with the roller thing. I figured he was just double-checking her measurements. He quietly turned off the machine, wiped the goo from my belly, and finally started talking. The first two words were "I'm sorry." My breath had frozen in my chest. He went on to explain there was no detectable heartbeat. The fetus was measuring at about nine to maybe ten weeks in size. I was just over eleven weeks pregnant. Eleven fucking weeks. I was so close to the safety zone. It was weird because I was devastated but kind of not surprised. I knew it was too good to be true. In my heart, I knew it was too good to be true. God was still pissed at me, and I just hadn't figured out why. What did I do that was so unforgivable?

Tuning back in to what the doctor was saying, he was explaining that I had two options: (1) let the fetus abort naturally or (2) have a D&C. I was not in a good place in my head and couldn't imagine walking around knowing my dead baby was still inside me. I opted for the D&C. The morning of the scheduled procedure was horrible emotionally. In my head, I knew my baby was gone, but in my heart, I felt like I was giving up on it. My mind still plays tricks with me every now and again. What if they were wrong? Did I give in too easily?

Shortly after my miscarriage, Dave and his wife found out they were pregnant with twins. One boy, one girl. Are you fucking serious? A perfect little family with no effort. I'm not going to lie—I was a little pissed and a lot jealous. Why do they get to have a family and we can't? Because of this, Dave and I grew apart a little bit. Dave and his wife were mad at me for not being more interested in their pregnancy, and I was mad at them for not being more sensitive and understanding about what I had been going through. We were at an impasse. I was happy for them and sad for us. It was an emotional tightrope that I was not doing a good of balancing on.

Will and I gave it several months before we were ready to try it again. Another round of six-hour trips to the clinic. Another round of legs in the air. Another round of drugs. Another round of intrusive ultrasounds. Yeah.

I was sitting in the waiting room at the IVF clinic one day, and there were about three other patients in there waiting with me. They were having a conversation amongst themselves, and I was secretly eavesdropping. They were trading stories about their infertility journeys. One woman was on her fifth attempt at IVF. They already had a second mortgage on their home. For this round, they had borrowed money from their family and church. The other woman was maxing out all their credit cards to pay for everything. If these people were lucky enough to get pregnant and have babies, they weren't going to be able to afford diapers. I made a deal with myself right then and there, if things didn't work out on this attempt, we were done. I didn't want a dream to destroy our financial future.

This round, we ended up with five eggs. Three fertilized; one of the three wasn't looking good for transplant. We transferred the two best embryos. They didn't take. We were done. We went back to normal life. Riding our motorcycles, goofing off in the hills, volunteering at the fire station. It was a comfortable life. It was quiet and predictable. And I hated it. I wanted more. I made a promise to Will and myself to let it go. We tried; it didn't work. But I couldn't keep my promise. I wasn't done. It took a while before I gathered enough guts to tell all this to Will.

I knew I didn't want to do any more rounds of IVF. I was still trying to shuck the perma-pounds from the first two rounds. I knew I couldn't do any more of the drugs. I hated the way they made me feel. I began thinking, *The goal is to be a mom.* I didn't really care how I got there. I wanted to adopt.

Will was not keen on this idea. He didn't know anything about it and could only concentrate on the horror stories people hear about on the news instead of all the beautiful families that are built through adoption. It's unfortunate that the feel-good stories are rarely shown. That's changing now, though.

I told him I would do some research, and if that's the route we went, he would fall into step. He would smile when necessary, answer questions when asked, and do whatever needs to be done. I stated that I would not live my life without children, and if he hates me for it later, he could divorce me after we have a child. That was the way it was going to be, and that was that. I think I took him by surprise. He was not used to me being so assertive.

I did a lot of research, slowly narrowing down what would work for us. We—well, I—decided on a domestic adoption for starters. I just felt that I would have more control of the situation if we were at least in the United States. Any amount of control over anything was better than nothing after what we had already been through. And I wanted to be as involved in the process as possible. This was a "learn as you go" situation, and I knew I would need to talk to someone often. It was just part of who I am. After making that decision, I needed to find the right agency.

More research. I found an agency that actually had a branch office in Prescott. Adoption is expensive. Thankfully, this agency did things a little differently. Instead of everyone paying one set price for all expenses up front, the cost varied per couple. It was based on a percentage of the total household income. And you paid as you went. There were steps that need to be done, and this agency let you pay as you go through each step, with the largest payment due at the end of the process. Putting all this down in black and white made it sound horrible, but the reality was, the agency had bills too. They helped cover birth mother expenses if needed; they have case workers to pay, lawyer fees, electricity, just to name a few. So yeah, adoption cost money.

I can only explain the things we had to go through at that time in Arizona. Things may have changed since then. I don't know.

First step, get fingerprinted. That was easy. A quick trip to the courthouse and a small fee for each of us. Botta boom, botta bam. Ink stains on my fingertips. Easy peasy. Now we waited for our background checks to come back. There's a lot of waiting in the adoption process. Waiting, for anything, is not on my list of positive personality traits. Eventually, it came back. Neither of us were convicted felons. Moving on.

Second step was to get a home study done. We got hooked up with a lady who was court appointed and not affiliated with our agency. The "home study" is when someone comes to your house and looks for things like pool fences and other safety issues. It's not a surprise—at least it wasn't for us—so if you lived like pigs, there was time to clean. We did not live like pigs, but for about a week prior to our appointment, I cleaned. I wasn't really sure what to expect, so

I went all terminator with a scrub brush on that house. I'm talking baseboards, vent covers, closets, under the sinks. No speck of dirt or dust was safe from my wrath. The day before our appointment, the home study lady calls and canceled. Blah, blah, blah, something came up and she needed to reschedule. Seriously? After all that? So we rescheduled, but this time, I just did a really good clean. No terminator on this job. She canceled again! Third time's a charm they say. This time? Fuck it. My house was clean. Usually is.

She showed up in an old ratty-ass station wagon that was packed with crap. I mean *packed*. Shit was shoved all the way to the roof. I saw loose papers, boxes, trash, clothes strewn all over, even a huge fake palm tree laying on its side from the back seat to the trunk area. Trash and file folders hiding in and among the plastic leaves. Junk. The only open space was for her skinny ass on the driver's seat. Even the dash was stuffed with crap. Empty fast-food wrappers and old soda cups folded in to fit more. This was the person who determined if we were fit to have a child in our home? This is whom I spent days cleaning for? This woman who drove a box of chaos on wheels? I was having a very difficult time trying to pretend I was not seeing what I was seeing and thinking what I was thinking. I needed to get my brain back on track and on to Nicey Nice Ville ASAP! But really, wtf? I wonder what it smells like in there? *Stop!* Nicey Nice Ville! Pronto!

Will and I were dressed in our Sunday best, looking at each other in amazement, while she wandered around the house with our file and a notebook. I have no idea how she found our file. She never opened a closet or a cabinet. All that work for nothing. How did she know I didn't have a hobby of stringing dead bunnies up and letting them air dry in the closet if she never checks? I don't, but the question still stands.

On to the interview part of the visit. We were sitting at the dining room table. She was asking Will all kinds of questions about his upbringing, his past, his hobbies, his job. Will was doing a really good job. He was answering all the questions, being polite, smiling when necessary. This was good considering he's really not a big talker. My turn. She turned to me, and the first statement out of her mouth was, "So tell me about your arrest." Well…shit.

LIFE LESSON #2074

Secrets don't always stay secret. Be prepared.

Will's head flipped to me so fast I heard his neck crack. His eyes were open blue saucers filled with shock. But his mouth was closed. He gets points for that. I never told him about some of the things in my past. Not fully anyway. I was going to be normal, remember? Normal people do not have arrest records. I don't know why it never occurred to me that that would come up when we got fingerprinted. I was not prepared. I gave her the Disney version of the story. I left out my drug addiction and a lot of other details, but she was satisfied. She left shortly after, pulling away in that chaotic station wagon, while Will and I stood in the driveway, waving goodbye. Time to talk. He wanted an explanation and I can't blame him. I explained that it really wasn't intentional. I had turned my life around a long time ago and had moved on. There was nothing else that he needed to know. He was not happy, but he was understanding. I was quietly hoping my past wasn't going to fuck up my whole future. All we could do was wait, again, for the report.

The report finally came in, and we passed. On to step 3. We needed to take a parenting class at the agency. Part of the class involved listening to other couples' stories. What brought them to adoption, how the process went for them, how things were going now, and how things were going with the birth mothers. At our agency, they only accepted couples that were infertile, so everyone's journey was unique. It was oddly comforting listening to other people's struggles. To be in a room filled with people who truly understood the pain, frustration, and embarrassment of infertility was a relief of sorts. And to hear everything was going to be okay was uplifting.

And yes, I said embarrassing. For those of us that have experienced infertility issues, we all know what's coming as soon as people find out. The stories, how to tell when you're fertile, you're not doing it right, you're not doing it enough, you're doing it too much. You're too stressed out about it, do it in the morning, no, do it at night, or the ridiculous suggestions on positions. And the inevitable story about an Aunt Sally who had been trying to get pregnant for years but finally had a baby. She had her husband tie her legs in the air for an hour after they had sex while she ate a kosher dill pickle. I should try that. The story and suggestions vary. The names change, but we've all heard them. It's like I'm going to have a sudden epiphany from their ridiculous suggestions: "Oh! That thing is supposed to go in that hole? No wonder I'm not pregnant!" It's embarrassing, and it gets old—quick. These people don't even know if I have a uterus. I know they are trying to help, but sometimes helping is simply just being quiet.

Step 4. This is a very important and expensive step. The "birth parent letter." This needs explaining. A lot of people, including myself, always just assumed there was some sort of list. Like a first come, first serve kind of thing. I know that sounds horrible, but I had no need to learn otherwise. In truth, that's not how it works at all. In truth, the birth mother has all the power, as she should. Prospective couples write letters about themselves; those letters go in a book for birth mothers to read. They decide from there whom they might want to meet, whom they might want to place their baby with and what kind of adoption they are interested in. Along with the letter is the acceptance paperwork. Now that makes you feel like a piece of shit. It's pages of questions of what you will and will not accept in a baby. Things like race, deformities, born addicted to drugs or alcohol, created through rape or incest. A lot of questions. Everything you can imagine really, except our agency would not allow couples to pick the sex of the baby. But all these questions help the case workers determine which birth parent letters to show which birth mothers. I feel ours was pretty restrictive. We just lived so far from any kind of specialists, and we didn't know what to expect.

We had a meeting with our case worker, turned in our questionnaire, got to read a few birth parent letters from other couples, and took a few home as reference to write ours. They were all generally two pages long with three or four pictures. But reading them? Some were disgustingly sweet, all "We got married in Disneyland at the princess castle" with pictures of a nursery all set up with the 101 Dalmatians theme, made me wanna puke. Other ones were all "This is us at our vacation chalet," with pictures of a room they were "thinking" about turning into the nursery. It was half the size of our whole house, for fuck's sake! I called our case worker in a panic. "We can't compete with that! I'm nobody special. A birth mother is never going to choose us!"

She told me to calm down and gave me some great advice. She said, "No matter what, be yourselves."

"But we like to ride motorcycles and won't birth mothers frown on that?"

She said, "Every birth mother is looking for something different, something that speaks to them. That's not always money. Be yourself."

So I was. I used a picture of Will and I on our motorcycles on the top of the first page. I wrote about being out in the hills and going fishing. I put a picture of Ned in there, wrote about Will's involvement with the volunteer fire department and life in a small town. It was who we were. Nothing more, nothing less.

Our letter officially went in "the book" in November. Now we waited—again. It was out of our hands.

As far as "the book" goes, there's really no telling how long a couple might wait for the right birth mother to come along. It could be months; it could be years.

While Will and I were waiting, Mom was moving. She decided to go back to Pennsylvania, move in with Dave and his wife, and be their live-in nanny for the twins. Dave sold that little row home in Philly and made a killing. Granted, he's a numbers guy. He bought the row home from the bank at a really good price. At that time, it was in a shitty neighborhood, but trends change. That shitty neighborhood became one of the new hot spots for real estate. The perfect area for young, educated, up-and-coming couples that were just starting out. He got into a bidding war and just smacked it on the sale price. He shit a golden twinkie on that one. If it were me and my luck? I would be begging someone to take it off my hands. In any event, they turned around and bought a ginormous house in the suburbs. It had a fully finished basement with a separate bedroom and bathroom like a small apartment for Mom.

I was conflicted with the whole decision for her to move. Part of me knew this would be good for her. She could save some money and have a purpose. But the other part of me was super jealous. First, jealous that they even had kids that needed a nanny; I knew I shouldn't feel that way but I did. Second, upset that now I wouldn't have any support while we wait.

We got a call from the agency in January, right after Mom left. It's very unusual for things to happen so quickly. A gal had come in. She was pregnant with a baby girl, and after going through the letters, she chose us. Our case worker is explaining that she was not sure if she wants to meet us or not. We would have to see at a later date. We were hoping for an open adoption but were willing to do whatever the birth mother felt comfortable with. An open adoption is when the adoptive parents get to meet the birth mother, maybe write letters in the future or have visits here and there, phone calls, whatever works out for everyone.

I told everyone! She was due in a little over a month, so I went shopping! We set up the nursery, which ended up looking like a giant had vomited Pepto Bismol on everything. It was a little too much, if I say so myself. Everyone kept asking what was going on and checking in with us. It was exciting. I would check in with our case worker at least once a week. They started having problems getting a hold of her on a regular basis. No worries. I was thinking she was just busy.

Another misconception about adoption is that all the birth mothers are young. Some are but not all. Generally speaking, young mothers are too irresponsible to realize the responsibility involved in raising a baby, so a good majority of the time, the grandparents step forward. Most birth mothers are older, maybe already have children, but know that love alone is not enough to raise a baby. Babies cost money. They need stuff. Diapers, clothes, formula, doctors. They need a way to get to the doctor and car seats and time. They need a warm, safe place to sleep every night. No matter how much assistance someone might get, it's never going to be enough. Every situation and circumstance is different and unique. But the basics remain the same.

So I wasn't concerned in the beginning. I wanted to believe everything was fine. I needed to believe everything was fine. I checked in the following week; they hadn't been able to get hold of her in two weeks. Now I was starting to get concerned. Another week and nothing. Our case worker's opinion was that he had changed her mind. She wanted to know if we wanted to go back in "the book." *Yes.*

I learned a few lessons with that. Do not tell everyone until you are sure and do not go shopping all happy-ass crazy. Good thing I kept the receipts on all that dumb-ass pink shit. I'm glad she never wanted to meet us. That should have tipped us off. But I was happy I couldn't put a face to the disappointment. It's hard to put into words, but it felt more like the death of the concept of becoming that baby's parent more than the actual loss of that baby, if that makes any sense.

While we waited—again—I read every baby book I could. How to get them to sleep through the night. How to create a realistic schedule that was age appropriate. What to feed them at what ages. Baby sign language. I even read parts of "what to expect when you're expecting" so I would better understand what a possible birth mom was going through. I became a professional parent without a child. I even thought about trying to produce milk to breastfeed. Talked to the doctor and everything. Apparently, there's a pill to get things started, but I would need to pump everyday too. And I would need to wear an SNS, which is a supplemental nursing system. It's a pouch filled with formula that hangs between your breast, then there are tiny tubes that come out of that, which are taped to your nipples. I opted out of that. What if I went through all of that and things fell through again? Plus, Will wouldn't be able to take part in the feeding, and that wasn't fair to him.

Life goes on while we wait. Will was busy with the volunteer fire department; I was doing little projects to keep busy and trying not to obsess over things. I even built a small water garden in the front yard. It was super cute with rocks and a small water fountain. It had lily pads and duckweed, other tall and spiky plants and goldfish. I fed the fish every day and would sit out there listening to the running water. It was very relaxing. I was proud of myself. Will and I went away for the day, shortly after I built it, and when we got home, all my fish and most of the plants were thrown out all over the lawn, all dried up from the sun. What the hell? I thought Ned had been a very bad boy! Turns out, the little boy across the street went fishing. Well, shit. That didn't work out for me. I guess I can't even have a water garden.

I had my good days and my not so good days. The waiting was like being pregnant without a due date. Everyone in town knew something about our situation, if not the details. That's one of the downfalls of living in a tiny town. Nothing is completely private. Half the time, the gossip isn't even the truth, but there's not much for the housewives to do. So the story goes on. I went to one of those home parties where they are trying to sell you some kind of shit— whether it was candles or cookware or sex toys, I can't remember. What I do remember was the baby there. The woman hosting the party was the grandmother. She was babysitting her daughter's baby that was maybe a little over a month old. Apparently, the mom was out at the bar with her friends. The problem was that the mom had been breastfeeding the baby, and the baby was hungry. It had never taken a bottle or formula before. The baby was wailing from hunger; Grandma is trying to shove a bottle in its mouth, and it wanted nothing to do with it. Grandma decided to put a bunch of sugar in the formula to try to entice the baby to eat. Nowhere, in any of the books I read did it say to put a shit ton of sugar in the formula. I walked away, but the baby quit crying soon after. I don't know if it drank any of the formula or gave up trying to get fed. But it puked everywhere. So Grandma undressed the baby, leaving it in only its diaper, which was already filled with poop. I could smell it. That poor baby got passed around for a good hour, while they talked about whatever it was they were selling. Someone tries to hand me the baby to hold. Ummm…no thank you. "But you need to get used to holding babies." Oh right, 'cause we are trying to adopt. Still, no thank you. All I'm thinking is that maybe someone should have changed it's diaper like forty-five to fifty minutes ago. Not because it smelled bad but because I was sure it's uncomfortable. Hadn't anyone else noticed? Where was grandma? I faked a headache and went home. What's going to happen in the morning after Mom gets home from drinking all night and the baby is hungry? Right back to breastfeeding? Why does she get to have a baby and I don't? I'm not saying I'm better than she is, but I would definitely treat my baby as more of a gift than an imposition, that's for sure. I was pissed off. Pissed off at her. Pissed off at the grandma. Pissed off at me and yes, pissed off at God. It wasn't fair. That was not a good day.

Time went on like that. Good days, not so good days, checking in with the case worker, waiting. Then in April, we got a phone call. In fact, it was *the call*. There was a gal that was working with the Phoenix office; she was placing her baby for adoption and she wanted to meet us. They gave us a little bit of her back story and wanted to know if we were interested. *Yes!* They had already set her up in an apartment, given her a cell phone, and gotten her to a doctor. An ultrasound was done, but the baby was in the wrong position so the sex was unknown. Secretly, I wanted a girl. The clothes are cuter, I already had a girl name picked out, and decorating the nursery would be easy breezy! We made arrangements to meet for lunch.

Talk about being nervous. This is the most important interview of my life. This meeting could potentially turn us from a couple to a family. I didn't want to blow it. I have no idea what to expect, what to talk about, what subjects were off limits. The pressure on this meeting was huge. I'm not always good under pressure. I can't seem to shut the fuck up and stuff comes out of my mouth that shouldn't. Plus, I'm opinionated. That doesn't always go over well. In short, I choke.

Will and I showed up early in an attempt to give me time to relax, catch my breath, and not come across as stupid. Whatever. A woman walks in, obviously pregnant, beautiful, dark hair, not real tall—surely that's not her. She walked up to us, introduced herself, and sat down. We started talking, a bit awkwardly at first, but soon it turned into a regular conversation, like two old friends that haven't seen each other in a long time. I liked her instantly. She made me feel comfortable in a very uncomfortable situation. Not that she thought that was her job; that's just who she was. We had the same sense of smart-ass humor; she said what she thought and meant what she said. I liked her regardless of the situation. I trusted her.

We dropped her off at the apartment after lunch. It was small but nice, clean. The agency also gave her a phone to use, so we traded numbers. She officially chose us to place her baby with. We were going to be parents! We started talking over the phone just about every day. I would drive to Phoenix to take her to her doctor's appointments. It was weird at first, but it got better. She was so open and determined when she would tell people who I was. It was comforting. Sometimes we went to lunch after, not always. There are very strict laws in the "do's and don'ts" during an adoption process. I didn't want to step over the line on any of them. Everything was taken care of through the agency. I was just along for the ride, so to speak. I didn't set up or pay for any of the doctor visits, dentist appointments, bills, food or living expenses. I wanted to do things to make her life easier but was afraid of breaking the rules, which is a tough one for me!

Birth fathers also have rights, and those rights need to be severed before a baby can be placed for adoption. There's several ways to go about that, depending on the situation. Our agency was working on getting his rights severed in two ways. They posted an ad in the paper and sent a certified letter. The birth father had thirty days to respond if they wished to contest the adoption. Or they could respond by not responding and let the thirty days lapse. We were waiting again for either of those to happen.

Our birth mom, AN, began having some dental issues in May. She went to the dentist; they tried to help her, but the baby's heart rate kept increasing under the local anesthesia, so they couldn't do much for her. She was in pain, and I felt really bad that there was nothing I could do to help. Then she got an abscess. Because of this, the decision was made to induce her a little early.

Holy shit! This was happening! The date was set. AN says we could be in the room when she delivered the baby. Holy shit! How amazing was that? What an unbelievable gift. I was trying to express my gratitude and she said, "This is your baby. I'm just carrying it for you." I gave her the longest hug because I didn't want her to see me cry.

We all go to the hospital on our given date. AN got checked in, explained who we are, got an IV, and begins the Pitocin drip to induce labor, and we waited. Nothing was happening. About three or four hours later, the doctor came in to check on her progress. Nothing. He decides to break her water to get things moving along. AN tells him he'd better stick around because things would happen fast as soon as he did that. The doctor scoffed at her and left. AN has had two children already; she knows her body. It always astonishes me when doctors don't listen to their patients. The nurse came in right after the doctor left and called for the anesthesiologist to come give her an epidural. He showed up about thirty minutes later. He didn't get a chance to administer the epidural. AN needed to push. The nurse started trying to desperately get a hold of the doctor. The doctor really listened to AN and had left the building! Even after she told him what was going to happen.

Three pushes. The nurse and the anesthesiologist delivered the baby.

It's a boy! We have a son! Blue cigars for everyone!

Our son was born on the afternoon of June 3. He is perfect.

SOMETHING I KNOW FOR SURE

*There is a special place in heaven for all birth mothers
who place their children for adoption. No matter the
reason or circumstance, it is a difficult and selfless
decision based on the love of an unborn child.*

As soon as the miracle of watching our son be born began to calm down and the tears dried up, the panic set in. *What the fuck was I thinking? This is a tiny human being. What happens if I break it? This tiny human needs me for everything. What if I fuck it up? There's no "do over" here! I don't know how to change a diaper on something this small. What happens if he doesn't like me? I need to take a deep breath here. In through the nose, out through the mouth. Repeat. And one more time. We can do this.* The nurse took JP, our son, out of the room to get cleaned up and what not. Will and I stepped out to give AN some privacy.

Out in the hallway, the tears started all over again. So did the panic. *I am a parent. A PARENT. Of a tiny, live human boy! Please don't let me fuck this up. I have got to get my shit together. I do not want to be seen as a blubbering idiot. Plus, I need to call my Mom!* Now she was crying. Will was on the phone with his mom; she was crying. It's a total boo boo fest.

In the state of Arizona, a birth mother cannot sign the consent to adopt until seventy-two hours after giving birth. That way, any drugs they may have been administered during delivery are out of their system and they are clear headed.

AN got discharged from the hospital before JP. JP had either ingested or breathed in some meconium during birth, so they wanted him to stay for observation for a few days. The problem was that we had no legal rights for information or decisions on his behalf.

They knew we were the prospective adoptive parents, but the law is the law. He even got circumcised without our knowledge. Probably would have chosen that anyway, but it still would have been nice to know what was happening to our son.

Seventy-two hours doesn't seem like a long time until you're waiting for paperwork to get signed. Paperwork that determines your whole future! We spent as much time as they would let us, sitting in the nursery with JP. He was so perfect. Gigantic blue eyes with thick, long eyelashes, bald and adorable. If we weren't at the hospital, we were shopping or hanging at the hotel wasting time. We had the basics, but since we didn't know the sex, we needed clothes. I had secretly wished for a girl because the clothes are so much cuter. But I did find the cutest blue and white onesie, blue and white slippers, and white knit cap to bring him home in.

Finally. Finally, the seventy-two-hour wait was over. AN signed the papers, JP was being released, our case worker had met with the hospital's legal team, and we were ready to take our son home and introduce him to the world. We were directed to a small, out-of-the-way waiting room to wait for the nurse to bring us JP. Everything was taking so long!

The nurse came in with our son wrapped in a blanket and began going over the post-op info on his circumcision. But oh no, it didn't end there. Since we were only the adoptive parents, we must be idiots. She changed his diaper and made us redo it to show that we are capable of this task. She swaddled him in a blanket, undid it, and made me redo it. She lectured us on how he should sleep, how much formula he should take, how often he should take it, how to hold him, how to burp him, how to bathe him, how often he should be bathed, what kind of lotion is best, make sure not to get soap in his eyes, and on and on. She even broke out the little blue boogie sucker, showed us how to use it, *and* makes us each do it too. What the fuck was happening here? It had been over an hour! I was getting seriously irritated. A fourteen-year-old crackhead just walks out of the hospital with her baby because it came out of her vagina. But because we're adopting, we have to be put through the third level of hell to prove we can buckle a five-point harness in a car seat? I couldn't decide if she was trying to be helpful or if she truly thought we're idiots. As far as I was concerned, class was over, and the information nurse could go away.

Pulling into our tiny little town with our son in the backseat with me was surreal. We didn't hear it, but we heard about it. The fire department made an announcement over the radio when we were pulling into town: "It's a boy!" and everyone responded with whoops and cheers. That made me feel good. We were not alone in this.

I had made some friends along the way. One was the wife of one of the other firefighters in the department; she had two young kids, and I knew I could lean on her for questions and support. I also made friends with a woman down the street who was in the department too. She had an older son so had already been there, done that. I think these two went into cahoots and had some of the other wives bring us dinners for a week so we could just concentrate on JP and being new parents. That was a very welcome surprise. Will's company offered "bonding time" for their employees who either have or adopt children that was two weeks' paid leave. That was so needed. And not to have to worry about cooking during that time was such a treat. These two also arranged a baby shower at the department's meeting hall. That was amazing! It was huge! Everyone got to meet JP, we got tons of necessary and much needed gifts, and it made me feel like a normal mom. I needed that more than I knew.

Will needed to know he could bond and love a child not created from his genes. That's why God picked out and sent us JP. They looked exactly alike, and JP was a daddy's boy. From day one, JP loved his dad. He would curl up on Will's chest and fall asleep almost instantly. Plus, JP was a really easy baby. Of course, I followed all the book's advice. I charted when he ate, when he was changed, when he napped, all so I could better figure out why he was crying. Worked like a charm. We were on a serious schedule. Will was great. He did diapers, even the poopy ones. He did midnight feedings, baths, naps—he was totally a hands-on dad. I'm so glad I didn't stick with the supplemental nursing system! Those 3:00 a.m. feedings are a bitch and to not have to do every one of them was a blessing.

I wanted some of those naked baby butt pictures, so off to Sears we went. The photographer got JP in the perfect position with his arms and legs all tucked underneath him with his naked butt up in the air. Super cute! He looked so peaceful and happy. In the amount of time it took the photographer to get up and walk to the camera, JP started to poop. I was trying to wipe as he went, but good night, it just kept coming! I know he pooped earlier, so where was this all coming from? My attempt at the wipe as he went thing was not going good. I couldn't keep up. I was apologizing, even though I didn't know why—he's a baby after all—and she was trying to tell me it happened all the time. Well, maybe a little, but this had turned into the never-ending fountain of poop! Time to throw in the towel on this photo shoot. Will and I are sitting on the bench in the hallway by the restrooms, taking a breather and getting JP redressed.

Some random old lady came up to us and commented on how cute JP is. I thanked her, but she was still standing there, staring at me. OK? She blurted out, "Aren't you a little old to have a baby?"

What the fuck? I'm like thirty-eight! People have babies at thirty-eight! I didn't think I looked that bad! I took a deep breath and decided to use this as a teachable moment to promote adoption in a positive light. First, I explained that I was only thirty-eight, but our son is adopted.

She asked with an attitude, "Oh? Where'd you get him?"

I'm getting a bit testy, forget the positive light bullshit. I answered, "At Babies-R-Us." How rude can this woman be? Annnnnd, she's still staring.

Then she noticed that I was putting socks on JP's adorable feet. She said, "Aw, look at that. You're doing everything a regular parent does."

I was insta-pissed. A regular parent? I felt like a "regular parent" at 3:00 a.m. when I was feeding and changing him, which might be the reason I looked like shit, by the way. I was thinking, *This irregular parent is about to kick some old lady ass in the middle of Sears.*

Will saw the look in my eyes and started pushing the stroller away from the soon-to-be-dead old lady. He was doing that "Honey?

Honey? Honey?" thing he does. This day was just getting started! But thanks to Will, that old lady lived to die another day.

JP was the perfect baby. Too bad he didn't have a perfect mother. I did some dumb-ass shit as a new mom. I bit him by accident once. I was kissing all over his belly, and he was doing the cutest giggle that I started laughing, and somehow, I bit him in the process. The day before a doctor's appointment, I bit my son and left a teeny, tiny bruise on his belly. At the doctor's the next day, I told him what happened and started bawling right there in the office. The poor doctor was looking at me like I'd lost my mind. He kept reassuring me that things happened, it was an accident, he was fine. I also, kinda, sorta, but not really, dropped him in the car seat. What happened was, I guess I didn't have the car seat handle locked in place, so when I pulled him out of the car, the car seat flipped upside down, and poor JP was dangling in his harness. I made quick work of righting him in the seat and even quicker work of looking around to make sure no one saw that dumb-ass move! I guess having things locked in place is an issue for me because I also launched him out of his crib. I was helping him practice standing up by letting him lean on the crib railing. He was using the side of the crib that lowers when you need it to. I guess it wasn't locked in place because it slammed down and JP went flying like a trapeze artist reaching for a swinging bar to grab. There was no bar, only Mommy, who thankfully caught him in midflight.

I may not have been perfect, but I was fierce. My son's birth father decided to fight for custody. Technically, not him as much as his mother. She wanted to raise him. The birth father had ignored all attempts of contact. He waived any rights of custody. His mother changed his mind. He was too busy doing heroin to respond to any of the attempts. But she wouldn't give up. Over my dead body was she getting my son. I heard that the birth father was willing to move the weight set in his room to make room for a crib if he had to. How hospitable. That's okay, don't bother. There was no way in hell that these people were going to take our son. They hired a lawyer. They made several time-consuming, stress-inducing attempts to overturn the custody. Didn't matter what happened, really; I was completely prepared to pack our shit and disappear. I would have done anything necessary to keep JP safe and happy. They lost. Twice. The laws are in place for a reason. The whole custody shenanigan just caused extra stress and time. It made us have to push back our "gotcha date." That was when the adoption was finalized through the court system. It was a really big deal. But we eventually got our date. Will's mom was there, and my mom flew in for the ceremony. Now he was not only our son in our hearts but by law too. Adoption day is a happy day for everyone at the courthouse. They are usually doing not-so-happy things, so when they get to make a family, they celebrate too. We even got to go in the judge's chambers and take pictures with him holding JP. It was a really good day.

Pretty much, every day was a good day. Well, except when he was teething. Those were not good days. Just saying. I was following everything in my books. Had JP sleeping through the night, eating off the approved list of appropriate items at the appropriate ages; I even taught him sign language. That ended up being the best thing ever. It was just the basics, but he could sign when he wanted something to eat or if he wanted a bottle. He could sign if he wanted Daddy or Mommy, all before he could talk. It made things so much easier. At one, I threw away the bottle and went to sippy cups. I was truly a pain in the ass, by-the-book mom.

And of course, we threw him a huge party for his first birthday. Looking back, I don't know why we do that as parents. And we all do it, but they don't remember anything. A simple cupcake and matchbox car would suffice. We're talking three dollars, max. But it's fun for the adults. Great for pictures. I turned into the paparazzi long before his first birthday. I got into scrapbooking so everything became a picture-worthy moment.

Sadly, Ned went to heaven shortly after JP's first birthday. He just got old and sick. It was his time. I'm grateful I have pictures of JP and Ned hugging and playing.

I was talking to my dad on the phone one day, catching up and talking about the weather, when out of the blue, he blurted out, "If you want to adopt another baby, I'll pay for it." Wait. What's this now? That was totally unexpected and came from left field. We had just assumed it was going to be the one and done. Our baby bank was empty after the two failed IVF attempts and one successful adoption. This was huge. I had to talk to Will ASAP because I was all in.

We were back at the agency. This time, it should be a tad easier since we don't have to do the fingerprints and deal with the crazy home study lady or the parenting classes. Straight to the new birth parent letter and the dreaded acceptance paperwork. This time, I've got this. Like I said, God knew what he was doing when he sent us JP first because this time, on all our acceptance paperwork, we wrote "will discuss" for everything. Because of JP, we knew we could love any baby God sent us and that that was the baby we were meant to have. The birth parent letter was so much easier to write this time. We are who we are.

Our letter went in "the book" in November. Just like the first time. We were picked by a birth mother in January, just like the first time, and she was pregnant with a baby girl, also just like the first time. What wasn't the same was that she wanted to meet us. We were told that she already had six children that were twelve and under, including two of the age of six that were not twins but that close in age. That she had been in an abusive relationship and was currently living in a shelter. She lived in Prescott; we made arrangements to meet at a park so the kids could run around. The agency had to bring them since we didn't have a vehicle, or two vehicles, that could fit everyone. Will and I bought several pizzas, sodas, and things so we could have a nice visit and get to know each other. It was a beautiful day, and our visit was nice. Not super comfy or enlightening or anything. But nice.

We talked on the phone some but not often. It was hard for us all to get together because there were so many of us. And she was due very soon, so there wasn't much time to work things out.

She called us in the middle of the night, shortly after meeting us, and told us she had had the baby. Things went really fast and there wasn't time to call us until after the delivery. We packed our crap, got JP up and loaded, made sure Will's mom could watch him, and headed to the hospital in Prescott. We finally got there in the wee hours of the morning. She apologized again about not calling sooner, but that was okay. We were here now, and that's all that mattered.

The baby was beautiful. We named her and cuddled with her as long as they would let us. They finally kicked us out so the baby and mother could rest. For me? Time to shop! Pink everything! We went back to the hospital that afternoon, and this time the twelve-year-old daughter was there. She was not happy with us, with her mother, with any of it. Will and I were a little uncomfortable. I felt bad for the twelve-year-old because she was so young and couldn't understand what is happening and why. Her mother was making a very difficult decision for many reasons. We decided to leave them be and come back in the morning. Will stayed with JP the next day so I could spend all day at the hospital with the baby and the birth mother. By now, the hospital staff knew who we are. A nurse came in to check on us and began questioning the birth mother, asking her if she was sure she "wanted to give her baby away." First of all, that's not how we say it. You're placing your baby with another family to raise as theirs. Secondly, placing a child for adoption isn't a decision made on a whim. It must be a very difficult, heart-wrenching, selfless choice that is made from love. It is not something someone wakes up on a Saturday morning and decides to do, so I would appreciate it if you would shut the fuck up! Oh! And thirdly, I was right there!

The papers were set to be signed the following day. I was out getting breakfast when I got the call from our case worker. The birth mother had changed her mind. She said the twelve-year-old was too upset she had already called the shelter to find a car seat and come get them. *But* she was keeping the name to remind her of what she almost did. The world stopped spinning for a second. I was heart-broken. And pissed. But in retrospect, not surprised. I never felt the same connection with her that I did with JP's birth mom. I was heartbroken that the hope that I was wrong was gone. Pissed that I spent three days away from my son to care for her and the baby when I don't think she was ever really invested in her decision. Super pissed that she kept the name. I loved that name. I had that name in my wheelhouse for years, and now it was tainted. I couldn't use that name again. Plus, I had to return all the shit I just bought—again. I begged a cigarette off a trucker. I hadn't smoked in years, and it tasted like shit, but I finished it anyway. Leaning on the side of Burger King, crying and smoking.

A couple of weeks later, our case worker called to see if we were ready to go back in "the book." I told her yes. I explained that this is exactly how things went with JP's adoption and she'd be calling us in April, just like with JP. She told me it didn't really work that way. I told her, "We'll see. That's the hope I'm hanging on to."

Meanwhile, I had a beautiful boy to take care of who was now walking and getting into everything. Our house was looking very top heavy since all items from the floor to about three feet up just kept moving higher and higher. We even spent a whole weekend child-proofing all the lower cabinets. That was a waste of time and money. I couldn't get in them to get a pot to boil noodles, but JP sure had figured it out. His favorite things to play with were any things that made noise. It was always a special day when the batteries died on his fire engine toy. Not big special, like I won the lottery. More like finding a twenty-dollar bill in the dryer kind of special. Like, I could ask Will if he lost a twenty, but I'm not going to. Just like I could put new batteries in JP's toy, but I'm not going to. That kind of secret special.

Then on April 30, we got the lottery kind of special day. Our case worker called, just like I knew she would. She started telling me a story. A gal had come into the Mesa office, was pregnant, and was thinking about placing her baby for adoption and needed some help. After getting her settled, she needed a phone, and they ended up lending her AN's old phone. Wouldn't it be funny if she picked our letter? She did. She wanted to meet us. Something else—her initials were AN, just like JP's birth mom. One more thing, both AN's had the same birthday. I had a good feeling about this. We made arrangements to meet for lunch.

I liked her. She was who she was and she was unapologetic about it. She was totally upfront, and that made me trust her. She already had two boys at home and couldn't do anymore children. She was also pretty far along. Again, no idea what the sex is because the baby was in the wrong position. I got to take her to the doctor twice before they scheduled a C section. Ready for this? Her C section was scheduled for June 3. JP's second birthday. What were the odds of that?

I started potty training JP the second we got the delivery date. The goal was not to have two kids in diapers at the same time. It wasn't working. He wasn't ready, and I was just throwing more stress at myself. I think I only tried for about a week or so. They say you shouldn't start and stop because it sends mixed messages that confuse the child. In my head, I knew that. In my heart, I didn't give a shit. I'll deal with it later.

We met AN at the hospital the morning of our delivery date. No idea what to expect. They took AN into a room to get her prepped for surgery. Out in the hall, I was handed a set of scrubs and head and feet coverings. What was this? The nurse tells me that AN said I could be in the room when the baby is delivered. Oh my god! Yes! Let's do this! We were all prepped and ready to go. The doctor came in—she was a short little thing—and started telling us what to expect and what happened when. Shortly after this, AN was wheeled into the room; I was waiting outside. A nurse leaned out and waved me in not long after. The doctor was up on a step ladder, getting ready to perform the C section, waiting for me to get into the position where they told me to stand. *I hope it's a boy. I know how to change boy diapers. We already have boy stuff.* I didn't want to look when the doctor got started, but it all happened so fast. "It's a girl!" *Holy shit, we have a daughter!* I got to hold her for maybe three seconds before they whisked her away and kicked me out.

Back in AN's room, I announced it was a girl! She was beautiful! She's a chubby little thing with a full head of dark hair. Our daughter was born on our son's birthday. They were two years, thirty-seven minutes apart.

LIFE LESSON #3671

God has a sense of humor.

Our daughter, Jae, was born in a small hospital in Mesa, Arizona. This hospital did not have a nursery. Babies stayed in the same room with their mothers. AN didn't want, or maybe couldn't take care of Jae through the night. I stayed in the room that night and slept next to Jae in a recliner. That was really hard. I knew what I was doing but was really self-conscious that she would think I was doing something wrong. I could tell she was uncomfortable every time Jae made a peep, and I didn't want to cause her any more pain. I barely slept. It was a horrible, stressful, and emotionally draining night. Jae was released the following afternoon. AN had to stay. That too was horrible. Walking out of the room with the baby and saying goodbye was bittersweet. It felt like we were stealing her baby. Not to mention the seventy-two-hour waiting period wasn't over. We had to stay in Mesa for another day. We were not prepared for that. Jae spent her first night with us sleeping in a dresser drawer.

It was brought to my attention, years later, that not only did my kids' birth mothers have the same initials and they have the same birthdays and that my kids have the same birthday, my social security number matched their birthdays. I never put that together. But it's true.

I do not consider myself a religious person. I believe in God, but my relationship with him is personal. I do not believe I need to show up at a certain place, at a certain time, on a certain day to prove that. After this information was brought to my attention? I get it. I have been pissed at God. I have ignored him and I have cursed him. And still, he silently walks beside me, probably shaking his head. He had my children picked out for me the day I was born. I just didn't know it. That's why my road to parenthood took so long. My kids weren't ready yet.

I'm still not perfect. My kids aren't perfect, thank you very much. But my kids are perfect for me.

Life with two kids seemed so much harder. No more following JP around making sure he's occupied, happy and safe. I had a screaming baby now. Bless the people who have a gaggle of kids. How do they do it and stay sane? Jae was a tough baby. Nothing like JP at all. She was either sleeping or crying. It is a rare moment when she's awake and okay. And then I'm afraid to make eye contact. As soon as I do, the moment is gone. Everything I read in those stupid books or did with JP was out the window. My mom said I was getting what was due since I was a tough baby. Whatever! I didn't think Jae liked me at all. She didn't seem to like anyone! I started walking around in my bra with her in only a diaper, holding her to my chest to get her used to skin to skin contact. This seemed to help but only a little. She wasn't bonding with me. I finally talked to the doctor about what was going on. He asked a lot of interesting questions, including about prenatal care. As far as we knew, AN didn't seek any prenatal care until she was eight months along. Jae was born clean, but we really had no idea what was going on the first eight months. Birth parents fill out medical history forms about themselves and their families. Sometimes, they aren't forthcoming or don't really know the information requested. For instance, we were told AN was Caucasian and the birth father was Caucasian. Jae was clearly not Caucasian, not that we gave a fat rat's ass. The pediatrician was concerned about what Jae may have been exposed to in utero. We didn't know. The doctor diagnosed her with a hypersensitivity disorder that she may or may not grow out of. For now, the world was just too much for her. She couldn't process all the stimuli around her. The noise, the light, the touch, the smells, everything. For now, we had to try to keep things as peaceful as possible. Give her some time to adjust to things.

Poor JP, all he wanted to do was touch her and play with her. He would peek over the edge of the bassinet when she was sleeping and

I would have to redirect him. "Please don't wake her!" As far as the bonding went, I started making her look me in the eyes when I was feeding her. In the beginning, she wouldn't look at me at all, always had her head turned away. I started making a short quick sound to her to take a peek at me. Then I started making the sound and repositioning her head to look longer. Then I would tell her to look at me and wait to let her have the bottle. Little steps at a time. The first time she reached up and touched my face made me cry. "Hi, baby girl. We got this and I love you." Things started getting better.

Off to Sears for some new pictures. No naked butt pictures! Been there, done that, and it was a shitty situation. This time, everything went really smoothly. Afterward, I was in the ladies' room, changing Jae's diaper. Some lady looked at her and then at me, back at her, and said, "Your baby is so cute. "Did you adopt her from China?" *What the fuck? My spouse isn't in here with us—how would she know if he's ethnic? What is wrong with people? Why couldn't she have stopped with "Your baby is so cute"? Wait, unless she's thinking I'm too old. I'm only forty! People have babies at forty!*

I was way too tired to get into it with this woman, so I looked her dead in the eye and simply said, "Nope. Mesa." She was obviously waiting for more information. I'm not giving it to her. The whole situation had turned into a surprise staring contest. I won. But this had prompted me to call the case worker to see if she can get any more information on Jae's heritage. Our baby girl had a thick head of dark curly hair, beautiful dark eyes, and an olive complexion. She was going to want to know someday when she's older. The case worker got back to us a few days later. Turns out, AN was half-Mexican, and the birth father may have been a 6'6" tall Mexican. That was good to know. For now, she was my little sumo wrestler. She had a roly-poly belly, huge, chubby, kissable cheeks, and no neck at all.

When JP was a baby, I bought him a bright silkie thing that had Winnie the Pooh attached to one corner. He always had it with him. Constantly rubbing it in between his fingers and on his cheek. JP was a thumb sucker, and he would hold that thing in his hand and drool spit all over it. Pooh would get so stinky and gross. When I realized how attached to the thing he was, I searched for a backup one. Never found one. Trying to figure out to find time to wash the thing was a pain in the ass. So for Jae, I found something a little different and got smart. I bought two! She couldn't have cared less for it. She never touched it. In hindsight, I'm grateful she didn't like it. JP's Pooh was hard enough to keep track of. Will and I went to town to do some shopping all day with the kids. After finally getting home, we were tired, kids are tired…no Pooh. I couldn't find him anywhere, and JP was having a total shit fit for Pooh. The last time I remembered seeing him was at Taco Bell when we went for lunch. This was not good. Will had to hop on the motorcycle and head all the way back to town, while I tried to reach them on the phone. This sucked. Now Jae was crying because JP was crying. Will couldn't find Pooh at the Taco Bell. This was a shit show! I. Needed. A minute. I stepped out to the backyard for some fresh air. There in the grass lay Pooh. All that time of agony, tears, and my suffering for nothing. JP must have run in the backyard during the two seconds we weren't watching him and dropped Pooh. ECS averted. But this fiasco got me thinking, *Pooh has to die!*

While I was working on the plans for Pooh's demise, Mom came to stay with us for a while. Dave and his wife were having a tough time, and Mom needed a break from the fighting. Mom was getting older and didn't have the stamina to put up with the drama. She said everything revolved around the twins. Dave couldn't do anything right. According to Mom, he would get yelled at for the way he carried the kids or how he read to them. Didn't bathe them right, nothing was right. He would even get in trouble for eating food out of the fridge after a long day at work because it was supposed to be for the twins.

Dave coped with this by popping more pills. He made a friend who worked in the morgue at a hospital. He wasn't a doctor or anything, just a worker. From what Dave told me, when someone dies in the hospital, their belongings go down to the morgue with the body. Sometimes, those belongings include all their extra medications they brought with them to the hospital. That's where the new friend came in. If there were any good pills like Oxycontin, he would take them and sell them to Dave. The problem with this plan is that it wasn't consistent. So Dave was either busy being super stoned and falling asleep at the dinner table or busy trying to figure out how to get super stoned. Couldn't be easy for anyone to live with. Mom definitely needed a break from all that drama. I mean, she's old.

Don't get me wrong—I love having my mom around, but she is a *slob*! What is it with old ladies and tissues? Is that in the *Old Lady Handbook*? Rule no. 3: Anyone over the age of sixty-five *must* carry and save tissues, both new and used, at all times. Walking in her room is the equivalent of a bad velvet painting of angle's walking on clouds. There's tissue everywhere! All over the floor. New ones, old ones—it looks like she had a fight with the box of tissues and the box won! How difficult is it to pull one tissue out of the box? And if she even brings her empty soda cans into the kitchen, she leaves them on the end of the counter. The fucking trash can is right below them! She could literally stand still, swing her arms, and get them in the can. Why? There's not even a lid to lift. Oh! And she drops her pills sometimes. I have two kids. I can't have them thinking that shit is a Tic Tac! So now I have to keep my eye on a baby that's crawling, a toddler, Pooh, and my mom.

It was nice to be able to hop in the car without loading everyone up and run to the store really quick. We had gotten a real grocery store by this point so you could actually buy fresh produce. No more mushy carrots! So I ran to the store for a couple of frozen pizzas for lunch one afternoon. In and out, I threw my bag on the passenger seat and got in behind the wheel. I was only in the store for ten minutes or less and someone had jacked with my seat. I couldn't see in the mirrors and the seat has been pushed way too far back. *What the hell?* I started readjusting things before I noticed all the crap in the backseat. *What the hell is going on? Holy shit! This isn't my car! I'm readjusting things in someone else's car! Mine is the next spot over. Please, please, please don't let me get caught.* I grabbed my bags and ran to my car. I sped off laughing the entire time. Now the person whose car that really was was going to come out of the store and wonder what the hell was going on in their car. That's funny stuff. I should have stuck around to watch.

Mom stayed for a little over a month, but eventually, it was time to clean the last round of shredded tissues out of my dryer, pack her up, and get her back to Pennsylvania. Rumor had it, things there were going from bad to worse, and Mom wanted to go see what was really going on and if there was anything she could do to help.

On the home front, Jae had developed a horrible self-soothing habit of rocking herself to sleep at night. She didn't even realize she's doing it, but she tucked her legs under her and got to rocking. Thing was that she scooted the crib across the room until it started hitting the wall every night. I had to get up and move the crib back to where it started. Every night. That was going on my list of things to do. Plus, it was time to potty train JP, and Pooh still had a price on his head.

I anchored the crib so that it would at least quit scooting across the room. I didn't know what to do about the rocking, if I should do anything at all. It soothed her. It was not hurting anything. Well, except her hair. She looked like a baby version of Medusa in the morning, and she was not a real fan of the hairbrush. I just bought a detangler by the gallon.

Next, JP's potty training. It took a weekend. I let him run around naked. Day 1, he did not like how it felt when he peed on himself. Day 2, not one accident. But he did poop in the backyard. Said he was camping. Ah, no, no more camping in the backyard. And that was that. Done. Who knew it would be so easy?

That left Pooh's death. Which kind of took care of itself, in a roundabout kind of way. We had gone to Phoenix to visit Will's brother, and his dogs played a game of tug-of-war with poor Pooh. Pooh got some serious booboos. JP was upset. Pooh needed to go to the ER. But this got me thinking, maybe Pooh didn't have to die. Maybe Pooh just needed protection. I stitched Pooh back together and put him in a shadow box behind glass. We sat down with JP and explained that I got his booboos fixed, but he needed to be kept safe, so he can look at him through the glass but couldn't hold him anymore. I still have Pooh hanging on my wall.

Mom was right to go back to Pennsylvania when she did. Things had gotten worse. I got a phone call from Dave's wife. She said Dave had passed out and she was looking through his briefcase and found a bag of white powder and didn't know what to do. I asked her to describe it to me, what the powder looked like, how big was the bag, and how much was in it. She said it was a small bag, maybe the size of her pinky, and the powder was kind of fluffy. I told her it was probably cocaine, maybe a couple hundred dollars' worth. I couldn't tell her what to do, but if it were me, I would flush it down the toilet.

About an hour later, Dave called me and was ballistic mad. He was screaming at me for telling her to flush it down the toilet. Yelling that I have no idea what I'd done. It wasn't his. I yelled back that he was taking stuff too far; he had two kids to think about and he needed to get his head out of his ass. It was ugly. He went on to tell me that that was five thousand dollars' worth of cocaine that he was supposed to deliver in the morning. What's he going to do now? He said it was a big bag of Coke. That is not what I was told. If I had known it was that big of a bag, I'm not sure what I would have said. Apparently, Dave had been delivering cocaine in exchange for oxycontin. Oh, well that makes it all better. Not. I hung up on him. I did not need this drama.

About an hour later, Dave called back and he was much calmer. His wife never actually flushed the drugs. She only told him she did and that I was the one who told her to. She actually hid the bag in a box in the pantry and gave it back to him. So now I'm the asshole. Perfect.

Will and I decided we needed a quick weekend getaway and decided to set out to Colorado on the bikes. We were planning on taking the scenic route there and the quick route home. Things never seem to go as planned. We were going to go through Jerome, which is a small old mining town with very narrow, very twisty two-lane roads. There is absolutely no wiggle room. A lot of the houses are built right next to the road on the side of the mountain, some on stilts. It's really a cool little town with a ton of history. Apparently an eighteen-wheeler got lost and attempted to make a U-turn. What they were thinking, I do not know. But it managed to get wedged across the road, blocking both lanes of traffic. We were turned around. Our plan for the scenic route got squashed. Straight to Colorado instead. It's beautiful there. We had a nice time, but I missed the kids and wanted to head home sooner than planned. On the way back, we rode into a huge, heavy rainstorm. There was absolutely no place to pull over, get under cover, and wait things out. Not even a tree! The rain was like ice darts hitting me at seventy-five miles an hour. There was a semi in front of us and a semi behind us. It was a horrible, stressful, and exhausting ride. I was not having fun. We finally made it to Flagstaff. I was freezing and completely soaked. I was done. We decided to call it quits for the day and went to pull into a hotel parking lot. This hotel was right next to a bar, and they shared the lot. When I went to turn in, a car was coming out on the wrong side of the entrance, heading straight at me. I swerved to get out of the way, hit a puddle, and laid down my bike. I missed the car—actually, they missed me, by inches. The car never even stopped to see if I was all right. They had to have seen me. No broken bones, thank God, but I really whacked my elbow, got some road rash, some bruises, and really sore muscles. All I kept thinking was that I had two kids at home that needed a mother.

The next morning, back on the bike with my battered body, I made it as far as Prescott to Will's mom's house. I was done. I was hurting and scared. Will had to finish the trip home alone to go get the truck and come back for me. We parked my bike in the garage and came back to get it later. I only took short little rides around town after that just to blow the dust off the bike.

I am no longer a badass bitch with a bike. I am now a fat-ass mom with a stroller. And I am totally content with it. Everything revolved around the kids. They keep you on your toes. They say there's seven wonders of the world, but parents know there's really eight. It's called the Power Tower of Toys. No parent has actually witnessed how this occurs because it only happens when a child is left alone for five minutes. It is the phenomenon when every toy is suddenly in a pile in the middle of the floor. The main question parents have is, "How did this happen in the amount of time it took me to pee?" They were in the toy box only five minutes ago, and now it appears that a nuclear bomb has silently exploded in the living room.

And the cleanup is a futile attempt of patience. Three toys go back in the basket; four come back out. Things get worse, not better. Then it always happens, I have the audacity to put the one toy away that hasn't been touched in an hour but is the one toy they wanted. Now we wait for the tantrum to subside.

We needed a vacation. My stepmom has a house way out in a tiny town in West Virginia that has been in her family for generations. They were having a big celebration there that summer, so I had this brilliant idea to tow the camp trailer and drive from Arizona to West Virginia. We wanted to take our time getting there, see some sights along the way, spend some quality time with the kids, and sleep in the trailer at night. We didn't really have an itinerary to follow as long as we were there by the party. It took me days to pack the trailer with food, snacks, clothes, and whatnot. Everything was organized and prepared for the drive down to a science. We were ready, we got this! I had visions of rainbows and unicorns on a family vacation!

Do you know how long kids can cry in the backseat of a truck? *Hours!* Where are the unicorns? I brought toys and things to play with, but they didn't seem to give a shit. All plans changed on day 2. New plan: get there ASAP, get the kids out of the truck, salvage any hearing we have left. Will spent some time reworking our route to the quickest way possible. It looked like a pretty straight shot. We finally made it into West Virginia and on the road the GPS suggested would be the fastest route. Almost there. The road started out well enough but slowly got narrower, curvier, and definitely ran at more of a decline down the mountain. My anxiety levels are increasing as the road gets impossibly narrower. At least the kids aren't crying at the moment. But the trailer is smoking, so there's that. We lost our trailer brakes about two-thirds of the way down the mountain. Cue a Xanax. I have learned to stick the pill under my tongue, suffer through the taste and let it melt because it seems to get in my system faster when I'm having a panic attack. Never really fast enough, but faster. Luckily, we found a small out-of-the-way RV repair place. I really needed to get out of the truck for a while. I needed some fresh air, and it was good for the kids to stretch their legs. It didn't even take that long for the repair. I assumed this repair place was used to doing emergency brake jobs for dumb-ass tourists that went down that mountain with a trailer.

We finally made it. We were alive and on flat ground although slightly hard of hearing from all the crying and screaming. I needed a drink. Dad's place was really cool. West Virginia was really green. The grass and trees were super lush and full. The house sat on the top of a hill; it was old and bright white against the green of the grass surrounding it. There was a front porch with rocking chairs, several detached outbuildings, and bright red flowers everywhere. There was so much character and history everywhere. We said our hellos, got the trailer set up, and were given a tour of the place. The house was beautiful. It still had the old wooden floors that creak in all the right places. Some modern amenities had been put in, but the bones hadn't been changed. It had the original slave quarters off the back of the kitchen. It was used for storage now, but to be standing on the floors and actually be touching the walls where slaves slept was kinda sad. On one hand, it was just a room that's filled with boxes. On the other hand, human beings were forced to lay their heads down at night in that room. It's…well, kinda sad.

There's also a huge building at the front of the property that used to be the general store. It was also the post office, feed store, and everything else people may have needed. It still has some stuff scattered around that was really cool to look at. Old pay records and postcards and such. I saw one card dated back to 1875! The floor was a tad sketchy, so we didn't hang out for long and there were maybe three floors up that I was too nervous to go up and look at. I could have poked around in there all day if the floor wasn't so creaky.

Up the hill behind the house was a small community cemetery. It was kinda creepy and cool at the same time. Some of the gravestones were really old and hard to read. It was not like a newer cemetery where there are evenly spaced rows. This one was a bit harry carry, so it was difficult to know where to walk. I didn't want to step on anyone's grave and be disrespectful. Plus, I didn't know if they just put the coffin right in the ground back then or if they used the concrete boxes like nowadays. If the coffins were just put right in the ground, wouldn't they rot? What if I stepped on a rotten one? Would

I fall in? I would *not* want to fall into a one-hundred-year-old rotten coffin! Unless there wasn't a body buried there but really pirates' stolen gold. Knowing my luck…it was a body. Ignoring all that that was rolling around in my brain, it was beautiful and peaceful up there.

My brother, his wife, the twins, and my mom were due in the next day. It's weird that my dad and Nancy let my mom come and stay. I'm not sure I would have been as gracious as Nancy was if I were in her shoes. But that's one of the reasons I love her. I think my dad always felt bad for Mom. She'd never really gotten her shit together. And Dad knew she wanted to see us. When they got out of the car, I was shocked. Both Dave and his wife looked like absolute shit. They were both so unbelievably skinny. Dave looked sick. He didn't even resemble himself at all. He had shaved his head, his eyes and cheeks were sunken in, and there was a grayish tone to the color of his skin. Even his teeth looked sick and yellow. What the hell had been going on? After seeing Dave, I got why she was so skinny. She was stressed out. Of course, she was carrying both twins. One on each hip. They had to be older than four. They could walk. Why make things harder on yourself? And how are those skinny arms even holding them up?

I tried to get Dave alone over the next few days to see what was going on, but he kept blowing me off and saying he's fine. He had things under control. Clearly not. He keeps disappearing too. His wife has always been a very private person, so I didn't even try to talk to her. I'm not sure she would have opened up to me anyway. Mom was saying things are bad, but she was not really sure what is happening. I didn't want to ruin my dad's celebration, so I thought I would let things go for now and get back into it later.

The big party went really well. It was great showing off our perfect kids to everyone. There were a ton of people there, but JP and Jae were the cutest, hands down. Jae wasn't fully walking on her own yet; she was a little behind on the baby milestones but catching up. She needed to hold someone's hand when she was walking to help with her balance; it was adorable. She was adorable. Full head of dark, curly hair, huge dark eyes, and the chubbiest cheeks. JP was just as cute. Blond hair, deep blue eyes with the longest lashes, and an easy smile.

It was a great week in West Virginia, but it was time to head back to Arizona. We were not going back up that steep and narrow mountain road. My Xanax prescription was running low. Our trip home went way better than the trip there. The kids only screamed and cried sometimes instead of all the time. I probably sang a million rounds of the ABC song and the wheels on the bus song. Poor Will, we all knew that singing was not my forte.

Thank God we made it home when we did. Three weeks, two adults, and two toddlers in a small, cramped camp trailer? Not enough space. Someone wasn't going to make it out alive. Someone who was over the age of three and not female. It took me forever to clean out the truck and trailer. Being seriously unmotivated did not speed things along. I don't even remember giving the kids animal crackers to snack on, but judging by the amount of half dead lions, tigers, and bears, oh my! I guess I did. And that shit turned into an edible version of Elmer's glue when it was once all spitty and then dried, stuck to vehicle seats and floor mats. I thought I was doing a good job of throwing out the trash every time we stopped for fuel; apparently, I was mistaken.

Long story which I will get into later, Mom ended up moving back to Arizona shortly after our trip to West Virginia. She was living in Prescott again. She didn't have a car, so I went into town at least once a week to visit and get her out of the apartment. She was still such a slob! Plus, she started all these projects and never finished them. So not only was her apartment messy with the normal tissues and soda cans but also with things like half-finished bead projects, weaving supplies, and other artsy-fartsy stuff. It was always something. It drove me crazy.

Mom was getting older, so every visit is different. It's like that famous box of chocolates, you never know what you're going to get. I took her to Walmart, and the whole ride over there, she was complaining that her pants were itchy and didn't feel right. I had no clue what she was talking about; I just chalked it up to her old lady brain farts. It happens sometimes. We got out of the car and started walking toward the entrance when I noticed something sticking out of the bottom of her pants. I brought it to her attention, so Mom, without a care in the world, propped her foot up on a random person's car bumper and began to pull out whatever it was. She was pulling and pulling, and it just kept coming like the knotted tissues in a magician's pocket. It was a pair of pantyhose. And it was taking so long to get out of there because they're so stretchy. I looked around to make sure no one was watching this odd old lady burlesque show. But they were, and they were giving us that face. You know the one. Head cocked to the side, one eyebrow lifted, quizzical expression all over their face. That one. Mom was totally unaffected. She finally got them out and held them up in the air like a trophy and shouted "Got 'em!" *Mom! Jeez.* She explained that she just picked the pants up off the floor that she wore the other day—not surprised—and put them on. But when she took them off a few days ago, she took off the pantyhose at the same time so they must have still been in there when she put them back on today. Oh, yeah. That happens to me all the time. Not. Who even wears pantyhose under pants? What is the purpose? I made a conscious choice not to ask those questions out loud. That is a rabbit hole I did not want to go down.

Back at Walmart on another day, Mom was walking smack dab in the middle of the parking lot aisle. Not a care in the world, swinging her purse like an innocent five-year-old. Taking her time, just twisting and swinging. Oblivious to Mom, a car had been slowly following her trying to find a parking spot. I was calling to have her move over, but she must have been in brain fart mode because she was not moving. The car behind her did a very polite little *toot toot* on the horn to get her attention. All innocence was wiped from her face in an instant and replaced with the look of the devil. Even I took a sharp inhale of shock. Mom stopped, slowly turned to face the car, making a show of putting her purse in the crock of her elbow, and threw them the middle finger. With both hands! Mom! Then she took her sweet time getting out of the way. She's going to get me shot! We need to talk about manners.

I would bring her home with me here and there to stay for a few days. Those visits were just as adventurous. We have javelina in Arizona. These are wild animals that look like small pigs, but they're not in the pig family. They travel in herds of about ten. Occasionally, a herd wanders into town. Mom always wanted to see one but never did. It happens to be one of the occasions that a herd had wandered into town and was grazing in the open lot in front of our house, and Mom was visiting. The perfect storm. Mom was out front before I could say boo. She was standing maybe twenty feet away, watching them with glee. I guess that's okay. But no, not for Mom; she wanted to get even closer. Mom! These were wild animals; they had tusks. They were generally herbivores but can get aggressive when they're threatened. Those tusks could do some serious damage. Mom was trying to get closer, and they were trying to walk away. What was she thinking? Quickly, the javelina picked up their pace. Mom was running after them to get a closer look, and I saw the big one in the back of the herd turn its head to get a look at her. It had that same look of the devil that Mom had at Walmart. She should know this look. This was not going to end well. "Mom! *Stop! Now!*" She did, but I think it was only because she was running out of breath. Crazy old lady.

I finally bought Mom a car. It was just a cheap old beater to get her back and forth to the store if I was busy. She called me from Walmart one day. What is it with Walmart? She couldn't find her keys and didn't know what to do. "I'm an hour away, my kids are napping, I can't come right now." I told her to look in the ladies' room and backtrack her steps. No keys. I had her ask at customer service to see if anyone turned them in. Nope. I told her to go see if she locked them in the car and I would get AAA out there to help. Turns out, she did not lock them in the car because she never turned the car off. She also never shut the door. She got to Walmart, put the car in park—thank God for small miracles—and skipped every other step. She shopped for forty-five minutes with the car like that. Mom?

Mom was losing it. Her health hadn't been the greatest for a while, but now her brain farts were becoming more frequent. I was going to have to figure something out. I got a call one morning that Mom had been taken to the hospital and was suffering with congestive heart failure. I didn't know what to do. Will was at work. I didn't want to bring the kids with me to the hospital. I figured I would wait until he got home before I headed that way. I had made some good friends in town and was telling one of them what was going on. She insisted I leave the kids with her and go right away. I'm so grateful she did that. By the time I got there, Mom was unconscious. She had had some complications, and *if* they could pull her through, she would need to go on dialysis and may not be able to walk or talk. They didn't know. My uncle's wife, mom's brother's wife, was on dialysis before she passed. Mom wouldn't want that. They asked if she had a DNR in place. Yes, but that was under my brother's control. He had not been very reliable lately, so good luck with that. The DNR question really brought the reality of the situation home. I spent the day talking to her, repeating all the funny stories from being kids, holding her hand, and listening to the low beep from the heart machine. Before I left, I told her if she wanted to fight, she needed to get busy, but if she was tired, it was okay to go. I told her I would be okay.

I got a call in the wee hours the next morning. Mom's heart had stopped. They had been doing CPR for forty minutes. Got her back twice but couldn't get it going a third time. I told them to stop. She wouldn't want it. I left the kids with Will and started driving to the hospital.

I know the exact moment my mom passed. The sun was just cresting the horizon when a javelina ran out in the road in front of me. I had to come to a complete stop. It was all alone, which is unusual, silhouetted by an orange glow from the sun, facing me, standing perfectly still and staring at me for a minute. I immediately knew that was my mom, saying goodbye. I don't know how long I sat in my car, in the middle of the road, crying.

I had Mom cremated. Dad paid for it. I didn't have a service. There wasn't anyone to come to one. There's always that tiny part in my brain that wonders if I did the right thing. Should I have told her it was okay to go? Does she think that meant I didn't care? Should I have fought with the hospital to try harder? Did I let her down when she needed me the most?

I had an amulet made with some of her ashes; the rest I drove around with in the back of my car for months. I would talk to her, and my friends would be in the car sometimes when I did. They looked at me like I was crazy. I didn't care. It made me feel better.

I eventually spread the rest of her ashes out in the woods. We had a favorite spot we would drive out to, have a picnic lunch, and relax. It's a beautiful spot with pine trees and open meadows. Wildflowers in the spring, a small creek nearby, and a herd of deer that were almost tame enough to feed. I got the best part of her in my amulet. I have her heart. That's what I tell myself. I hope she's happy there. I question that too sometimes.

Unfortunately, our time spent in West Virginia would be the last time I would ever see my brother. And his wife and kids, for that matter. Through phone calls with my brother and mother, the story I could piece together goes like this: Dave got tired and lonely from being left out of his wife and children's lives. He solved that by going out and finding a girlfriend. His first of many mistakes. They would go out partying, and Dave was having a hard time getting up for work the next day, so she introduced Dave to crack. He already had a drug problem that was manageable, and why he would even try it is beyond my comprehension, knowing how addictive it was. He was in his forties. He should have known better. He was instantly addicted. That's where he kept disappearing to in West Virginia; he needed a hit. His girlfriend was from Liberia and somehow convinced Dave to invest in an import business with her family back home. And invest he did. Lots of money. The problem was that they were sending things that Dave was paying for that are illegal to sell in the States. Things like elephant tusks and leopard skins. Of course, the business wasn't going good. Dave had a crack addiction; he was stressed out and was missing work from lack of sleep. So this wonderful woman introduced Dave to heroin to help him sleep. I guess it was supposed to be crack in the mornings, heroin in the evenings. Dave was instantly addicted to that now too.

In the cookie cutter version of the story, she got arrested on a stolen motorbike and got deported. I'm sure there's more to that than I know. Dave got fired, and within six months, he blew through all the family accounts, the kids' college funds, got credit cards out in my mom's name, unbeknownst to her, maxed them out, and the big, beautiful house was in foreclosure. Six months. Between all the drugs and the "business," Dave was ruined.

His wife kicked him out, rightfully so. What wasn't right was that she blamed everything on my mother. It was her fault because she didn't raise him right and she kicked mom out too. Right then and there. She literally threw my seventy-something-year-old mom out on the street. Now I was pissed. I had to figure out how to get Mom to Arizona ASAP. This is how Mom ended up back in Arizona. I had to figure out where she was going to live, how to get her things here, how to get her here all in record time. Which I did. I found her an apartment at a retirement complex, had her stuff shipped, and bought the majority of furniture she would need to get started. The rest I would figure out later. After getting Mom here and settled, I wrote Dave's wife a letter. I'm not sure about everything I said, but I know I told her she needed to take some of the responsibility for his behavior. She was on the front line. She was the closest person to him and should have stepped up a long time ago. Instead, she was so wrapped up in the kids that she forgot all about Dave and took the easier route of ignoring all the signs. She enabled him by giving back his drugs and turning a blind eye. She must not have liked hearing that since she hasn't spoken to me since.

Dave spent his time holed up in a shitty apartment that my dad paid for, doing crack and heroin all day. This pisses me off too. I get that my father can't stomach the thought of his son living on the streets, but I don't get why he always seems to get special treatment even when he's a fuckup. Dad tried to have several interventions, but Dave wasn't having any of it. I pretty much checked out at that point. I was mad that he did this to himself and his kids. I was mad that Mom was getting the blame. I was mad that Mom was getting credit card bills she couldn't afford to pay. I was mad how badly his wife treated her. Most importantly, I missed my brother. We were best friends, and he let me down. I couldn't even talk to him on the phone anymore. It hurt my heart to hear how stoned he always was.

He got cancer. He thought it was an abscess from shooting up his heroin and didn't go to a doctor. By the time he went, it was bad news. He got a form of cancer called synovial sarcoma. The problem was that he was too high to make it to any doctor's appointments or chemo. It traveled fairly quickly to his brain, and he passed. So yeah, technically, Dave died from cancer. Realistically, he died from drugs. I didn't go to his funeral. I had mourned the loss of my brother long before his physical body was gone.

The loss of my brother crushed my dad. He was never really the same. Everyone says parents shouldn't bury their children. They shouldn't, but sometimes they do, and it sucks.

At least my mom was there to greet him.

I had made a handful of good friends. We were like the Musketeers. One I met through the fire department. I usually spent Sundays at her house drinking a few beers and smoking a few secret cigarettes. We both liked this series on HBO, so we would watch that and gossip. It was my Sunday Funday. Another gal I met on the first day of kindergarten. I had dropped JP off and was skipping back to the car with joy in my heart. There was this poor, sad woman walking back to her car, crying. I was perplexed. Why the tears? This was a happy day. Our kids were growing up a little bit; they were learning and making new friends. Blah, blah, blah... Who gives a shit about any of that? My day just got that much easier! One down, one to go! I did feel bad for her though. I let her have her moment and approached her after school that day. We became fast friends.

The Third Musketeer, I met through her husband. I had gotten a part-time job at a tiny sandwich shop. I loved that job, and I loved the owner, Lisa. Her husband was also on the volunteer fire department. She eventually closed the little sandwich shop and moved to a much larger building. That building had a restaurant on one side, a bar on the other side, and a takeout window in the center for pizza's and things. I followed her there and worked part time as a waitress and bartender. Jax's husband had been coming into the bar for dinner while she was still back home finishing up and getting things ready to move to our tiny mining town. Her husband was telling me that she would be showing up to town right near her birthday. Amber and I put together a birthday party for a woman we didn't even know. Amber got toasted and started smearing icing from the cake in places icing shouldn't be. It was hilarious. Poor Jax had no idea whom her husband had introduced her to. Welcome to town! We had become fast friends.

Amber had one kid, Jax had three, and I had two, all around the same age. We would meet up at our local park at least three times a week to let the kids run around and play on the playground while we sat and had a few beers. Mommy bonding time. There was always something or someone to talk about. That's one of the downfalls of living in a tiny isolated town. Everybody knows your business, whether it's true or not. It's like living in a fishbowl.

Will and I sold my motorcycle and bought a couple little two-seater sand buggies instead. We would tow our camp trailer to the river, which was only about twelve miles out of town and didn't always have water running. We would spend the weekend goofing off with the kids in the buggies, cooking hotdogs on sticks and visiting with friends. It was close enough for people to come to camp for the day and drive home at night. It was always a good time. We always had the kids wear helmets while the adults took turns driving them around. Wearing a helmet had no bearing on the time I almost killed Amber's kid, though. There was a big hill behind where we were camping, and I really wanted to ride one of the buggies up it but was afraid it wouldn't make it up. Everyone kept assuring me it would make it, so I gave it a try. Amber's kid was in the passenger seat. We were all strapped in with our five-point harnesses, sitting at the bottom of the hill. I gunned it. The buggy got to the top of the hill a lot faster than I expected. I didn't expect there to be a giant hole at the top. When we reached the top, the front tires fell into the hole, and the buggy flipped upside down. The hole was slightly bigger than the seating space of the buggy and deeper than the height of it. We were hanging upside down by our five-point harnesses, the wheels holding us up on the edge of the hole. Holy shit! Amber's kid looked at me like this was just another day, unhooked her harness, and climbed out. I, on the other hand, needed a minute.

We sold those sand buggies shortly after that incident and bought a Polaris side by side with a backseat for the kids. Jax's family bought one too. Now we had it going on! We spent just about every weekend riding out in the hills. We explored some beautiful country, cool old abandoned mine shafts, and watering holes for catfishing. We would pack coolers of food and drinks and head out for a whole day. We even did a night ride once or twice. They are not my favorite. I do not like not being able to see beyond the reach of the headlights. Especially when I had to pee. You basically have two choices. Pee in the light where everyone can watch you or pee in the dark where you can't see what's watching you. I always chose the light.

Sometimes there were a lot of us that went on the rides, sometimes only a few. My single friend even got herself a four-wheeler and would come along for the day too.

Only once, the weather did not work in our favor. There were a bunch of us on this ride, and we were way out in the middle of nowhere, heading home after a long day, when it started to rain. At first, it was really nice. Cooled us off, washed off some of the dirt from the roads, and was kind of fun. Different. But then, it started coming down in buckets. That's when it got really cold. We were not prepared for this. All I really cared about was the kids. We had to cross an open, flat dirt mesa that the rain had turned into a mud bog. It was fun at first, super messy. We were slipping and sliding; mud was flinging everywhere. By the time we reached the middle of the mesa, the mud got thicker and deeper as it continued to rain. All our rigs started slowing down because the mud was building up and getting packed in the wheel wells and tires. If you stopped moving, you were screwed because you would never be able to get enough traction to start going forward again. My friend's four-wheeler got buried in the mud. Jax's husband tried to tie it to the back of his rig and pull her out, but it was so stuck it broke the back of his rig. She had to abandon ship at that point. That thing wasn't going anywhere. We had to go back later to pull it out. We ended up coming across a rancher on a big o' horse who pulled it out for her. That was kind of fun to watch. We all messed up our rigs that day in one way or another.

On another memorable ride, Jax invited one of her friends to join in on the ride for the day. She had her own four-wheeler. I had met her once or twice before; she was one of those people that just rubbed me the wrong way for no real reason. When she showed up in bright white Daisy Duke shorts, full face of heavy makeup, no food, only two bottles of water, and two beers for the entire day in the Arizona heat, I found my reason. I secretly nicknamed her Fancy Pants. Everyone was told to bring supplies. "We will be out all day, and bring enough food and water for yourself." And she had a kid with her. So that's one bottle of water each for the whole day? And no food? Not even for the kid? She had all the information and chose to ignore it? Or was she expecting everyone else to take care of her? I was irritated. This woman had to go. This was going to be an interesting day.

First rattle out of the box, we had an issue. We were taking a trail that had a very steep, rocky incline in the beginning but then flattened out. She was scared and didn't want to ride her rig up the hill. Fan-fucking-tastic. And so it began. Jax had to ride her four-wheeler up the hill, walk back down to get Fancy Pants's rig, and ride it up while she and the kid walked. When she got to the top of the hill, she started running around in circles, flapping her arms and screaming, "Bees! Bees! There's bees!" Well, no shit. We are out in the country. Bees live outside. I asked if she was allergic. No, she just didn't like bees. Huh. Now I was feeling kinda snarky.

Will and I were in front of the pack; Fancy Pants was about four rigs back. I told Will to pick a spot up the road, make sure Fancy Pants can see us, slam our rig in park, jump out, and start shooting. Will was like, "Shoot at what?"

"I don't care. Shoot at the dirt, but pretend you're shooting at a rabbit or something." We always have a pistol with us in case there's a rattlesnake or something, and Fancy Pants made a comment that she doesn't like shooting. She should not have said that. Will did exactly what I said, and she started screaming again then started demanding to know what we were doing. "Will got a rabbit," I told her. We drove off in the middle of her tirade with a small smirk on my face. Gotcha.

A couple hours go by, we pulled over in some shade for a break. She was having a meltdown over her bright white Daisy Duke shorts that were now the color of Arizona dirt. What did she think was going to happen? It's dry and dusty in the desert. Hello? It's not a fashion show. I didn't have the heart to tell her that all that heavy makeup on her face was now one-fourth inch thicker with dust too. Hair too. And of course, their one bottle of water each was long gone. I couldn't let the kid suffer from his mother's stupidity and gave them each more water before we took off again to find a nice place to park for lunch.

Lunch was my final straw. Couldn't eat in front of them. Couldn't do that to the kid. So of course everyone fed them. Now her two beers were gone and she wanted more. Shocking. Since we fed her, I guess she thought we would be supplying everything and started helping herself to everyone's coolers. So did the kid. I usually pack a little extra stuff but not enough to supply two extra people for a full day. I also brought a few secret cigarettes for myself, and she started helping herself to them too. But what really pissed me off was when she started bragging about how good of an outdoors woman she was. Between the bees, the dirt, no food or water? I'm not buying it. She was going on and on about how good of a camp-fire builder she was. Arizona was under a fire restriction at the time. We hadn't had any rain in a very long time, and it was dangerously dry. It was illegal to have fires because of the risk of sparks creating a wildfire. That wasn't a secret. It was all over the news, and there are signs posted along all the trailheads stating this. Jax and I had to go pee and came back to a raging campfire! What the fuck? That dumb bitch was going to burn down the forest! Any yahoo with a lighter and a stick can start a fire! What was she trying to prove? I dumped our cooler of ice and water on it with some not so nice words. I was done with Fancy Pants. Will and I packed our crap and hightailed it home with whatever beer she left me in our cooler that now had no ice or water left.

That woman ended up being pure drama with a capital D. I had nothing to do with her anymore, but poor Jax worked with her, so I got to hear all the stories. She didn't last that long in the mining town. I think she got fired for drinking on the job. Don't quote me on that, though. I don't think Jax kept in touch with her after she left.

For the kids' birthday, we got them some rides of their own. JP got a tiny little dirt bike, and Jae got a tiny little pink camo quad. Both had governors so we could control how fast they got to go, and Jae's had a remote kill switch. JP caught on fairly quickly until he tried to load it on the trailer by himself. He never hit the brake when he got to the end of the trailer, so it smacked into the little side wall and sent him flying in the air. No serious injuries, just a bruised ego that taught him he had more to learn. Jae, on the other hand, didn't catch on as quickly. She kept getting distracted. She would take a hand off the handlebars to readjust her helmet. Then she would take a hand off to push up her safety goggles. Then it was to fiddle with her protective gloves. If it wasn't one thing, it was another. Then I don't know what she was thinking because she took both hands off the handlebars at the same time! Heading straight toward a small cliff! Thank goodness for the emergency kill switch. They weren't allowed to bring them on our rides; that would have been too stressful. When they rode, it was a day just for them, but we did find some flatter ground for them to play on. I liked watching the kids goof off, doing their thing.

Most days were about the kids. Rarely did I get to go to town by myself. It was a real treat when I got to do that, but I always had to hurry to get out of the house before the kids noticed something was different. On one of the days I got to go to town by myself, I got up, did my hair and makeup, grabbed a T-shirt, and snuck out of the house. I was having a great day. It was one of those rare days when everything seemed to be in your favor. Parking spot by the door. Everyone was being so sweet and pleasant. Every store I went to, random people were smiling at me and being extra helpful. It was as if God himself was shining a ray of sunshine directly on me. So much so that I could feel the warmth on my shoulders. On my last stop for the day, I had to use the restroom. After doing my business, I was washing my hands and glanced in the mirror above the sink. Well... shit. My t-shirt was inside out and backwards. The printed label was at my throat for everyone to see. God wasn't shining a light on me. I was nobody special. People were quietly laughing at me. I looked like an idiot. I should have known better. It turns out that solo trips to town aren't always a good thing since a normal person's wardrobe malfunction isn't half as interesting or newsworthy as Janet Jackson's. A normal person's wardrobe malfunction falls in the dumbass category. I seem to find myself in that category more often than I should.

On a family trip to town, I found myself back in the dumbass category. This time, I blame Will. We were about halfway through our errands, and I started getting a massive headache and asked Will to pull into a gas station so I could buy one of those easy packs of aspirins. I'm standing at the counter getting ready to pay when the cashier lady starts giving me that sideways look with one eyebrow raised. I was thinking, *What the hell are you looking at?* Now I was all paranoid. *Do I have a boogie hanging? Is there something in my teeth? Is my shirt on backward?* I've been there. I paid for my aspirin, and the first thing I did when I get back in the truck was flip down the passenger side mirror. Seriously? One of the lenses in my sunglasses had fallen out. That's why I had such a bad headache and why the cashier was looking at me so funny. Yep, back in the dumbass category. I was looking at Will like, "What the hell?"

He was all, "Sorry. Didn't notice." How do you not notice that?! I developed a habit of tapping my sunglasses to make sure both lenses were in after that for a while. I'm sure if anyone saw me doing that, they would wonder what my dumb ass was doing!

Everyone knows raising kids can be tough. There are good days, and there are shit days. I was having one of those shit days. I had to do some shopping in Prescott, and the kids were entertaining themselves by picking on each other. All day. They were both on full-on brat mode. The stupid books say that when your kids are misbehaving in public, you should just leave and go back another time. That's easy to say when it doesn't take an hour just to get to the real grocery store. So I didn't leave. I just gritted my teeth and put on my big girl panties. Things were going from bad to worse. The kids were getting under the racks, knocking things off the shelves, and doing a really good job of driving me bat shit crazy. Then JP pinched his sister, and she started screaming like he had ripped her arm off. I gave him a tap on the butt to get his attention, and some lady started throwing the stink eye at me. She started telling me that I shouldn't spank my kids;

I needed to leave instead. "Bitch, today is not the day." I probably should not have said that out loud, but it was already out there. Exit stage left! I got only what we had to have and decided it was time to head home. I made one last stop at the bookstore so the kids could each pick out a book to entertain themselves on the ride home. Yes, I know I shouldn't reward them for bad behavior, but I needed some peace, and the kids needed to still be breathing by the time we got home.

The first twenty minutes of the ride home was bliss. It was the ear-piercing scream coming from the backseat that made me glance in the rearview mirror. JP had a handful of Jae's hair. Jae had a hand-ful of JP's hair. Their heads were rocking back and forth, depending on who was winning the hair tug-of-war at that moment. One of them wanted to trade books; one of them wanted both books, I'm not sure which. I don't care. I got to the first pullout I could find. I didn't know my SUV could skid out. I told the kids to get out! They couldn't have been but four and six, maybe five and seven. I don't care. Well, well, well. Now they're a team. A united front. Ha! JP is telling me all about how Jae didn't even have shoes on. Jae was concerned that JP needs a jacket. *Out!* I had them stand over by the bushes, gave them their shoes and a jacket. JP was asking if I was calling Dad to come get them. Nope. And the worst part was that it was going to be dark soon so they were going to have to hold hands! I stomped back to my car like a two-year-old and got in. I watched them holding hands by the bushes for almost ten minutes. I needed a mental moment. I got the kids back in the car, and neither of them made a single peep the rest of the way home. About a week later, there was a story on the news about a woman who did the same thing I did, except she drove off. She was arrested for child abandonment and child endangerment. I'm so glad I didn't even put the car in drive.

Good days, bad days, and funny days. Jax was at the house; we were sitting in the garage watching the kids play. JP was swinging a stick around, so I called to him to bring it to me before someone got hurt. He was pulling a flat-out *no*. Excuse me? Bring me the stick. No. Now I was annoyed and demanded the stick. He marched in the garage, full of attitude, and threw the stick, which bounced and jabbed Jax in the leg, drawing blood. I was no longer annoyed; I was mad. I picked up the stick with the intent of giving him a swat for being disrespectful and for hurting someone. JP took off running around the house. I was chasing him with the stick. Two times around the house. I was fat. I was old. I secretly smoked and I was losing. He finally stopped running, and I went to give him a tap on the butt with the stick. It was so old and rotted that it just crumbled on impact. It would have been more effective if I had tapped him with a roll of paper towels. I was standing there, out of breath and a bit frustrated, when Jae walked up and handed me a new stick. "Here, Mom, use this one." The whole scene was so stupid and futile that I couldn't help but burst out laughing. JP started laughing. Jae was pissed I didn't take another whack at her brother. I never was a good disciplinarian. I can probably count how many times I've spanked the kids on one hand, combined.

There are also days that we learn something. I was in the shower, shaving my legs, when JP walked in. No such thing as privacy anymore. I had run out of my shaving cream and was using a bar of soap. My very observant son noticed this and told me to wait a minute. He ran to the sink and grabbed his dad's can of shaving cream for me to use. Thanks, buddy! It was Cooling Aqua Velva Gel. I shaved my legs, and it was a really close, smooth shave. I liked it. I was going to shave my pits. Great shave. I was going to shave my vag! I loaded her up with that Cooling Aqua Velva Gel and just started getting things going. My vag was seriously getting cool. About half-way through, the cooling sensation on my vag was kind of starting to burn. Uncomfortably so. Forget the vag! I rinsed off, making sure all the shaving gel was gone, but I shit you not, I could taste Aqua Velva in the back of my mouth. I don't know anything about biology or how the body works, but I do know that Cooling Aqua Velva Gel tastes like shit! And I know my vag is only one half shaved, which is an interesting look. That day, I learned to never *ever* use anything other than female shaving cream anywhere near your vag. Period.

LIFE LESSON #3807

Life is a learn-as-you-go kind of situation.

*****

Years ago, when I was working on being normal, I had my tattoos removed. Normal people do not have tattoos. Getting tattoos removed hurts. Way more than getting them. Not to mention, it's super expensive. Way more than getting them. And it's not a one and done situation. It takes several trips. The machine basically burns the ink out of your skin. Then more ink rises closer to the surface and you go back for another round. It stinks and it hurts. So why would I go back and get another tattoo? Because my facade of being "normal" was slipping.

I tried to do all the things I thought normal people did. I even went to church for a while. Personally, I found it to be a little hypocritical. People know things about people when you live in a tiny town. I felt that just because you show up to church on Sunday, sing along with all the hymns, and bow your head when you're supposed to, it doesn't excuse the things you do the rest of the week. I joined a women's only bible study. Boring. I took up cross stitch as a hobby. I liked it, but it sure takes a while. I made four-course meals no one ate. I volunteered at the school. I hosted dinner parties and game nights. I never cursed. I rarely had a drink. I wore cotton briefs and sensible shoes. I kept my mouth shut and my head down.

And I was dying inside. I was so busy trying to be what I thought was normal that I lost myself. I was no longer creative or outspoken. I forgot that my opinion mattered and it was okay to get mad. No matter how hard you try, a person can only hold their breath underwater for so long.

Not surprising, Will and I started going through a rough patch. First, I got my nose pierced. He didn't like that. He said if it got infected, he wouldn't drive me to the hospital. I didn't care. Then I got a big tattoo with the kids' names. He really didn't like that, and I really didn't care about that either. So I got another one on my foot. And then on the back of my neck. We still went on our rides in the hills, but I no longer spent my time trying to make Will happy and making sure he was having fun. In fact, I got my own four-wheeler so I didn't have to sit in the rig with him the whole time, never even having a conversation. I was too tired to worry if he was having fun or not. I was having fun, and the kids were having fun. My four-wheeler was built to have two riders. The driver and a seat behind with its own foot pegs and backrest. The kids would take turns riding with me. Jae would almost always fall asleep. Her helmet had a small visor on the front that stuck out, and when she would fall asleep, her head would constantly fall forward and whack my back with the visor. I would come home with a small horizontal bruise every time, but it was worth it.

The Musketeers started taking girls weekends to Laughlin, Nevada, whenever we got a chance. Actually, Jax always wanted to bring her husband because she still liked the guy. Amber and I always poo-pooed it. Looking back, I don't think we were very nice about that. Who were we to tell her what to do? I think it was just because we weren't happy at home and didn't want to see other people who were. Or maybe we just didn't want any extra witnesses to our foolishness. I'm not sure, but with the kids safely tucked away at home, we always drank too much and acted like idiots. Just a handful of normally calm housewives blowing off steam like college girls on spring break. We only lost Jax once. Amber and I decided we needed a nap because we are not college girls anymore and left Jax at the pool. I'm not sure what happened while we were gone, but by the time we found her, she was drunk and had pissed off a couple at the pool. Something about showing her boobs? Whether on purpose or by accident, I'm not sure, but the wife wasn't happy. We thought it

163

was funny, and Jax was hilariously drunk. We had our own personal entertainment for the evening. That was so much fun! She wasn't having as much fun the next morning on the ride home, though.

Will decided it was his turn and wanted to take a vacation by himself to Sturgis on his motorcycle. I decided I better get to work stashing some cash of my own in case things went sideways. And things weren't looking so good. I started working every bartending and waitressing shift Lisa would give me. I'm not happy. I'm not sure if he's happy. Hell, I don't know if he even liked me anymore. I did know he would rather spend time away from me instead of with me. We talked about going to a counselor, but that never went anywhere.

I packed up our stuff and moved a few blocks away on a Sunday afternoon with the kids and the cat. Amber and her husband helped me with the big stuff because they had a truck. I felt like a failure. I couldn't make it as a normal person. Whatever that was, it wasn't me. I had to shoulder the majority of our failure. Will was who he was. He was the rock and never pretended to be anything different. I was pretending to be someone I wasn't. I became what I thought he wanted and needed. Or rather, I tried to become that person. I needed more attention, more affirmation. I knew he wasn't that kind of person when I married him, but I thought it would be enough. I never really told him what I needed. I'm not sure I really knew.

At some point, I had to figure this out. The first go-around, I desperately tried to fix him. This go around, I tried to fix me. Neither of these approaches were working. At least we didn't fight. We could have coasted through life like we were, but it wasn't enough for me. You only get to go around this life one time. There are no do-overs, and I wanted to spend my time here happy. Not complacent.

Of course, living in a tiny town, the rumors started flying. I heard all kinds of things. I heard I was having an affair. I heard I was having a lot of affairs actually. I heard Will was sick, so I left him. None of that is true. Yes, I worked at the bar. Yes, I went out with friends. Yes, some were male friends. That is my crime. I didn't really care what people were saying. I knew the truth.

Being a single mom is tough! And I probably had it a little easier than some, and it was still hard. Since I didn't work for the mining company, I couldn't rent a house in town. Will bought us an old, beat-up mobile home, and my car was paid for. I still had lot rent and all the other bills to pay, not to mention food.

I worked as many shifts that I could as long as Will could watch the kids. Babysitters cost money, and I didn't really have any to spare. Any extra money went toward fixing the house, which ended up being a cute little house in the end.

I met a guy at work right about the time Will and I started falling apart. We would hang out at the bar here and there, dance the two step, and talk. But that was it. He was a contractor that lived in a different state but was in town for a little while doing a job for the mine. Right when the kids and I moved into our little house, he got into a fight with his boss, quit his job, and needed to go back home. He asked if he could move in with us until he worked something else out. Ahhh, no, that was not going to happen. I just split up with my husband. The kids needed time to adjust, and so did I. I couldn't do that to them, and I didn't want anything like that. Sorry. Not really. He was leaving the next day back to Texas, but on his way out, he found a dog wandering around all by himself in the middle of nowhere. Of course, he brought the dog to me. It was a little red miniature pinscher. Jae wanted to keep him, and she named him Frisbee. He was a cute little thing. And he fit through the small doggie door that was built into my little house. How convenient.

I stayed in touch with the guy after he got back to Texas. We talked on the phone quite a bit. Kept each other up to date on what was going on in our lives, how work was going, normal bullshit.

My little house had a little front porch that was just big enough for all the girls to hang out. We would get together every chance we could and sit around the table talking about everything and nothing at all. We would laugh and vent, tell stories, and talk about work. We traded gossip we heard about other people and ourselves. My little handful of girl friends are what kept me strong during some hard times.

Texas and I started talking on the phone more and more. It made me feel good to know someone gave a shit about me and would call just to see how we were all doing. I took a vacation and flew out to Texas to visit. And I hate to fly! I put it all on a credit card and figured I would deal with it later. Which in reality, was going to be tough because I was broke. Waitressing and bartending in a small town doesn't leave a lot of room for extravagances like vacations or food for that matter.

I had the school bus drop the kids off at the restaurant when I worked a day shift. I would have the kids sit in a back room and do their homework while I finished up my shift. Sometimes they helped with my side work or setting tables while they told me about their day. It was sweet. I usually fixed them a snack of pepperoni and crackers or a cheese sandwich to split with some soup. I didn't pay for it, and my boss, Lisa never brought it up. She was a good friend. She knew things were tight. She always let me work the big parties or the dance nights at the bar when there were big tips. She let me pick the shifts that worked around the kids and were the good money makers. She also knew when I needed a night out and would have her daughter come babysit for me. And she paid for my drinks. We used to have so much fun! There was another gal that worked at the restaurant too. Her name was Liz. Lisa and Liz had been friends since they were kids. Listening to their stories was hilarious! And they knew everyone in town. More often than not, a Friday night at the bar was a reunion of sorts. The other manager at the restaurant was Shelby. Shelby was the sweet, motherly type. She would sit with my kids sometimes and help them with their homework. I appreciated that. I would make a horrible teacher. I have no patience. Plus, there's always that one kid. The one you want to beat the shit out of, but you can't, because you're a teacher.

I loved that job. We were a family. Albeit a dysfunctional one but a family nonetheless. Those were some days.

Almost a year after I left Will, I was working the night shift at the bar and some guy came in for a few drinks and dinner. The place was dead, so we got to talking. It was early on a Thursday night, and I always worked that shift. He was all depressed because his wife of almost thirty years packed her crap and moved out the previous Sunday. We bonded over our failed marriages. We chatted for over an hour and a half before we even introduced ourselves. His name is Joe. I thought he looked familiar from waiting on him but didn't have a name to go with the face. It was a good talk. We traded phone numbers before he left. He said we should get together sometime, maybe get some dinner. Sure. He was not my usual type. I liked them tall, the taller the better, but a free dinner sounded pretty good. It took us two weeks of calling and texting before we could get together.

Meanwhile, Texas was starting to drive me crazy. What I thought was really nice in the beginning was becoming overwhelming. He called me constantly. Then he started wanting to be on speakerphone when my friends were at the house. Then he wanted to be on speakerphone when I was having dinner with the kids. I would try to take a nap before my bar shift on Thursdays and would tell him that, but he wouldn't wait more than twenty minutes for me to call him back. It all ramped up so slowly before I realized it. I was basically checking in all day. And I mean all day. If I had to run to Prescott, I had to call when I was leaving. Then call when I got there. Then call when I left one place to go to another. Then call when I was leaving town, heading home. Then call when I got home. Once, I called when I was leaving town and then decided to get gas. I called when I got home, and he was interrogating me as to why it took so long. I had to get gas. Was he timing me? I was an adult. What is going on? I didn't see it at the time, but he was grooming me for total control.

Joe and I finally met at a bar/restaurant outside town. That almost didn't happen. Gotta love small town gossip. Everyone was telling me that Joe and his wife were swingers and she still lived at their house. And Texas kept calling and calling. I called Joe to cancel on my way there, but he insisted I go and listen to his side of the story. I was hungry. Free dinner. Turns out, his wife had moved out and only came to the house on Tuesday's to do the yard and earn some money. All that drama and I ended up paying for dinner. It was only five dollars.

Joe and I started spending more and more time together. I liked him. We had the same smartass sense of humor and he's funny. Joe is the one who made me realize what Texas was up to with the never-ending phone calls. He wasn't concerned with my safety. He was keeping tabs on me. He wanted to be on speakerphone all the time to make sure he didn't hear another man's voice.

I couldn't take it anymore. I told Texas I needed a breather and he needed to stop calling me. Things blew up, and he went batshit crazy! He called everyone I knew and told them horrible lies about me. He told them things I said about them that I never said. Somehow, he got Joe's number and started calling and threatening him. He even got Will's number and called him. Told him a bunch of bullshit stories about how horrible I am. His end goal was for everyone to hate me and then abandon me so that I would have no one left to lean on but him. If he couldn't have me, no one could. Win by default. It didn't work.

Texas stepped up his game to a new level. The phone calls were becoming violently threatening. I was getting really scared. Texas is only a one-day drive. He started sending pictures of guns and his car on the road. Joe finally told him to come on into Arizona. He wasn't scared. I sure was. I went to the courthouse for a restraining order. I had to bring Jae with me that day. The judge wouldn't let me bring her into the courtroom when it was my turn, so I had to leave her in the hallway. When the bailiff came to get me, I told Jae in a very loud, stern voice, "If anyone tries to touch you or talk to you or even looks at you…you scream as loud as you can and I will be right there. Got it?" She was nodding when I noticed an armed guard reposition himself to stand directly across from her. I was very grateful to her secret protector. It took about eight minutes for the order of protection to be granted. I mouthed a silent "thank you" to Jae's guard who gave me a quick nod before walking away. Now I had to find someone to serve the paperwork. That was going to cost money I didn't have, but I got it done.

When I said he went bat shit crazy before, I was wrong. After getting served with the order of protection was when he really went bat shit crazy. The phone calls were relentless. All hours of the day and night. Threats about there not being enough cops to keep him away from me. A piece of paper can't stop a bullet. Hell, he didn't even need a gun to kill me. Threats about him being a patient man and can wait to get me later. Threats about him always getting even if someone wronged him. It never stopped. I was so stressed out and worried for my kids. It got so bad that I ended up in the hospital for 3 days with my blood pressure going stupid. Thank God my divorce wasn't final yet and I still had insurance.

Joe had a chat with Texas while I was in the hospital. I don't know what was said; I don't want to know and I honestly don't care. But things started to slow down. Thankfully. Over the next couple of weeks, I found out some interesting and scary things about Texas. The most frightening thing was that his name wasn't what I was told it was. It was an alias he had been using because he had been in prison for attempted murder. That was not good. This man had been around my children and in my home. I had gone to his home. I found out that he didn't quit his job as a contractor. He was fired because they found out his real name and he couldn't pass the background check and was escorted off the property. That's crazy scary. He had a friend in town that I didn't know about that would drive by my house and take pictures of me sitting on the porch. They also took pictures of me when I was at work. Whoever this was was giving Texas regular reports on where I was, whom I was with, what I was doing, and even what I was wearing. And that had been going on for months without my knowledge. I felt duped and completely stupid. How did I not see any of this? How did I allow this to go so far? Looking back, I see the red flags. Like when I went to Texas to visit and he suddenly got ill the night before I was leaving. Now I think he was trying to work out a way to make me stay. Like I would walk away from my kids? And if I had stayed, I don't think I would be alive to tell this story.

I can't believe Joe stuck around through all that drama. I really started to like him. He made me feel safe. I thought we had the start of something good, but as they say, "All good things must come to an end." Joe and his wife had a previously arranged thing planned from before she moved out. I didn't want to be the kind of person to tell him he wasn't allowed to go. And we weren't really there yet in our relationship. So they went and got to talking while they were there. She wanted to try to work things out, but first, he needed to dump me. Which he promptly did. I was heartbroken. On one hand, I didn't want him to throw away twenty-nine years of marriage. On the other hand, I was sad for me. But I understood.

Joe's plan was to get her stuff the next day and move her back to their house. She had taken the travel trailer to live in when she left, and they owned a home in a tiny town about thirty miles outside the mining town where I lived. Apparently, that wasn't what she was thinking. She wanted to still live in the travel trailer and talk, text, and go on dates with Joe. Joe may have gone for it if the neighbor hadn't told him her boyfriend was still living with her.

Guess who got a phone call a few days later? Me. Guess who was kissing ass? Joe. Guess who has trust issues? Me. Guess who had to work really hard to get back into my good graces? Joe.

I like ass kissing Joe. He's just that much sweeter than he already was. He also understood that I was holding back. Especially because of the kids. He was still living in his house thirty miles out of town so we didn't see each other every day. It took a while before I let him sleep over here and there. The first time he spent the night at my house, he went to the fridge for a snack, and it was pretty much empty. He went to the pantry which was pretty bare too. I made enough money to pay the bills and get groceries for a day or two at a time. I couldn't do a week or two's worth of shopping at one time. Joe suddenly had an errand to run. Okay? That was out of the blue. He was gone for a while and came back with a truck full of groceries. I can't afford to pay for all that! He explains that it is all a gift. He says he liked to eat, and he liked to have choices. Okay. then. Later that evening, we were sitting on the porch with the girls, when Jae comes out with something in her hand, asking if it was an apple. Seriously? This makes me look really bad. In my defense, fresh fruit is expensive and it doesn't last long, so I don't buy it often.

And that damn little dog was costing me money I didn't have to spare. Frisbee got out of the yard when I was at work and I got a ninety-dollar "dog at large" ticket. Dog at large? He was smaller than a racoon! The ticket should be half that. The ticket should have been a "weenie on the run" ticket. He's a sweet little guy most of the time, until you have to take something away from him that he shouldn't have. Then he turns into a total asshat. He gets all snarly and bares his teeth and gets the beady little devil eyes. It's kind of scary. Jae had a bag of Reese's Peanut Butter Cups on her bed that she was snacking out of. Frisbee jumped up and snatched the whole bag. Joe was at the house that day, Jae was trying to get the bag back, but Fris was doing his devil dog routine. I was not really sure if he'd hurt her, so I took over trying to get the bag back. I know chocolate isn't good for dogs and he'd already eaten a couple, paper and all. But every time I went to grab the bag, he was now lunging at my hand. Joe was watching the doggie shit show and got in on the action. He had to put his boot on Frisbee to hold him back so he could get the bag without getting bit. The dog went crazy aggressive and bit his boot. But as soon as Joe got the bag away, Frisbee flipped back to being a sweet little guy. Like a switch had been turned off. Now I had an idea why he was found in the middle of nowhere all by himself. I couldn't have that level of aggression around my kids. Joe and I hatched a plan that the next morning: Joe would take Frisbee into Prescott in the morning and drop him off at the shelter. So the following morning, kids would go off to school, and Joe would load up the dog to head to Prescott. On the way, he made a quick stop at the post office. One of his cousins was there, and they got to talking; she noticed the dog in his truck and made a comment about how cute he was and how she always wanted a miniature pinscher. How convenient! Joe explained that he was on his way to the shelter and asked if she wants him. Yes, she did! He told her he had a little food aggression, and she said, "No worries." Okey dokey. That worked out well. When the kids came home from school, they asked where the dog was, and I told them he ran away to go live at the zoo.

LIFE LESSON #3198

I have now officially become an iffy parent like my mother.

Being a single parent has its ups and downs. An "up" is being able to eat cereal for dinner and taking the whole blanket in bed. A "down" is when your kid lights the backyard on fire. No one to blame but yourself when that happens. Also, no one to help you put it out. So technically, that's a "down" on top of a "down." Apparently, JP pocketed a box of matches from my work and thought it was a good idea to light them and flick them over the fence into a dead bush. I was in the bathroom getting ready for work when JP came running in screaming about a burning bush. I was pretty sure he was not making some kind of biblical reference, so I was immediately alarmed. He had my full attention. He started dragging me outside; mind you, I was only half dressed. I smelled the fire before I saw it. Holy shit! It really was a burning bush, and unlike in the bible, it was spreading really fast! Everything was so dry back there that it was hopping from one patch of dead grass to another in no time. Standing in my underwear and bare feet, I had the hose in one hand and the fire department on the phone in the other. I thought I was going to be late for work.

Another "holy shit" moment was when the kids decided to hold a "Midnight Madness" party. I have no idea how I slept through all the hoopla. I could only put together the events of the evening from the evidence that was left behind. I woke up in the morning and shuffled into the kitchen for a cup of coffee to find two broken eggs on the floor in front of the stove. They had had enough time to harden where they fell and turn into a natural glue. The shells were stuck to the linoleum. There was a pan on the stove with another broken egg next to it. This egg had been cooked on because the burner was still on low. What was I looking at? What the hell? The refrigerator door was slightly open, and there was a trail of spilled chocolate milk down the hallway towards the kids' rooms. As I passed by the bathroom, I smelled cigarettes. When I smoke, I do not do it in the house. The sink was full of water, burnt matches, ashes, two burnt cigarette butts, and about six or seven unlit cigarettes floating in the pool. My beautiful, smart, funny little angels were in so much trouble! They were sleeping so soundly, with the chips they spilled all over the floor, before I woke them up. Awwwww. They are going to look so cute scrubbing the floor in their pajamas. If you want to play, you gotta pay!

Joe was spending more and more time at my house. He still had his house outside town, but it was easier to stay at my place during the week. Less travel time. I liked having him around. More important than me though, was the kids. He was really good with the kids. It took Jae a minute to warm up to him but when she did, he became her best bud. She followed him everywhere. I knew we were good when she crawled up in his lap and fell asleep.

The kids loved spending time at his house outside town. He had a little dirt track out there and a little buggy for the kids to ride. His house was on five acres, so there was a good amount of space for kids to goof off. Joe would set up empty soda cans for the kids to shoot bb guns at and barbecue burgers on the porch. The porch is my favorite part of the house. I'm a sucker for a good porch.

The more Joe stayed at my house though, more of his crap showed up. He brought over his side by side and trailer, more clothes getting hung in the closet. More clothes in the laundry. Then he bought a small chest freezer and filled it with food. He bought a real dining room table to eat dinner at every night. *I think he's my boyfriend.*

Of course, that got out in a small town. First thing everyone kept bringing up was that Joe was a serious hunter. That's okay, I liked to go camping. I don't particularly care for game meat; I've only had it once or twice, but it wasn't my thing. Joe grew up hunting and fishing to feed the family. And he was pretty good at it. He even won some championships and made record books in archery.

Then the rumors started. The main one was that Joe left his wife for me and I was a homewrecker. That was simply not true. It irritates me that people think this. I have done plenty of things in my life that I could be judged on, but don't judge me on something I didn't do. I'm pretty sure this rumor is why things didn't go so well the first time I met Joe's kids.

Joe had three grown children with kids of their own. He started really young, and I started really old. Or so I've heard from random old ladies. Joe's grandkids and my kids are all around the same age. But his kids really didn't want anything to do with me. I'm sure it was difficult seeing their dad with someone other than their mom after all those years, especially if they were told I was the reason they split up. I get it, but it still hurts my feelings.

It also hurt my feelings that my girlfriends started ditching me. Maybe they were doing to me what we had done to Jax. They didn't like being around a happy couple, or maybe some of the lies Texas had told them stuck. I don't know. I wish I did. I tried to throw out an olive branch once or twice, but it was never returned. I thought we were tight, but I guess I was wrong.

Jax was the only one who stuck around. She actually saved me one night. This was before Joe. We were sitting on the porch and had a gal from town coming over to do our nails. She brought her husband. He was kind of sketchy. He made me a drink, and that's all I can remember. Jax told me later that after I finished that drink, I went in and fell asleep on my bed. They wouldn't leave. They were trying to get Jax to go home and said they would stay to keep an eye on me. Jax stood her ground and said no. Eventually, they left, and Jax locked everything up and went home. I woke up several hours later and called her to ask what the hell had happened. She was shocked that I sounded so good. I felt fine—no hangover, not drunk, nothing. She filled me in on the evening, and now I was shocked. I think I was drugged. I should have had my blood tested the next morning. Thankfully, she stayed. I think she saved me from something horrible. When Joe and I got together, we told him the story, and he too thought something fishy had gone on.

Joe and I had reached that pivotal point in every serious relationship. We could poop in front of each other. Men typically reach this stage long before women. In my experience, poop and farting, for that matter, comes with trust, comfort, and love. The first time we went away together, all I was worried about was how was I going to poop in the hotel room. We had reached the point that that was no longer a concern. I was kind of forced into the situation before I think I was completely committed. We had a guest sleeping over and using the spare bathroom in the morning, Joe was in the shower in my bathroom. My body turned into an impatient traitor. I had no choice. The shit was out of the bag, so they say. There's no turning back now.

While my divorce was in the paperwork phase, Joe and his wife were just beginning to split things up. At that point, she didn't want the house. She did want some cash out of the 401(k). So Joe took out a loan to give to her and refinanced the house to include all the miscellaneous bills. She changed her mind the day before the check from the 401(k) showed up. She wanted the house after all, one half of the 401(k) and alimony. Joe couldn't just send the money back and tell them he changed his mind. I'd never seen him this mad. I'm not sure I've even seen him mad at all. It was unnerving. He was super still and quiet, but I could see the muscles in his jaw working. Grinding. I could almost smell the tension in the air. They say you don't really know someone until you live with them. I believe that is so true.

Joe worked out a plan while he sat there seething in anger. Since he couldn't send the money back with an oopsy-poopsy letter, he used it to pay off everything that he owned, all my bills and credit cards, and then took us on a vacation to Florida to see my dad. Just between me and you, I didn't like that house anyway. Mainly because it only has one bathroom. But also because no matter what, it would have always been thought of as their house.

I should have thanked his soon to be ex-wife for the Florida trip. It was amazing, well, after we got off the plane. I hate to fly. I definitely drugged up to help with the anxiety. If I could open a window it might have helped, but then, you know, we would all die, so there's that. Best part about that flight was when Jae farted. She was sitting next to Joe, and everyone thought it was him. So funny! It was great to see my dad. We had begun to repair and work on our relationship since my brother's passing. I needed Dad and Nancy to meet Joe. If this relationship had any kind of future, I needed their approval. They loved him.

Joe is a total redneck. Born and raised in Arizona. The oldest of four. Raised a country boy, hunting and fishing. His father died when Joe was seventeen. He took on three jobs after that to help pay the bills, while going to school and playing baseball. Baseball was his love, and he was really good at it. He was a left-handed pitcher and even got drafted after high school to the majors but had to turn it down when his now soon-to-be ex-wife got pregnant. They barely knew each other when they got married, but it was the right thing to do since she was pregnant. He had to take a better paying job to support his family. He continued to play for the minors, though. Won a world series even. He's been working for the copper mine for over thirty years now. He was smart, funny, and likeable. He was a true stand-up kind of person. Of course they would like him.

We did all kinds of redneck tourist things when we were in Florida. We rode in an open-air swamp buggy through the wetlands. That was fun—we had to climb to the top of a tall platform to get in the thing. We took an airboat ride. That was a blast! If I ever live in Florida, I'm going to need one of those. We went to a roadside zoo where the kids got to ride on the back of a gigantic turtle. We got to hold a nine-foot python and a baby alligator. Yes, I was just as afraid then as I was when I was a kid. But I wanted a picture on Facebook! And we went deep sea fishing. That was a go, no-go situation for me. When the boat was moving, I was fine. When we were anchored to fish, it was horrible. I'm not sure I like deep sea fishing. I was so sick to my stomach. The best part about that day was the scenery. Some young man took his shirt off while we were fishing, and I completely forgot about my upset stomach. I mean, *ba bam*! Holy shit. His muscles had muscles. Of course, I had to strike up a conversation. "Where are you from?" Who gives a shit? "Aren't you here with anyone?" I don't care. "Do you like fishing?" It doesn't matter. I was asking the questions, but I was not paying attention to any of his responses. He could have said he was from the moon, he was there with his imaginary friend, and he hated fishing. I don't know. Then I got an early Christmas present. He asked me if I could rub sunblock on his back! Why, yes! Yes, I can! Annnnd I'm pretty sure he's going to need some on his chest too. Hehehe. Turns out, I love deep sea fishing! I think the kids caught some fish; I was slightly distracted.

We spent the rest of our time in Florida swimming in Grandpa and Grandma's house. It was a much-needed vacation. We both needed a break. And to add some icing on the cake, Joe got a call from his lawyer on the last day we were there. His divorce papers were signed. His soon to be ex-wife had become his official ex-wife while we watched a baseball game in the Florida sun. Joe ended up losing the house and one half of his 401(k), having to pay back the original 401(k) loan for three years and alimony for five years. We secretly called the alimony payments child support because her boyfriend was so much younger.

On the flight home, I got stuck next to a chatty Cathy. I had to shut her down by snapping at poor Jae. She asked me a question, and I snapped about "Mommy hates to fly, the takeoff is the worst, please talk to me later!" Chatty Cathy never said another word to me the whole flight. I was left in peace. Just me and my anxiety.

Joe and all his junk moved in with us after he lost his house. My little house isn't big enough anymore. Joe put in for a company house, but that's a long list that doesn't move very fast.

Now that Joe was living with me and sharing the bills, I didn't have to work as much. I got with Lisa to see if we could work something out. What I really wanted was to give up my bartending shifts and be the straight daytime waitress. Bartending made better money, but I started hating my shifts. Once again, the general public can be a fickle bitch. And working at the only bar in a small town has its own set of unique issues because you know everyone. When I have to cut someone off, I very well might run into them at the grocery store the next day. In a big city, you will probably never see them again. Then there's the wife swap issue. This gal used to be married to that guy. That guy was now married to her old best friend. The ex-wife was now married to her ex-husband's boss, and they hated each other. Mix that whole messy soup together and throw in some alcohol on a Friday night, and it turns into a shit show. Plus, there was no taxi service or Uber, so I needed to make sure everyone can walk or drive home. And there was no security. If a fight broke out between the exes, it was on me. The cops could be an hour away. It was too stressful.

I had a friend of a regular come in one night, he was already toasted and demanding shots. Not going to happen. In the state of Arizona, if a bar patron gets drunk and drives and gets in an accident, they can sue the bar and the bartender personally. I can't afford that! So I told the guy I would give him some water and we'll reevaluate the situation later. He got insta-pissed! Started calling me all kinds of nasty names. Going on about how no bitch was going to tell him what to do. I feel bad for his wife, whoever the hell she is. As a bartender, we learn how not to escalate any situation. I was calmly explaining that he could stay with his friend but I would only serve him water. Technically, by law, I shouldn't have even done that. I should have made him leave. But...small town and all. He was not happy that "a fat c**t was telling him what to do." I was a woman, and I needed to do what he says. Excuse me? Now I was insta-pissed and told him, "This bitch *is* telling you what to do, and right now, she's telling you to get the fuck out of her bar!"

He threw his water in my face. Now my mascara was running. "Get the fuck out!" He was acting like he was going to climb over the bar and I was ready to throw down. His friend got the message and dragged him out, kicking and screaming like a little girl. I should not have lost my temper. It is what it is.

Another shift, a group of kids—I called them kids but they were twenty-one—just came into the bar and ordered a round of Southern Comfort shots, my nemesis. One of them did her shot and went running for the exit door. Oh no. This wasn't looking good. She didn't make it quite far enough. She puked all down the door. Southern Comfort of all things. I do not need this shit. I do not want to bartend anymore. Plus, it was really hard to get up in the morning to get the kids off to school. I was over it.

But I *loved* waitressing during the day. And I was good at it. That was my thing. I felt like I was getting paid to socialize. I got regulars; I knew what people wanted, what they liked, how they liked it. The cook was fast, and I was busy. I loved taking care of big groups when they would come in from out of town. I got to meet new people from different places and make them happy. I like making people happy. Who doesn't?

I also liked being home every night. I went a little "suddenly single" crazy there for a while after Will and I split up. I was partying too much, drinking too much, doing dumbass shit. Don't get me wrong, I had so much fun at the bar with Lisa, Liz, Jax, and the girls. We had some really memorable nights. Vodka was my drink of choice. Vodka has the least amount of calories, and that was important since I had lost a ton of weight on the divorce diet. But I have a tendency to go overboard, and it was time to get back on track. In my case, time to get back on track again. Being home every night was a step in the right direction.

It was nice having a man around the house again. It's just that the man I had around the house was Joe. Joe hates spiders, so I still have to kill those. He's a foodie and wants a real cooked dinner every night—no more cereal for me. He said from day one, he does not do dishes and he does not do windows. What else he does not do is put the damn toilet seat down. It pisses me off! It really makes me contemplate if it's worth having a man around. Sure, they cut the grass and take out the trash when you tell them to, but I can hire someone for that, and it never leads to my ass hitting cold water at 3:00 a.m.

I came up with an ingenious idea. It was a win-win. I bet Joe that if he kept the toilet seat down, I would cook. If the seat was up, he cooked or we ordered out. Joe has a motto, "Win when you can. Lose if you have to. Cheat whenever possible." He cheated. He literally glued the toilet seat down. I didn't know this for a week. I was too busy cooking dinners and patting myself on the back for coming up with such a good plan. And of course, he never said a word. He was too busy acting all high and mighty over winning the toilet seat crown. It wasn't until I went to go scrub the bathrooms that I found out. I went to lift the seat and was like, *What the hell?* I thought the seat was stuck. That never happened before. It took a minute for me to realize the thing was glued down. Cheater! I had been cooking for a week under false pretenses! That asshat. So funny, ha ha. Joe and the kids thought it was hilarious. A few more days went by, and Jae asked me how we could unglue the toilet seat so Joe could cook. Traitor! I'm a good cook but Jae was obsessed with Joe's pork chops. I get it. They are delicious. I ate three myself the first time he made them.

Things are going really good with us. I met his family; there sure were a lot of them. Every time I turned around, there was another cousin or something. When I met his mother for the first time, Joe had me so worked up and stressed out. He said she was going to bombard me with questions and I definitely needed to watch my language. I do have a potty mouth, but he said she wouldn't even like me if I said the word *butt*. I was screwed. We met for lunch, and she only asked me a few questions. That's all you got? I was ready. I told her everything Joe had told me about meeting her, and she just laughed. I liked her. She made me feel comfortable. We had a really nice lunch.

I liked all of his family. I liked them as individuals, and I really liked them as a unit. It was so obvious that they truly loved each other. And the spouses. They were each recognized and appreciated equally. There was not one "odd man out." These guys had each other's backs, no matter what. I wanted in. I wanted to feel that kind of acceptance for who I was.

No more fixing him, no more fixing me. Just me. As I am. Good, bad, and ugly. Poor Joe.

Poor Joe's whole family! I held a fiftieth birthday party for him at the bar and got a bit toasted. One of his friends gave him a package of Depends as a gag gift. I decided to put a pair on and give Joe a sexy strip show with Depends. I crack myself up sometimes and thought it was hilarious! I was completely enjoying myself. So much so that I forgot I was giving Joe a lap dance, wearing a pair of Depends, in front of his family, including his mother! They're going to welcome me into the fold with open arms. Right?

Joe and I decided to get married. Our joke was that I needed health insurance and he needed a tax deduction. We loved each other, but that stuff is true too. In my opinion, a marriage certificate is just a piece of paper to keep in your safe. It means nothing if you don't have the commitment in your heart. We were committed, but you can't get any benefits without that piece of paper.

We also decided we should buy a house outside the mining town instead of wasting our money on rent. It was a buyers' market at the time. We looked at a ton of houses. Some were beautiful houses, but I couldn't picture myself living in them. Some didn't have enough usable land or were too far for Joe to have to drive to work. Some were exactly what we were looking for, but we would have been macaroni and cheese poor trying to pay the mortgage. Slightly frustrated, driving home from another house tour, Joe spotted a For Sale sign on the side of a dirt road not too far from the mining town. Joe was excited. I was not. I did not want to live down this dirt road. I'd never been down it, but I'd heard of it. It was not even a town. It was a three-mile-long dead-end dirt road with maybe twelve houses and only a handful of those are occupied. He made an appointment to go look at it as soon as it was possible. I was not interested but figured I would go just to shut him up.

We went to check out this stupid house, which was a waste of my afternoon. I was kind of pissy the whole ride there. Driving down the dirt road, we passed five houses. Each house sat on acres of land and was not visible to one another. The house we were looking at had two acres. We parked at the gate and walked onto the property. The first thing I saw was a double-decker porch shaded by trees and surrounded by grapevines. I didn't even care if there was a house attached to that porch. I was in love. I'm a sucker for a good porch. I felt at home on this porch. I could see myself getting married there. Growing old and dying there. The house wasn't bad either. It had some very unique features, a small kitchen, three bedrooms and two bathrooms. This would work. They gave us a tour of the property. There was a separate pump house because the house was on a well. A large detached garage. A wood shed because the house had a wood burning stove for heat, two more sheds, a feed barn, a chicken coop, a pigpen, and a duck pen. Yes, yes, and yes. A small creek ran through the back of the property, and the property backed up to ranch land. I could pee in the yard if I wanted to, and no one would be able to see me. We had our realtor put in an offer before we got back off the dirt road.

Our offer was accepted! Now the work started. All the paper-work, holy shit. It probably didn't help that we weren't married. We opted for a fifteen-year mortgage in the hopes that the loan would be paid off by the time Joe retired. And I had to sell my little house. That is easier said than done. Since the house was on company owned land, I had four options. I could sell it to an outsider, but they would have to move it. I could sell it to a preapproved mine employee or a preapproved mine contractor. Or I could sell it to the mining company itself. No one was going to pay for the cost of moving it. Mine housing was so cheap—why would anyone want to buy a house without land? Contractors came and went. So I sold it to the company. There was no haggling on the price. They offered a price; you either took it or you didn't. I took it but had to make a deal to be able to rent it back from them until our house was ready. The couple we bought our house from still needed to find another place.

You would think I would have spent my time slowly packing the unnecessary items and going through things in a stress-free process. That's what normal people would do. Pish posh. I am not normal. What I did was have Joe buy me a baby pot belly pig. Makes total sense. She was pink, tiny, and adorable! I named her Petunia. Joe said if we were going to have a mini ranch, I needed a mini pig. He was so right! The kids loved her too. Joe's dog? Not so much. When Joe's divorce was final, he lost his house, but he got the dog. I think it was a good trade. Trench was a big, old black dog. He was a good boy, no bat shit crazy attacks like Frisbee. But he didn't know what to think of the baby pig. It was funny watching Trench try to keep a good four-foot berth around Petunia. But I had her housebroken in no time, and she could fit through the old doggie door, which was perfect.

Joe kept joking that since we were buying a mini ranch, he was going to get me a pair of bib overalls and knock out some of my front teeth so I would look the part while I walked around holding my pig. His stupid joke came to fruition the night before we were scheduled to close on the house and sign all the papers. We were in the car driving home, snacking on chicken fingers. I bit into something hard and spit it out the window. At the same time, Joe said something funny so I smiled at him. He's got this odd look on his face... "Ummmm... babe? What's up?"

He proceeded to tell me that I have no front tooth. Oh, holy shit. I just spit my tooth out of the window! What was I going to do now? The dentist was closed, the next day was an important day, and I made a living smiling at people.

The next morning at the title company, signing my name a billion times and going through two trees worth of paperwork, I did the best I could to cover my mouth. After everything was done, I couldn't help but smile. I was so happy and proud. The lady that we had been working with all morning gave me that sideways look of surprise. I forgot about my missing tooth. I had to explain the situation and Joe's stupid joke that jinxed me. We went out for a celebratory lunch, and the waitress gave me the same look. Something had to be done ASAP. As soon as we got home, I went straight to the local dentist office. This was a satellite office and was only open two days a week. It doesn't have everything on hand that a full-time office would have and it was really late in the day. But the dentist fixed me up. He did the best he could with what he had on hand and built me a temporary crown. It was bright white, really thick, and slightly longer than my other front tooth, but it would do for the time being, and I was grateful. I felt like a human cartoon character. You know when a cartoon character smiles and this star shows up for a second with a ding sound? That was me.

Now that everything was set and signed with the house, I gave my notice at the restaurant. The plan was to start packing and sorting, but without an actual moving date, my motivation wasn't where it should have been. In fact, Joe and I decided to spend a long weekend in Laughlin instead of packing. We were on fire! Sitting at the poker table, we couldn't lose. That never happens. We ended up having an amazing weekend and actually came home with some money in our pockets for a change.

That following week is when I lost my ring. Not my engagement ring but a ring that was very sentimental to me. My first husband was Dumpster diving and came across an old tool box. Inside the box was a pair of diamond earrings that he gave to me. I rarely wore them because the posts were really wide and hurt my ears. They sat around in my jewelry box for years until my mom suggested I have them turned into something else. We took the earrings to a jeweler in Prescott and decided to have them turned into a ring. Mom picked out the center stone. It was a smoky zircon, a warm chocolate color. We had it set in white gold with the zircon in the center and the diamonds flanking the sides. I loved that ring, and it always made me think of mm. I can remember how much fun we had that day, picking out the stone and hitting the ice cream parlor after. I set it on the kitchen windowsill like I have done before, and then it was gone. It just vanished. I hunted everywhere for that ring but never found it. Losing that ring still makes me sad. I keep hoping it will magically appear somewhere. I don't think that will happen, unfortunately.

Right after I lost my ring, we got a call that the folks at our house had found a place to go and were all moved out. Now I have to pack. No more goofing off! Ugh.

When we finally got access to our house, I thought I would spend a week or so to paint and clean before moving all the stuff in. Joe had other plans. He and a friend started hauling stuff while I was painting. Things weren't packed or organized at all. I thought I would have more time. And I don't care if you are moving next door or across the country; moving sucks. The older you get, the heavier everything becomes. Pushing a mattress around in your twenties was as easy as rearranging the throw pillows on your couch. When you're in your forties? It's like trying to push an oil tanker that's full. By the end of a long day of moving, even a box of bras is too heavy.

As soon as we had a chance, we headed over to Sears to order the appliances, patio furniture, and a ride-on lawn mower. Our house started out as a mobile home, but through the years, additions and extra bedrooms had been built on, so it's really not mobile anymore. The kitchen is in the mobile home part of the house, so the refrigerator space is a few inches smaller than that of a newer modern house, so the fridge needed to be specially ordered. In the meantime, we had my old garage fridge on the porch. Everyone in the mining town has a spare fridge in their carport or garage, usually for beer and extra milk and things. The kids in town were known to go "fridging," which was when they went around town stealing beer and snacks out of people's refrigerators. Back when I was in town, they snatched some beers and frozen pizzas from mine. It was the pizzas that really pissed me off. I marched my happy ass right down to the store and bought a small, cheap bottle of vodka and a brand-new bottle of Visine eye drops. It took about a week for that bottle of vodka to disappear. I bet those kids didn't have as much fun at that party that they thought they were going to have. I don't have to worry about those kinds of shenanigans anymore.

When the new fridge finally came in, and the Sears guys delivered everything, the fridge didn't fit. It was too big. We tried to tell them that was not what we ordered, but they didn't give a fat rat's ass. They said that was the one on their paperwork and we needed to take it up with the store and our salesman. They stretched the plug across the floor and left it standing in the middle of the kitchen. Seriously? Back at Sears with our paperwork, and of course the guy we were working with had since been fired. New guy figures out that old guy transfixed the last two numbers on the form. We were told that we could use the one we had until the right one came in and got delivered.

About a week later, the delivery guys were back. First, they took out the wrong fridge and then brought in the new one. This fridge was way nicer than the one we ordered, but it fit. Again, I was telling them that was not what we ordered. Again, they didn't give a fat rat's ass. It was the one on their paperwork, call the store, blah blah blah. We never called.

Petunia loved the new house. But there wasn't a doggie door, and we couldn't get one. It was not a good idea to have one in the country because not only would she use it but so would a random skunk or racoon. I had to come up with something for her to let me know when she needed to go out to pee, so I installed a doorbell for her. I put the button down low on the inside of the door and taught her to push it with her nose to let me know when she wanted out. I could be anywhere in the house and know when she had to pee. And she got a new playmate. Will's mom brought each of the kids a new dog. JP got a chocolate lab puppy from a church friend that wasn't prepared for how much work a puppy was that he named Rocky. Rocky was the name of one of the dogs that ate his beloved Pooh all those years ago. I guess he never forgot. Jae got an older Lhasa Apso from a woman who was too ill to take care of it anymore. I forget that dog's name because it was only with us for about a week before I took it back. The old lady that had that dog hand fed it. It wouldn't eat unless I hand fed it. I don't have the time or patience for that shit.

My dad called right after we moved into the new house. He was going to be at a church convention in Vegas. I think that's an interesting place for a church convention, but who am I? His preacher was going to be there too, and he wanted to know if they should all take a detour out to us after the convention and have Dad's preacher marry us. Ummmmm…okay. Sure. Babe! I think we are getting married.

Talk about pressure. Now I had less than three weeks to finish painting, unpacking, and planning a wedding. No big deal. The tiny town that Joe's old house was in is about ten miles down the road from our new place. He had a friend out there who had a separate outbuilding on their property that they turned into a small bar for them to hang out in. A bigger, more professional version of a man cave. And she was an amazing cook. Joe talked to her to see about having our reception at her place. And we made an agreement for her and her hubby to prepare a pit BBQ for us. She even helped me print out some invitations. There was no way I could have done all of that by myself. This was going to be a "no frills" event, and I was happy with that.

Because everything always went according to plan, our water pump died three days before the wedding. No water pump meant no water to shower or even flush a toilet. This was not a good situation. Teetering on an ECS, and since we lived in the middle of nowhere, repair men were not around the corner. In fact, repair people hated coming out here because of the time it took to get here and back. They always charged us extra. But it got done just in time, and everything worked out in the end.

If at first you don't succeed, try, try, again. I got married, for the third time, standing on the porch on a rainy afternoon. A clap of thunder struck right as we said I do. They say it's good luck if it rains on your wedding. I don't know who "they" are, but I will take it.

I wore a simple black-and-white sundress I got from JC Penny's for forty dollars and a matching pair of flip flops from Payless. Joe wore a cowboy shirt, jeans, and boots. We had my dad sit off to the side holding a shotgun just for laughs. I don't think Dad's preacher friend had ever been to a redneck wedding. For me, the only thing that was really important was that we were married, not what we were wearing. The poor preacher didn't know what was happening when Petunia and Rocky got into a scuffle in the middle of the ceremony. I dressed Petunia up with a big pink bow for the occasion; Rocky wanted the bow. Have you ever heard a pig scream? It's really loud. Quite distracting during a wedding ceremony. Kind of funny, though. As soon as the ceremony and pictures were done, I changed into some jeans and a T-shirt. I'm not really a dress kind of girl.

So many more people showed up than I expected. The food was amazing. The music was amazing. Joe's brother, Paul, plays the guitar and sings, and he's really good. The cake was amazing; Joe's mom made it. And the pictures turned out amazing. Joe's sister, Sohnja, took them for us. This was my best wedding yet! The family welcomed me into the fold, and I couldn't be happier.

The next morning, not so much. We had way too much fun and drank way too much whiskey. The next morning, we both felt way shitty. Joe was asking me to make him breakfast but the thought of smelling eggs cooking made me want to throw up, so I threw a box of Pop Tarts in front of him and told him to have at it. I would have never done that before. I would have made the damn breakfast, feeling like poop and resenting every flip of the spatula. It took a while, but I was starting to feel good about being me. Joe was helping me with that, and he didn't even know it. That's what made it even more special. He loved me for me. He knew I was not perfect, and he didn't expect or want me to be. It was okay if I got mad. He liked that I was opinionated and a smartass. He held my hand when I had a panic attack for no reason and brought me a tissue when I cried over a dumb movie without being asked. He thought it was funny when I got distracted easily. Those are just some of the things that I hated about myself. He just doesn't care. He loves me. And I was almost getting used to liking me. It felt good for a change.

It was time to embark in my new life with the new me. I seemed to have moved further and further from civilization, and I couldn't be happier. I did have a lot to learn about being in the country but I got this. I was out in the back part of our property and came across a strange looking pile of poop. I called Joe over to take a look at what I found. He stared at it for a few seconds, kicked at it with the toe of his boot, and proclaimed that it was a pile of bear shit. He knew because he'd seen it before. Bear shit? We had bears just roaming around? Maybe I don't have this after all. He started laughing as he walked away. "It's cow shit," he said over his shoulder. Ha ha, so funny.

Jae wanted baby chickens, so I got her twenty-five chicks. I figured it would be a good thing to teach them some responsibility by caring for them on a daily basis. I wanted fresh eggs right away though and found someone who was downsizing their farm and selling off their chickens. Grown, laying hens are more expensive than you would think. I got ten. I loved watching them do their thing. It was like a redneck fishbowl. My favorite thing to watch was when one of them found a big, juicy bug, and the rest of the chickens turned into a vicious gang trying to steal it. The hen with the bug was weaving and ducking, desperately trying to keep her prize, the rest were trying to guess where she's going. It's funny. The kids loved digging through the laying boxes for the eggs every night. It was like a never-ending Easter egg hunt. And they were doing a really good job taking care of the twenty-three and a half chicks we had left. We had a few learning experiences along the way. We learned that Jae needs to pay attention to where she was walking in the chick pen. She flattened one like a pancake. The half chick was the one that got its leg broken when the kids were closing the gate to the coop. I actually got some advice from another farmer on how to doctor it up. I used some toothpicks and medical tape to make a splint. It healed, but it always walked with a limp and ended up being a rooster. No eggs from him.

You never know what the day is going to bring when you live in the country. Sometimes it's something totally unexpected. Joe had to leave for work before the sun came up, so after I packed his lunch and got him off to work, I usually went back to sleep for a little bit. One morning, I got woken up by a cow's moo. It sounded really close. We don't have any cows. Was I dreaming? Maybe I didn't really hear a cow. I heard it again. Nope, not dreaming. That's definitely a cow. I crawled out of bed and peeked out the window to see a huge cow right outside the window. When you drive by cows in a field, they don't look that big. When there's one right outside your window? Huge! I'm not a cowboy. I don't know how to wrangle a cow. I was kind of hoping it was going to meander out the same way it meandered in. No such luck. It didn't seem to be in any hurry and as very happy eating the grass right where it is. Well…shit.

I was working on a plan as I was getting dressed. I still really didn't have one when I went out on the porch. What. The. Fuck? Yeah, there was one cow at my window in the back of the house, but there were like twenty in the front of my house. This was above my pay grade. I needed to use a lifeline and phone a friend. I called Joe at work and told him we had a cow situation. He told me to get out there and started waving my arms and yelling. He says they'd move off. Are you fucking kidding me? I was not walking into the middle of a herd of cows and yelling at them! That didn't seem to be an appropriate way to make friends. Plus, they're huge! And there were momma cows with babies in the mix. I didn't know anything about a cow's protective behavior! Would the mommas try to run me over to protect their babies? Did cows bite? Or kick? I felt a panic attack coming on. I didn't know Joe was in the middle of a meeting, and he put me on speakerphone. Again, he was telling me to get out there and make some noise. Oookayy! Here went nothing. I said, really loud, "Shoo, shoo, moo cow. Shoo, shoo!" What was all that laughter I was hearing? I was too annoyed to address that right now. Louder, "Shoo, shoo, moo cow. Shoo, shoo!" They actually started heading out our gate! I couldn't believe it was working, so I said it again, even louder. Now they were running out the gate, but some of the babies got separated from their mommas and were freaking out. They were trying to go through the fence to get to them. Poor babies. Poor fence. After several frantic moments, everyone was reunited, uninjured. I'd deal with Joe and the fence later. All this action before coffee was just too much.

We moved into our house in the beginning of summer, so when I wasn't busy being a cow wrangler, the kids and I spent a lot of time goofing off on our property and riding on the dirt road. Joe bought the kids some bigger used four-wheelers since they grew out of their old ones. Jae's was really too small for her, and it wasn't running. It was one of those knockoffs that you can't find parts for. Joe had a friend over one day, and he asked what the deal with Jae's little pink camo four-wheeler was. Joe explained that it wasn't running and we couldn't find any parts for it. The guy offered to buy it, but we told him he could just have it. He felt bad about just taking it without paying for it, so Joe said he could buy me a bottle of whiskey to make it an even trade. Done. I didn't need the whiskey, but it made the guy feel better. Jae told her dad I sold her four-wheeler for a bottle of whiskey. That didn't sound good, and that's not really how things went down. Kids have their own perspective on things and don't always get things right, especially when the parents are divorced and stories get relayed. That was the first of many stories that needed some background information when my ex would call.

As for Joe's ex, she called fairly regularly, asking questions about the house, asking if he could come fix something, just random things. She also came by our house here and there to pick something up or drop something off. I would never interfere with that relationship. Regardless of how things ended up between the two of them, they had a long history that included two children that I had grown to love. There would be celebrations and events, graduations for the grandkids, and weddings in the future that we all would need to be at. I don't want any animosity when we are at those events because it's not fair to everyone else there.

Having said that, which I truly believe, I am not a total angel. Joe told me stories about how she hates the F word. I normally have a potty mouth but whenever she was around, I dropped the F bomb as much as I could. I went into full-on sailor mode. I couldn't help myself. I know it wasn't nice, but it was fun. Fun for me anyway. My halo was slightly tarnished.

Even though Joe's kids and I had a rough start, once we all got to know each other, everything changed. I *love* being a stepmom. To be fair, Joe's kids are all grown, so all of the tough stuff is already over. Now I get to participate in the lives of three amazing adults.

The oldest, Joey, is what I call an observer. Nothing gets by him. He is loyal, smart, strong, and really funny. He looks exactly like Joe only bigger, so of course he is handsome. Joey is the guy you want in your corner when the zombie apocalypse goes down. I know I could count on him to keep zombies at bay and put food on our table. And he's also a great teacher. He takes the kids out hunting with him and they always come home with some kind of new skill.

Then there's Shana. She is the poster child for the definition of the word *sassy*. She is lively and spirited, very intelligent, and stunningly beautiful. She is also a total smartass like me. I think we bonded over poop jokes. Shana will be our medical support during a zombie apocalypse. She knows her stuff and can get it done without any bullshit. As an added bonus, she grew up hunting alongside Joe and her brother. We won't go hungry.

The youngest is Jenny. Jenny is Joe's daughter but not his ex's. Long story that's not mine to tell. Jenny is the creative one. She is also beautiful, smart, and kind. Joe has some really good genes. Jenny is full of life, always so happy with a big smile that is contagious. She exudes positive vibes. Jenny would never purposely drop the F bomb in front of someone knowing they didn't like it. You know you can count on her. She's also an amazing cook. Which is imperative during a zombie apocalypse. We have a good team!

Each of Joe's kids have kids. Joey has two, Shana has two, and Jenny has one. All around the same age as mine. Here comes the Jerry Springer shit: since JP and Jae are Joey, Shana and Jenny's stepbrother and sister, they are technically their kids' aunt and uncle. Which means that Jae is younger than most of her nieces and nephews and JP is only a year older.

Shortly before Joe and I got married, Shana and her husband split up. She got a cute little apartment in Prescott. Joe and I spent a lot of weekends picking up her kids from school on Fridays so she could work all weekend. Picking up the kids from their school was so different than what I was used to. They went to a huge school with a gazillion kids. To get them at 3:00 p.m., I would have to be there no later than 2:45 p.m. to get a good place in the pickup line. The line of cars was ridiculously long and would wrap around the school and even go down the street. I hated it. I would always have to fight back the panic attacks while I was waiting. I felt so boxed in, but I couldn't bail. There is no way I could do that every day. I would lose my shit.

I was used to the school in the little mining town. It is a small school with small classes since each grade only had about thirty kids. Then when we bought the house, the kids switched to the country school, which is about ten miles down the road. Actually, it's right next to Joe's old property. The country school went from kindergarten to eighth grade. It is a two-room schoolhouse with a separate building used as the lunch room and auditorium. There was a total of twenty-three kids. JP was the only fourth grader at the time. The two rooms were cut up with first through fourth in one room and fifth through eighth in the other room. There were only two teachers and two aides. That's it. When there were kindergarteners, they used a small room off to the side. There wasn't a lunch program; I had to pack a lunch for them every day, and they had a small bus that would pick up and drop off the kids at the end of our two-mile dirt road. On the rare occasion that I was running late, the bus driver would call me to see if he should wait. If I missed the bus in the afternoon, he would wait for a minute but couldn't leave them. I never missed the bus.

When the science fair project time rolled around, I was so excited. Normally, I hate the science fair projects. They are a parent project, not a kid project. I didn't have time to do it. But this year, I did! We came up with an awesome project. I helped with the experiment, I charted everything, I put the board together, I printed out all the results, and I actually had a blast. He won first place. I was so proud of him, and myself. I worked really hard on that project. It never crossed my mind that he was the only fourth grader so of course, he would win first place. We could have tested bubblegum and won.

After winning at our school, the top three winners from each grade got together with all the other small schools from the surrounding areas and had to present their projects again. JP had to do this every year until he graduated eighth grade and moved on to high school. He hated it! Sorry, buddy.

I always tried to do my errands and grocery shopping once or twice a month when the kids were in school. Shana and I started meeting for lunch just about every time I went to town. We tried to go to different places and try new stuff. We went for sushi once. I like sushi, but I like the boring white girl sushi. California rolls, avocado rolls, veggie rolls, that kind of stuff. Not Shana. I don't know what the hell she was eating. She even knew how to pronounce it right. It looked like little pieces of baby octopus or maybe raw squid. And she keeps trying to get me to try some! Not going to happen. I know I was staring at her while she ate, watching her chew and chew and eventually swallow. I wanted to see if she really liked it or if she was just pretending to gross me out, which she would totally do. I think she really liked it, though. Going out to lunch with Shana is good. She has some kind of juju and is so beautiful and friendly that our drinks never get a chance to run dry.

Joe has some of that juju too. It must be a family thing. We went to Red Lobster for lunch, and both ordered the crab legs. The waitress was a cute twenty-something-year-old girl. Joe is kinda sorta but not really flirting. When our plates showed up, she asked Joe if he knew how to crack the crab; he said he thought so. He knew! She never asked me. The waitress stood, with her back to me, cracking and picking all of Joe's crab, and putting the meat in neat little piles for him, all ready to dip in the melted butter and shove in his big, fat mouth. Seriously? It was so offensive it was funny. Joe was soaking up the attention. Like he had a shot with the twenty-year-old! Maybe it wasn't juju. Maybe it was pity.

Pity came in to play when Joe and I went out for sushi. We had just started dating and went to a sushi bar for dinner. I ordered my boring white girl rolls, and Joe ordered some tuna rolls. I didn't know he had no idea what he was ordering. He never said anything. Our plates arrived, and he spent a good thirty seconds staring at his food. First thing he did was pick up his fork and eat the entire glob of the wasabi. At the time, I was thinking he must really like that stuff. Poor guy had no idea what it was. It only took a few seconds for it to hit. His eyes were really watering, his nose was running, and he was trying to suck in the snot and look sexy at the same time. It was not working. He's a hot mess. Things got a little scary when he started having a hard time catching his breath. The waitress was practically pouring water down his throat and rubbing his back. As soon as he could speak, he asked, "What the hell was that and why didn't you say something?" Like it's my fault? I thought he knew. I explained that it was a horseradish sauce and I thought he really liked it! We had our food boxed up to go. I felt really bad for him. So did everyone in the restaurant who were watching.

Anyway, after going to town one day and having a lovely lunch with Shana, it was time to pick up the kids at the end of the dirt road. One of Joe's many cousins lives down the dirt road too, and her kids go to the same school as mine. She asked if I could grab her kids too and drop them at her place. I don't mind doing that once in a while. I don't want to be responsible for it every day, but here and there it's okay. I pulled up to her place to drop off her kids, and a pack of dogs came running from the side of the house. Front and center of the pack was a little red miniature pinscher. "Mom! Look! That's Frisbee!" Dead silence. "You lied. You said he ran away to live at the zoo." Well…shit. I guess the zoo wasn't quite far enough away.

Life Lesson #2074 Revisited

Secrets don't always stay secret.
Be prepared.
I was not prepared. I've got nothing. I lied and I
got caught by my kids. I blame my mother.

As I said, Joe is a big hunter. I haven't bought meat from a grocery store since shortly after getting together with him. I've had deer meat before and didn't really care for it, but Joe had his processed a little differently, and he was very meticulous with the meat before it even got to the processor. Elk and deer are my family's main protein source. In Arizona, hunting tags are drawn pretty much like a lottery. A person can only get one elk tag and one deer tag a year. One deer will not feed a family of four for a year, and if Joe doesn't get drawn, we don't eat. I like to eat. So do my kids. I could go buy meat at the grocery store, but at this point, it tastes funny and makes me sick. I'm not sure if it's what the beef was raised eating or what's been added to it in processing. I don't even like the way it smells when it's cooking. Elk and deer is a very lean meat that has never been given antibiotics or growth hormones or any other unknown substances.

Having said all that, we were running low on meat, and it was time to put in for the hunt. I have never hunted. Never wanted to. Not even sure if I can. But when Joe asked if I wanted to be put in for the draw, I said yes. I figured I wouldn't get drawn, but I did.

The hunt was in October in northern Arizona. We spent some time practicing shooting the rifle before we headed to Mormon Lake for the hunt. We stayed at a friend of Joe's cabin, which was a blessing since it rained the whole night before opening day. The next morning, we were up and out before the sun, heading to the forest. It's still not light out by the time we unloaded the side by side and started driving in. It's cold and started to drizzle about a mile down the road. I told Joe it was no big deal; it would stop raining by the time the sun came up. And it did. But I know God has a sense of humor, and I should have been a bit more specific because it did stop raining, but it did start snowing. Our side by side doesn't have a full windshield or doors or a heater, and it's cold. To make things even worse, I thought it would be a good idea to pick out a pair of "licky panties," which were red lace. If those were the panties from the past, my little heart-shaped mood indicator would have been black. My ass was frozen, and I could no longer feel my toes. About five miles into the forest, the snow started coming down so hard we couldn't see but maybe ten to fifteen feet in front of us. Out of nowhere, we saw a big white truck coming toward us. It pulled up next to us and rolled down the window. A huge cloud of marijuana smoke came pouring out, mariachi music was blaring in the background, and the five guys in the truck were asking how to get to a grocery store. What the hell? We were literally in the middle of a forest, on a dirt trail, in a snowstorm. The closest grocery store had got to be a least twenty miles away. I was not having fun. Joe said this would be fun. This was not fun. I wanted to go back to the cabin, warm my feet, and change into some good old-fashioned rotten cotton granny panties.

Day 2. No rain, no snow, just a whole bunch of red dirt mud. We are deep in the forest by the time the sun came up. Joe pulled the rig off the road and parked. He told me to get my stuff; we were walking. Walking? Where? He said he heard a bugle, so we were going to walk toward it. But I was not hunting bull elk, I had a cow tag. He says they would be together. Okaaay. Not even fifty yards into the trees and the bottoms of my shoes were about 2 inches higher and ten pounds heavier with caked-on red mud and dried pine needles. It looks like I had stepped on hundreds of dead spiders. Joe's shoes were fine. What's up with that? He started telling me I needed to walk on the rocks. Let's just add another challenge to this day. So there I was, carrying my rifle, a backpack, canteen, looking for elk, and aiming for the rocks. That was a lot of things on my menu, and I was falling way behind. Joe was ahead of me, waving for me to hurry and catch up. He saw some elk. I finally caught up, but I didn't see shit. He told me to look through the scope on the rifle and I would see them. Oh yeah! I see them, I shoot. I couldn't have hit the side of a barn for a million dollars at that point. I was shaking so bad. Back to walking on the rocks. He spotted another herd, and the same thing happened. More walking. Another herd, but this time they were running. A moving target was above my skill set, but I tried anyway. More walking. Now I was repeating in my head, *Aim small, miss small, feed the family* over and over again. We walked damn near five miles in the red mud, aiming for the rocks, carrying all my gear. "Aim small, miss small, feed the family." Joe spotted another herd and told me to aim between these two trees. There was no elk between the trees. He used the *P* word and told me to be patient. I hate that word but I waited. He said one would walk between the trees and stand there. Whatever. Damn if he wasn't right. First a bull walked by, then two more bulls, then a cow. It stopped just like he said it would. I shoot. I asked Joe how I did, and he said he wasn't sure and started walking in the wrong direction. I was arguing with him that he was going in the wrong direction when I saw it. I got it! I thought I was going to cry, but instead I started jumping up and down while Joe was trying to grab the rifle. I was so happy I didn't have to go out and walk another five miles the next day, and I was even happier that I provided for the family. Before we did anything else, I knelt down next to the elk and said a prayer. I thanked it for its service to my family.

After field dressing it, Joe headed back out to get the rig and left me there with the elk. I don't like being alone in the woods. It's kind of creepy. My mind starts playing tricks on me and I hear things. Twigs were snapping. I started wondering if bears or coyotes were attracted to the scent of fresh blood. Now I have to pee. I was afraid to pee, which made me have to pee more. Where was Joe? I knew there were other hunters out there. What if they caught me going pee? Worse, what if a bear came in while I was peeing and had my pants down around my ankles? I didn't want to die with my pants down! Where was Joe? Right around this time was when the first *Hunger Games* movie came out, so I started picking out a tree to live in. I also took inventory of all my supplies. I had almost a full canteen of water, a half bag of fruit snacks in my pocket, and seven rounds of ammunition for my rifle. I can make it a day. Maybe two. Where's Joe? I did not like being alone in the woods. My anxiety was beginning to spike out of control. Just about that time, I started hearing an engine in the distance. Finally. I didn't have to start rationing out my fruit snacks, and I was suddenly very thirsty. Now all we have to do is load this elk in the back of our rig and head out. How the hell was that going to happen? Joe had a plan. He tied one end of the rope around the elk's head and the other end to a small come-along he'd set up in the back of the rig. While he was wenching it up, I was on the ground, trying to lift the back end. That thing is heavy and I'm not doing a very good job. So then I started freaking out, thinking the head was going to pop off, and I was going to get sprayed with matter. I didn't want to get sprayed. This was the moment that Joe called me a Horriblizer for the first time. I was trying! We finally got it loaded and started driving the three miles across country to get back to the road. I was not sure if we should be off the road so I'm yelling at Joe to hurry up. Now I have earned the title of Horriblizer. As soon as we got to the road, there was a big white truck coming down the road toward us. When it pulled up next to us, the window rolled down, and a huge cloud of marijuana smoke came pouring out. Mariachi music was blaring in the background, and five guys were asking us if we had seen any elk. Ummmm…yeah. As I was pointing to the elk in the back of our rig, Joe told them there was a herd of about sixty that crossed the road a mile back and the guys were congratulating him on getting his. Hello? That's my elk. They didn't say any congratulations to me as they drove away. Maybe if they weren't so stoned, they could have spotted the huge herd of elk themselves. Whatever.

After processing, we got about 175 pounds of healthy, lean meat. I did that. I provided that for my family. I'm kind of proud of myself.

I started referring to our house and land as the Compound. The Compound was a popular place for our friends and family. We were always hosting BBQs and weekend getaways, which is just fine by me. I would rather be at the Compound than any place else. I felt safe and comfortable here. Home was definitely where my heart was.

During hunting season, we had people here just about every weekend. I'd met some really great people through Joe's old baseball days and hunting buddies. They never made me feel like an outsider, even though most of them knew Joe when he was still with his ex. I loved hearing all the stories from the olden days. We had some really good times. Memorable times. Even the times when things didn't go as planned were funny. We had some friends staying in JP's room for the weekend, and they brought a bunch of snacks with them. They left for the day to go hunting and unfortunately forgot to close the door. Petunia loves a good snack. She meandered in their room and proceeded to have her own personal pig party. She destroyed their stuff, rooting through it for snacks. She ripped open packages, spread Captain Crunch all over the floor, and left pig snot on their clothes in the process. Happy pig. Not so happy friends. Oopsy, poopsy!

Then Shana showed up with a present for her dad. A kitten. A girl kitten. She was cute but crazy. We named her Pita, short for "pain in the ass." Pita and Trench did not get along at all. Rocky and Petunia just gave her a wide berth. Before I got a chance to get Pita into conversion camp at the vets, which, by the way, is the only conversion camp that I think is useful, she got pregnant. I had no idea cats could get pregnant so young. But that is why I try to only stick with male pets, whom I still send to conversion camp. I feel it really helps with their attitudes. It seemed that Shana's gift to her dad was the gift that kept on giving. Yeah. Now I had to find homes for six kittens. I found homes for the kittens and made an appointment for Pita's trip to conversion camp at the vet about ten weeks after the kittens were born. She was already pregnant again! How? How did that happen so fast? Of course, the price to get her fixed doubled. But it would have cost anyway because she was already on the table, opened up. Over three hundred dollars! Ouch! That was a lot of money for an indoor/outdoor barn cat. That ended up being a total waste of money. About three weeks after I paid all that money to get her fixed, she disappeared. She unfortunately probably became a snack for a mountain lion or coyote.

Sometime after Pita disappeared, Petunia started getting really aggressive. At first, she stopped listening to anyone but me. We had a dog bed in our room next to my side of the bed, and Joe would tell her it was bedtime, and she would waddle her little butt in there and go right to sleep. She started only listening to me telling her to go to bed. Then she started corralling people away from me. She would wiggle her way in between me and anyone she thought was getting too close. Something switched. She was no longer my pig. I became her human. She took it up another notch when she started biting Trench when he got too close to me. She would bite him on the butt and not let go. It was horrible. When she bit Joe, I started getting concerned. He came in for a kiss, she didn't like it, and she bit him on the calf. I couldn't have this. I had two kids that I liked to hug, and I couldn't risk her biting them. We found a new home for her, not at the zoo but at a nice little farm right down the road from the kids' school. She got famous in that little town pretty quick because she kept breaking out and wandering the streets. Everyone learned to just tell her to go home and she would waddle her way back. No harm, no foul.

Then we had to put Trench down. He was getting so old and was hurting. It was time for him to go to heaven. That's when I met the love of my life. I thought it was Joe, but it turned out to be a 110-pound redhead named Dude.

After we got Petunia rehomed and Trench went to heaven, Rocky was all alone. He had never been the only dog and was getting really lonely and depressed. Joe was at work telling people that we needed a buddy for our dog. One of his co-workers said she had a dog that really needed a new home. We went that following weekend to meet him. He was a big, big sweet snuggle bunny. He looked like a Rhodesian ridgeback/chow mix, and he really did need a home. The gal told us that she dognapped him from someone's backyard because they were kicking him around and only feeding him occasionally. She was living in a small, single wide trailer, and the dog grew. And grew. So she put him outside in a pretty good-sized chain link kennel. But Dude figured out how to climb the fence and get out. So she put plywood around the inside of the kennel. Then he figured out how to open the gate, so she put him on a chain wrapped around a tree in the kennel. She would spend time with him and stuff, but he lived in a plywood box chained to a tree for a year and a half. She didn't want him to have to live like that. He needed a home, and I had one. We told her we would take him for a week to see how everyone got along. I was a bit wary because of his size. I was head over heels in love in less than twenty-four hours. He was a huge, sweet, happy ball of fur. He loved being in the house with everyone, and his appreciation was evident in every kiss and belly rub. It took him a little bit to get used to some of the normal household noises like a toilet flushing and kids running in the house. Since I was the one who was home all day, Dude became my protector. No one was allowed to raise their voice to me without him coming to stand next to me, just in case things went sideways. I pity the fool who would ever try to attack or hurt me. I love that dog.

The one problem with Dude, whom I call Dinky Do, is that he's a runner. He's fine when I'm home, but when I have to run to town for the day, he's gone. He digs under the fence; we put concrete in the hole. He climbs over the fence; we make it higher. He squeezed through two posts—how he got his head through, I have no clue— but we block the space. It's a game of cat and mouse, and he's really smart. He watches to make sure I remember to lock the gate, just waiting for me to forget. And Rocky follows him everywhere. So I have to worry about both of them. They have become a canine tag team.

Wildlife comes with country living. Sometimes it's great, some- times not so much. We seem to have a racoon problem. I think hav- ing the creek on the back of our property doesn't help. I think they're really cute, and I always secretly wanted one for a pet, but in reality, they are a pain in the ass. They are kind of destructive assholes. And since they are nocturnal, all their shenanigans go on at night. I have to make sure we secure the lids to the trash cans or I wake up to trash strewn all over the road. I have to make sure the kids don't leave any kind of food on the porch at night because that's an invitation. But they come up on the porch anyway. They steal the fruit off of our trees and eat the grapes off the vine and then poop everywhere.

They make a mess in the dog bowl washing off their treats, so I'm constantly having to scrub it out. It's a pain in the ass but what really makes me mad is when they break into the hen house and eat a chicken or two. They don't even eat the whole thing. They only eat the butt half. Why is that? We started trapping them for relocation, but the zoo didn't want them, so we took them far, far away.

Trapping them doesn't always go as planned. We caught our cat once and a skunk twice. A pissed-off skunk stuck in a live trap is not fun. They don't get taken anywhere. They get covered in a towel and run to the creek as fast as possible! But we still set the trap when we start seeing the poop. We set the trap, go to bed, and see what's going on in the morning. This time, at about 3:00 a.m., the dogs started going crazy at the arcadia door. I got up to see what all the ruckus was, and there was a racoon in the trap. I got Joe out of bed to go move the trap or the dogs would never shut up. His plan was to move the trap outside the fence for the night and take care of it in the morning. We had a small fenced-in area off the back porch that was surrounded by the rest of our property. Joe was going to put the trap out beyond the fence, thinking out of sight, out of mind for the dogs. It would have been a good plan if Dinky hadn't taught himself how to open the arcadia door. Joe was standing in the middle of the yard, holding a live trap with a seriously pissed-off racoon in it, wearing nothing but a pair of whitey tighties, when Dinky decided to see what was going on. Of course, Rocky followed him. Jae and I were watching the whole thing through the arcadia door. It all went down in super slow motion. As soon as Joe saw the dogs coming, the look of "Oh…shit!" came across his face, and it was classic. He lifted the trap as high as he could, but Joe was not a tall man. I gave him credit for trying, though. Dinky took a flying leap at the trap and knocked it out of Joe's hand. When it landed, the door popped open. Now the pissed-off racoon is out of the trap. I figured it would run, but it didn't. It was getting ready to fight, and the dogs were all in. Joe was standing in the middle of a knockdown drag out that is about to go down. Who knew a nearly naked redneck could run so fast? Jae and I had closed the door because we didn't know what was going to happen. Joe was screaming like a ten-year-old girl, "Let me in!" The dogs and the racoon started fighting. Rocky would circle and distract it so Dinky could attack. I was yelling at the dogs trying to get their attention, but they weren't listening. There was nothing we could do. It was a total shit show. The dogs ended up killing the racoon, but it went down fighting. That little racoon did some damage. I had to run Dinky to the vet in the morning for repair. His ear got ripped in half, he had numerous puncture wounds on his face and his lip was torn. After a good clean up and some antibiotics, the wounds were only cosmetic and would heal but he would be scarred.

That's how Dinky got his Indian name. Some Native American Indians have beautiful names. Their names have true meaning to their heritage or nature. Proud names. When I give someone an Indian name, it's more Hollywood style like Dances with Wolves or Stands with a Fist. After Dinky's run in with the racoon, his lip never healed back together, so I gave him the name Two Lips a Dripping.

LIFE LESSON #4011

Just because something is small in size, it
doesn't mean it isn't mighty of heart.

Joe and his ex used to host a big BBQ every year at the end of hunting season for all their friends and family. I inherited this tradition after we got married. It was a ton of work to get ready for it. Thankfully, Joe had some great friends that would help and even do some of the cooking. I had no idea what to expect the first time but Joe and his friends had pretty much figured things out years ago. It was a lot of fun, but with so many people in my house and down by the bonfire, my anxiety would ride the rails. Big crowds are tough for me. It's hard to keep an eye out on everything that's going on around you without eyes in the back of your head. I generally stuck with a smaller crowd of friends and family. We haven't had one in a while now, and that's okay by me. We still have BBQs but not ones that big anymore. I think the last one we had I counted eighty-four people. Too much work. Not to mention the incident from the last year we hosted it. We woke up in the morning to find a guy passed out on the living room couch, sitting up with his pants down around his ankles. His penis in full view. He had come with one of Joe's cousins as her date. Now I don't mind the sight of a random penis. I will always look, but I don't want to touch it! My kids don't need to see it, though. I was wondering why. Did he have to pee and never made it that far? Did he pee in the living room somewhere? Or worse, did he have nefarious intentions? Whatever the case, I didn't really care. He needed to get up, cover his penis, and get out. This is a job for Joe. His cousin was asleep on the other couch and she said they were going to poke but never got that far. On my living room couch?

Where I lay my head to watch TV? Ummm, no thank you! They're lucky the kids were still sleeping and didn't see anything. I'm not sure how their morning wakeup would have gone if they did. I'm not as non-confrontational as I used to be.

Another thing I inherited through Joe and his ex was participating in the Youth Outdoors Unlimited organization. Their goal was to get kids outside and learn about Arizona wildlife, conservation hunting, and fishing. It's run by an amazing group of people who volunteer their time to teach things that they have learned through years of experience. But you don't have to be a hunter to participate. I wasn't a hunter when I first went there; neither were my kids. Just being outside and learning things about the wildlife, listening to the stories and trading experiences was fun. When Joe's brother, Paul, would get to go to camp, he would always break out his guitar and play around the campfire. He's good. Really good. Shana usually comes to the camp too. And she brings her kids, who, by the way, are not allowed to call me Grandma since my kids are the same age as hers. They call me Melzor. Well, they're supposed to call me Melzor, but they usually call me Grandma Mel Mel. I really don't care; I love them no matter what they call me.

Shana started dating a guy after her divorce, and they had come to the point of moving in together. Guess whom she calls? Yuppers. Dear old Dad. So we made plans, hooked up our trailer, and headed to town that following weekend. Of course she lived on the second floor. I hate moving. At least she had pretty much everything packed up unlike I did. After about two hours and not quite finished, I was no longer having fun. Up and down the stairs and back again. My thighs were on fire! Finally done, now we had to drive it across town and get it in the new place. I was on the fence with this guy; he never seemed happy. But I had no idea how he was when we're not around. He could be the exact opposite.

After a long day of lifting and moving boxes, the main thing I was looking forward to was the hot tub we had waiting for us at home. There was nothing better than having a few adult beverages and getting in the hot tub after a long day. Since the kids were at their dad's for the weekend and we had no neighbors, we got in naked. It's so beautiful in the hot tub. We don't have street lights or any street noise; the only light comes from all the stars. There are so many that when you look up, it almost makes you dizzy. I got out of the hot tub to dry my hands to have a ciggy and slipped off the steps. I knew I was going down, but there weren't any handrails to grab on to. It was a freefall. I bounced off the steps and smacked my face on the side of the tub, leaving me naked and on all fours next to the tub. Joe didn't realize what had happened and gets out to stand behind me, grabbing my hips and making sex jokes. Not funny. I'm hurt! When I turned to look at him, he was shocked to see all the blood pouring from my nose and lip. He felt so bad and helped me into the house to doctor my face and get some ice. It took a few days before I decided to go to a doctor. At first, I figured I just had a black eye, but after a couple of days, every time I blew my nose, my teeth shifted. That started to make me nervous. The doctor was afraid I broke my orbital bone and sent me for an emergency X-ray and MRI. It turned out that I didn't break any bones, but the impact had bruised and seriously inflamed my sinus cavity, which was putting pressure on my teeth. Fantastic.

About a week later, Joe and I had to go to Walmart to do some shopping. By that point, my face looked horrific. Most of my eye and cheek were still a deep purple, but some spots had that green hue going on. Joe was asking me if I thought we needed something, and my response was a little curt when I said, "Do whatever you want." Some old lady got a look at my face right when I said that and must have assumed he had done it. She was going to kick his ass! I was going to watch, just for fun.

When Joe and I got together, he brought some friends with him. Jon and Shannon were some of those friends. Joe had known them for years; I met Jon when Joe and I were just dating and they each had a deer tag. I met his wife a little bit later. They are my kind of people. They are no-nonsense kind of people who do not pass judgment. If we have different opinions on something, we sit around the table, have an adult beverage, and listen to each other. I like them. They have two kids and are really into horses and hunting. I don't know diddly squat about horses, but I get the hunting side. So there's a yearly rodeo not far from here, and one of the events for the kids is to catch a greased piglet. Not an easy task. Plus it was dirty and stinky, and you can never be sure if you just slid in mud or pig poop. But whoever catches the pig gets to keep it. Jon's kid caught a pig and brought it to our house. We already had a pigpen set up from the previous owners, so it was a no brainer. The plan was to raise it, butcher it, and split the meat. But when the little guy got here, he had something wrong with his eye, so I had to make friends with it to be able to doctor it. I would rub his belly with one hand to distract him, while I washed and doctored his eye with the other. I started calling him Bacon Bits to remind myself that he was headed to freezer camp.

Jon built an automatic feeder so he could eat whenever he wanted to, but we also fed him all our organic scraps. And Joe made arrangements with the local restaurant in town to save their scraps for us too. We bought a couple of trash cans, and Joe would swing by every other day to swap out a clean can for a full one. It was a win-win for everyone. The restaurant didn't have as much garbage, and we got some good organic scraps to feed the pig for free. We fed him anything but meat products. Every once in a while, I would give him a fresh egg from the hen house as a treat. He loved them. We knew everything that went in his mouth. No artificial bullshit at all.

The kids hated Bacon Bits. The pigpen had a built-in cement pond for him to get in and cool off and it stunk. Stunk bad. If I couldn't pay JP to, I would shovel it out about once a week to give him fresh water to dip in, and the first thing he always did was poop in it. Raising Bacon Bits was very different than raising an indoor mini pot belly pig that got regular baths and had small poops. Big pigs have big poops. Big pig poop does not smell like roses. Especially on a warm summer day with a breeze.

When Bacon Bits was about 275 pounds and his snout was a good 4 inches wide, he would still come running when he heard my voice. When he got that big, the kids refused to go in his pen any-more, and I had to do all the work by myself. I went in to muck out the pond, and as usual, Bacon came running to me, rolling over to scratch his gigantic belly, knocking me right into his poop pond. I was dripping with liquified pig shit. It's disgusting! It was in my hair, all over my clothes, and some got in my mouth! Bacon Bits looked pleased with himself and still wanted a belly rub. Not going to happen today, buddy. When I waddled myself back up to the house, trying not to throw up, Joe refused to let me in. In fact, he refused to even let me on the porch. After he was done laughing, he gave me two choices: (1) let him hose me down in the yard or (2) strip naked on the porch and then I can go take a shower. I choose option 2. I thought he would get way too much enjoyment out of squirting me with a hose, and for some reason, I was mad at him. I'm not sure why he didn't push me in the poop pond, but somehow it was still his fault.

The day the butcher came to take Bacon Bits to freezer camp, I stayed in the house with the TV blaring and the vacuum running. He was the first and last pig we ever raised for butcher. I knew that was why we were raising him, but I ended up with a freezer full of meat I refused to eat.

Live and learn. At least hunting season was coming up and I drew my first deer tag. Joe drew one too. We both filled our tags and our freezer. Which is a good thing since we always have people at the house and I'm always cooking something. I like to cook. Actually, I like to make stuff up in the kitchen or take an existing recipe and tweak it to how I like it. I'm not a good rule follower in pretty much anything I do. Most of the time, things turn out fine, but not always. Our visitors are my test subjects. One of Joe's friends came out for a visit from the city for a little weekend getaway, and I threw some experimental recipes at him. The food was good, but the drinks were better. Joe's friend, Stan, was tossing them back with a vengeance. Somehow, when we were all preoccupied eating an okay but not great meal in the house, one of the rancher's cows went rogue and ended up on our property, happily eating grass in the horse corral. I'd already done my cowboy cow wrangling, and my "shoo, shoo, moo cow" technique left some damage. It was Joe's turn. Joe and Stan took a walk down to the corral, working on a plan. Joe was holding the gate open wider for her to get out but she was not moving. Stan was standing just inside the gate, holding his drink. Joe cheated and called Dinky over. Dinky just stood there next to Joe and waited for Joe to tell him to get it out. How Dinky knew what was being asked of him or how to do it, I will never know. But Dinks started circling the cow to get it facing in the right direction of the gate and then started nipping at her heels to get her moving. Stan was watching the whole thing while standing right in front of the gate, enjoying his drink. Joe was yelling, "It's coming out!" but Stan doesn't move. The cow plowed right over Stan like he was a small bush in her way. She knocked him to the ground and rolled him out of her way. Dinky stayed on the cow's heels until she was off our property like he had done it a million times before. Stan was now up and jumping up and down like a little kid who just got off a roller coaster ride. He was dirty and bruised but super excited about not spilling his drink. And he kept going on about how big she was in real life. No shit. Been there, done that! There was nothing more entertaining than a city boy hanging out in the country for some good old-fashioned fun.

Not long after Dinky saved the day with the cow, I lost him. I had to make a quick trip to town for supplies, and he got out while I was gone. When I got home, both Dinks and Rocky were gone, but Rocky came home. Dinky didn't. They always stuck together. I was getting really worried and taking trips back and forth on the dirt road, calling his name. I kept praying for the best, but the best didn't come. Dinky did though. He made it home to say goodbye to me. He must have gotten into a fight with a herd of javelina. They ripped open his throat from ear to ear. I could see his esophagus moving as he was panting for breath. One of their tusks degloved his whole side, and I could see his ribs moving too. There were at least fifty deep puncture wounds in his hind quarters. We were an hour away from the closest vet. He didn't make it. I was sobbing when he left me. It's been several years since that day, and writing this story still makes me cry. I loved that dog, and he loved me. There will never be another Dinky. God doesn't make one like him every day. He's got other things to do.

That year was going to be the year of the garden. I had already started to can stuff. I made some apricot jam from the apricots off our tree. I went out in the desert and picked prickly pears and made jelly. I went to an abandoned pistachio farm not far from here and picked pistachios to roast. That, my friends, is a pain in the ass. I have a newfound respect for the cost of pistachios from the store. Before you can even get to the roasting stage, you have to take the outer skin off the shell that's underneath. It's bright red and really sticky. It's a long process. I pickled asparagus I bought from the local farmers market. I was becoming a real homesteader. I wanted to expand my horizons and try my hand at growing and canning my own veggies. I made Joe go buy a used tiller and spent days prepping a good patch of earth. He hates when I come up with new ideas because he knew it meant he's going to have to do some work. But he's usually a pretty good sport. I even bought us garden hats with extra-large brims to protect us from the sun. Every self-respecting gardener has a good hat. One of my mottos is "Fake it till you make it"! I planted my seeds and put special markers on all the rows so I could remember what was where. It looked so professional. All that was left to do was water it. How hard could it be? I had such big plans! The day I saw the first tiny sprouts coming up, I was so excited. I got this!

I didn't have it. I didn't even close to have it. The weeds! So many weeds. I felt like I had spent an hour pulling weeds, go in the house for a glass of water, and they would grow right back. That fast. I couldn't keep up. And the gophers were a totally separate issue. The bastards would dig under the plants and steal the whole thing, pulling it down into their freaking hole. They were eating better than we were. All that work, sweat, and money, and I never harvested a single green bean. My friends and neighbors are growing things. Why can't I? It's so frustrating. I figured I had probably wasted one hundred thousand dollars over the years at fifteen dollars a shot trying to grow something. I didn't know what I was thinking. I did know there's a farmer's market about thirty minutes away, and I would gladly pay whatever they want. That tiller I made Joe buy hasn't moved since. "Gardener" is yet another title that will never be under my name. I'll add it to the list.

At least I was trying, and it kept my mind off losing Dinky. But Rocky didn't have a garden to keep him distracted, and he seemed to be getting more and more depressed. He needed a new friend. We are not the "go out and buy a dog" people. There's always a dog somewhere that needs a home. It just so happened that our friend had that dog. It was a yellow lab about 1 1/2 years old. She used to work from home but had recently opened a business in town, so he had to spend his days outside by himself and was becoming super destructive. He was bored and lonely, and she felt bad that he wasn't getting the attention he needed. That's where we came in. I was home all day and could give him the attention and distractions he needed. He still pulled some bone head moves but not that bad. In my opinion, labs have scrambled eggs for brains until about the age of two. Bow is no different. Over time, Bow has become one of the most expensive free dogs ever. It started shortly after we brought him home. He ate the normal stuff like his water bowl, a couple of hoses, and a welcome mat or two, but the bigger bills started when he broke my ribs. Well, technically, I broke my own ribs, but it was his fault. He followed me to the bathroom in the middle of the night, and I didn't know it, so on the way back to bed, I tripped over him and fell on my side. I don't think they were broken at that point, only bruised. My side was sore, but I went back to sleep without any problems.

The next morning when I woke up, my back was killing me. I didn't think it had anything to do with the fall. I thought I must have slept wrong, so I had Joe crack my back. That turned out to be a huge mistake. As soon as he did, I heard the cracks and couldn't breathe. Broken ribs are extremely painful. I had to have Joe drive me to the ER for an X-ray, and just the bouncing of my boobs while we were driving almost made me pass out. That was an expensive bill to pay, only to find out there is nothing they can do for broken ribs. Time is what it takes, and in the meantime, things like brushing my teeth or coughing, forget about sneezing, it all makes you want to pee your pants.

Nothing was really safe from Bow. Not even the arcadia door. I got up in the middle of the night, this time for a glass of water and felt a chill. I couldn't figure out where it was coming from until I realized there was no glass in the side part of the arcadia door. What the hell? All the glass had been smashed out and was on the porch outside. Another 3:00 a.m. wakeup call for Joe in his tightie whities. After getting Joe up, we came to the conclusion that Bow had probably seen a racoon on the porch and tried to get to it. Actually, he did get to it. Our arcadia door was really old, not tempered glass, and a lot wider than the standard ones you can buy at a home improvement store. We set to work trying to figure out how to cover the hole when I saw a little bit of blood outside on the porch. Not much though. That's when I took a good look at Bow. He had sliced his chest wide open down the center, leaving a good ten-inch slash. Fan. Fucking. Tastic. I knew where I was going in the morning.

While I was driving to the vet, watching Bow's skin flap jiggle like a raw piece of cheap steak, Joe was on the phone with Jon. Jon was always there if we needed him. He picked us up a new arcadia door and brought it out here to help Joe install it. Turns out, Jon installed it, and Joe kind of helped. The problem was that the hole in the side of our house was bigger than the new door. Jon was really good at building things. He was one of those kinds of guys that could just look at something and then know how to make it. Joe is a car guy, so for him to do woodworking, it was a lot of measuring and then remeasuring. Jon got the door installed fairly quickly, but there was a gap between the old frame and the new one and we didn't have any insulation on hand. We ended up stuffing it with an old cut-up Styrofoam cooler and some old blankets before Jon trimmed it out. That's redneck ingenuity right there!

All in all, this escapade of Bow's cost about $1,500. Our free dog wasn't really free.

Joey was coming to visit and we were preparing for a family BBQ. First stop, Walmart for supplies. I brought Jae with me because I knew I was going to need 2 carts. A big pack of TP, paper towels, paper plates and a fifty-pound bag of dog food is one cart. Why is it that when you're in a hurry, the kids always want to push the cart but when you need them to push a cart, they don't want anything to do with it? So I was pushing my cart in front; Jae was behind me pushing her cart, whining and complaining the whole time. About the third or fourth time she rammed my heels with her cart, I popped. I can put up with the complaining, but my heels were getting blood-ied and I'm done. I stopped and turned on a dime in the middle of an aisle, people everywhere, and said to her in a very calm but stern voice, "If I need you to push a cart, you are going to push that cart. And when you do, you better do it with a smile!"

Some guy walking by heard the whole exchange and stopped to say, "Way to go, Mom!"

Jae never said another word; she didn't run into my heels again, and she followed me down every aisle. She didn't smile, but I will take two out of three.

About a week or two before the family BBQ, I bought Joe a new BBQ grill. I went to Sears and picked out an okay—not great—grill, but it was on sale. I had to make arrangements to come back and pick it up that weekend when we had the truck. When we got there to pick it up, the grill was on clearance and fifty dollars cheaper than what I paid for it three days ago. I was mad. I was all ready to give them a piece of my mind, but they had no problem refunding me the fifty dollars. Sweet! Back out to the loading area, fifty dollars richer with a smile on my face, I handed the guys my paperwork, and they started loading up this really nice grill. I told them that was the wrong one. While I was in the store showing one of the guys the grill I bought, the other guys were loading up the fancy one in the back of our truck. I told them, "That's not the grill I bought." They checked my paperwork, said that was the one on my form and to take it up with someone else. My next stop was Walmart for some ribs to grill on that fancy new BBQ grill.

This kind of thing seems to happen to me all the time. One year I ordered ten cookbooks for all my friends and family, paid for them online, and made arrangements for them to be picked up at the store, which I did. About two weeks later, I got an email stating that since I never picked my order up; they had put them back on the shelf and refunded my money. Once, I ordered two folding camp chairs that rock. A couple weeks later, they came to our house. A week after that, another one showed up. A few days later, another one. I called to tell them they sent too many. They looked up my order and said they saw that I ordered two chairs and they were sent out. I said, "Yes, that's right, but you sent two more."

"No." They said I ordered two and got two.

"Okey dokey then."

Just as recently as a few months ago, I ordered a taco shell fry basket, and two showed up. I always try to make things right, but so far, it hasn't worked.

Back to the BBQ grill, we cooked up a couple racks of ribs for the family BBQ, and they were delicious. All the food was good, but the company was better. I love Joe's family. I love listening to all their stories about growing up. About all the crap they pulled. Joe's lucky to be alive and out of jail! Then his kids started telling their stories about growing up, stories about Joe being their dad. Stories about uncles and cousins. Hunting stories and—let's be real—hunting lies. Everyone is laughing, kicking back, and eating way too much. In the middle of all the action, I noticed Shana giving Bow a rib bone. Not a good idea. I gave him one several weeks ago, and he spent the night puking all over the house. Which means I spent the next morning scrubbing the carpet. They never seem to puke on the tile. Anyway, I figured, *Crisis averted*, and went back to listening and laughing with everyone.

Later that night, all snuggled into our cozy bed, dead asleep, I am awakened by the sound of a dog getting ready to puke. If you have a dog, you know that sound. It's unmistakable. Someone should make that the sound on an alarm clock because nothing wakes you up and gets you out of bed faster than that sound. I'm up and out of bed in .02 seconds, trying to zero in on the sound like the bionic woman. Target located. There is one goal: Get dog on tile ASAP. I clipped my foot on the corner of the bed and broke my pinky toe on the way to my target, but I did not, could not, abort my mission. With my target in hand, I hobbled to the bathroom tile just in time. As sweat dripped from my brow and my toe throbbed, I flicked on the bathroom light to see how bad the mess was. What the? There's no puke. Poor Bow had the look of "What the hell?" on his face. Well... shit. I dragged the wrong dog to the tile. I had just assumed it was Bow because that's whom I saw Shana giving bones to. She never told me she gave some to Rocky first. And surprise! He didn't make it to the tile. Shana was buying lunch next time. She doesn't know that yet, but she will.

Whether you're a dog mom who drags the wrong dog across the bedroom at night or you're a people mom who sends their kid to school with a broken arm, or both a dog mom and a people mom, we all have our moments of regret. I regret not taking a closer look at JP's arm before sending him off to school. In my defense, he lied. He woke up for school one morning complaining that his arm hurt and he didn't want to go to school. I asked him where it hurt and what happened. He told me he fell in the playground at school. The playground is sand, so I took a half-assed look at his arm, didn't see anything, and figured he was full of poop. As a last-ditch effort, he said he couldn't put his socks on because it hurt too much to pull them up. Whatever. I put his socks on for him and got him down the road for the bus. Around lunch time, his teacher called me, the school doesn't have a nurse, and she asked me if she can give JP some ibuprofen and an ice pack. He was complaining that his arm hurt. I told her "Sure," but I was thinking that he was really working this one. About thirty minutes later, the teacher called me back and said JP wanted to talk to me. This should be good.

First thing out of his mouth was, "I lied. Don't be mad." Fantastic. He proceeds to tell me that he didn't fall in the playground. He crashed his four-wheeler the night before. He didn't want to tell us because it was a little damaged. "I don't give a damn about the four-wheeler! We can fix that." I wouldn't have been so dismissive about his arm if I had known he crashed. Since they were taking the bus to their dad's for the weekend, I had to call him and ask him to get JP in for an X-ray after school. Here went another one of those phone calls that needed a little more explanation than just "Hey, by the way, I sent JP to school with a broken arm." Turns out, it was broken. Now, I feel like a crap mom, and I feel bad he went a whole night and day with a broken arm. As for JP, he had to spend six weeks in a cast and couldn't ride his four-wheeler. Then, we grounded him for six weeks for lying. Three months without being able to ride his four-wheeler.

Right after JP got his cast off, Jae broke her arm. She was wearing a long skirt and twirling and dancing, got twisted up in the skirt, fell, and slammed into the coffee table. This time, I took her straight to the ER. Her timing couldn't have been worse. She had her first deer hunt in two weeks. It took a lot to get her there. We had her take the Hunter Safety course through Youth Outdoors; we bought her a youth rifle and spent weekends practicing. And she was lucky enough to get drawn, which doesn't always happen. She was excited. Opening day came. We packed everything up and set out to see how things would go. She wanted to at least try. Just as the sun came up, Jae got it done with one arm. Joe and I were so proud of her. More importantly, she was proud of herself. She set a goal, she did the steps to get there, and she accomplished it. Every time I made dinner after that, she would always ask if that was her meat. She got a new bump of pride every time I said yes.

Shana and I have become really close over the years. We talk at least two or three times a week and throw each other a text just about every day. Usually, it's a poop joke. She is so funny and nothing, I mean nothing, grosses her out. I'm not sure if it's because she's in the medical field or if it's her personality. Or a combination of both. But if she came across a floating dead dog balloon, she would pop it on purpose. Not because she's mean, just because she's curious.

She's also super busy. She's working, going to school, taking care of the family and the house. I think she's a little stressed out. And she's head over heels in love with this guy she's moved in with. She's a different person when he's around though. She is so preoccupied with making sure he's happy. I'm not sure if he's ever really happy. I think I've only seen him genuinely smile and laugh maybe once or twice in all this time. Maybe things are different when they are home, I hope so. Maybe he just doesn't like us. I don't know but he's always so serious and none of the rest of us are. Maybe he thinks our dumb redneck asses are beneath him. And maybe I'm reading too much into it. The only thing that really matters is that she's happy and that she and the kids are cared for.

Joe and I went to her house for Christmas dinner one year. We had already done the Santa thing with our kids, and they were off to their dad's for the rest of the day. It was nice not to have to spend the day in the kitchen preparing a huge meal that would only take ten minutes to eat and another thirty minutes to clean up. To backtrack for a second, Shana had been to our house several weeks before Christmas and treated us to her deep-fried tacos. I gotta say, I love her deep-fried tacos. Mine are okay, but they are a pain in the ass to make, and I always manage to burn myself in the process. Shana's are perfect. Anyway, when she was cutting up some veggies, she was using one of my favorite knives and made a random comment about how she really liked the knife. She said she liked the weight of it and how perfectly it fit in her hand, which is exactly why I liked it. So Joe and I special ordered her one for Christmas. We were super excited to give her something that we knew she would like rather than a random gift card. And she was happy when she opened it. The guy immediately started giving her shit. Asking her why she would want another knife, they had plenty. She started telling him why she liked it, and he thought that was stupid. She said it was really sharp, and the guy started giving her shit that he could sharpen the ones they already had. Hello? We were right there. Having to listen to him berate her over a gift we just gave her pissed me off. I'm trying to give the guy the benefit of the doubt, but I'm wondering what it's like when we aren't there.

Time to eat dinner, and Shana pulls out a roast she's been cooking all day, and it smells delicious. Then he started berating her because the ends are crispy. First of all, that's my favorite part. And secondly, we are right there! Lastly, holy fuck, dude! Back off—it's Christmas. After we finished eating, she still cuddled up to him on the couch. At my house, after all that, Joe would be lucky if I didn't put Nair in his shampoo the next day. She wanted us to hang out and have an adult beverage with them, but I couldn't take another round of the "Let's bash Shana game" or I was going to lose my shit.

I thought it was funny when she secretly hired a maid service to clean the house. I wish I could hire a service, but no one would come out this far and I would probably clean before they got here just like my mom. But it made her life a little easier, and I was all for that. Then she graduated, which is fantastic, and the kids were doing good. Now that she wasn't so busy, we decided to take a weekend and get out of town. Joe, the kids and I had been going to Mormon Lake for the last few years to go to their yearly Volunteer Fire Department fundraiser. Joe has a friend, Marty, who has a cabin up there and he lets us stay there. Marty is a good guy. I really like him and have the second we met. He's my kind of people—what you see is what you get. Joe made arrangements for us to stay in the cabin and Shana to park their trailer on the property.

The fundraiser is an all-day thing. It starts off with a huge yard sale, then you can buy a lunch plate, bakery goods, raffle tickets, and T-shirts. After lunch, they hold an auction. It's an all-day social event. Groups of people park their butts on the used furniture for sale, drink beer and bullshit. We love going and have met some really nice people every year, and I usually come home with some good stuff. I learned after our first time that kids can nickel and dime a person to death at a yard sale. From then out, I started having the kids do extra chores for their yard sale money several weeks before we go. They each get twenty dollars for the yard sale and ten dollars for the baked goods. When that's gone, it's gone. It is amazing the amount of crap a kid can buy for twenty dollars! At the end of the sale, they sell grocery bags for one dollar, and whatever you can fit in it is covered. That's when the real junk starts showing up. The kids don't know this, but most of that stuff ends up at Goodwill within a few weeks. They don't miss it. I forewarned Shana about this problem so she would be prepared.

Our group consisted of four adults and five kids. We showed up early in the morning, so all the good furniture wasn't gone yet. All the tables were set up in the two bays of the fire station and the driveway. I let my kids do their thing while we wandered the tables, made some good buys, and scoped out the stuff on the silent auction table. The guy kept snapping at Shana's kids for touching stuff. They're kids—of course they're going to touch stuff. And if they break something, who gives a shit? It's not a high-end antique store; it's a yard sale. Whatever they might break will only cost a couple of dollars. Sometimes kids need to be kids. As long as they're safe, let them explore.

After making a few rounds through the sale tables and buying some cookies, we found an old couch to sit on and get the bullshit party started. My kids keep stopping by to show off their latest purchases; the guy won't let their kids wander around. After a while, lunch was served. No one is wan any hurry to move things along to the auction. Apparently, this was unacceptable to the guy, and he was getting irritated. He thought things should move along like clockwork. Yard sale, check. Lunch, check. Auction, check. Raffle, check. Done. Home, check. No time for dilly dally. No time for socializing or fun. His bitching and complaining was giving me anxiety and ruining my day drinking buzz.

When any auction starts, I have to really pay attention to Joe. he is very competitive and will keep bidding on something if he really wants it or not. He just wants to win. And his competitive juices start flowing even before the auction. He *has* to get his lucky number 13 paddle. Every time I see that number 13 paddle fly up in the air, another bead of sweat forms on my brow. I have to be ready to pump the brakes every so often. He loves the bidding, and I love telling him no. It's a win-win for us. The guy didn't even bid on anything. I don't know why he was so impatient for the auction to start other than that he wanted it to be over.

At the cabin the next morning, all five kids were running around, goofing off outside, enjoying the cooler weather and fresh air. All the kids were doing the same thing, but for some reason, the guy got mad at Shana's two and sent them to sit in the trailer, by themselves, for the rest of the time we were there. His daughter was allowed to stay outside. This pissed me off. This was supposed to be a nice, relaxing family weekend, and some of the family wasn't allowed to participate. But when we were packing up, Shana's kids were allowed to come out of the trailer to work like pack mules. His daughter didn't have to do anything. This pisses me off more. I have nothing against his daughter; she's a sweet little girl. I do have a problem with them not being treated equally. I don't want to go camping with them again.

The next time I met Shana for lunch, I overstepped my bounds and told her how I felt. I told her it wasn't right that there were two sets of rules and the kids were treated so differently. She told me she treated his daughter differently and that's what happens in blended families. I don't know what it's like to blend two families together when there are little kids involved. But I said my piece.

I'm not sure if she's happy, though. We talk all the time, and she won't give any specifics, but I think she's putting a whole bunch of pressure on herself to be perfect. I'm not sure if she's trying to be perfect for him or herself. She even started going to a doctor to lose weight. She does not need to lose weight. There's no such thing as perfect. I think the pressure is starting to get to her.

Then she called and said she was done and wanted to move out but didn't know where to go. We talked and told her she could come live with us. She could enroll the kids in the country school; I could get them back and forth with mine. She could work whenever she wanted to because I was home for the kids. We would figure things out as we went.

The following weekend, Joe and I hooked up the trailer with the plan to head to her early the next morning. We would pack and get whatever we could in the time we had. The rest we could go back and get another time. She called and cancelled before we got to the end of the dirt road. She wanted to try to work things out.

Then she was gone. Shana took her life late on a Monday night. The guy called us around midnight and said we needed to get to the hospital immediately. Shana was in the ICU.

When we got there, we were ushered into a side room and told what had happened and what was happening. Surely there had been a mistake. We went in to see her. Surely they were overdramatizing the situation. She was going to sit up at any moment, pull that thing out of her throat, and want to go home. She didn't get to go home. At first, I was in shock. That quickly turned to anger. Which quickly turned to sadness, where I stayed for a very long time.

She had been at our house on Sunday. She brought the kids, and they all stayed over. We had a great impromptu visit. Joe had called her that afternoon to ask her to pick up a part he needed for the truck before the store closed and he could run and get it from her. She offered to bring it out to us. When she showed up with the part, she brought a pizza for dinner, a twelve-pack of Corona beer, and a dozen cupcakes for her son's birthday. We spent the evening shooting the breeze on the porch. The guy had told me stories about how she was depressed and had taken a handful of Tylenol not long ago. We even talked about that. She said it was a mistake and she would never do that again. We ate the pizza and sang "Happy Birthday" to her son and went to bed. She got up in the morning, took a shower, and went on their way. Nothing seemed out of the ordinary.

The guy and his friends made all the arrangements for the memorial. I am grateful for that. We would have had no idea where to begin with that and weren't in any frame of mind to figure it out. I am also very grateful to Joe's brother, Paul, for never leaving Joe's side. I was trying to be strong for him, but I was barely keeping myself upright. It was a lovely service; I barely remember any of it. I know there were a lot of people there, but I don't remember whom, except for a small handful of friends that I stuck to. I do remember trying not to throw up.

In fact, I spent a good three months trying not to throw up. Grief is a hard thing and hits everyone differently. Me? I couldn't eat. I tried, but it usually didn't stay down. Right after it happened, old friends I hadn't spoken to in years reached out. I thought it would be a good distraction from the sadness to get together with someone who didn't know Shana and I extended an olive branch again, but it was ignored again. So I kind of crumbled in on myself. Joe wasn't doing any better. We got suspended in sadness.

We began to question everything. The night she came to the house before the incident when she brought beer. We don't drink beer, but her brother does. We sang "Happy Birthday," but her son's birthday was over a week away. Did she already have a plan? We question if we missed something. How could we have not known something? Anything? Why didn't she talk to me? Did she try and I missed it? Could I have done more? What could I have done? I felt betrayed, and that doesn't make any sense. I know the guy said something, but I never saw any signs of being that depressed; she always seemed so happy. I didn't know how to help myself or Joe or her kids or mine. I was lost.

Going to town was pure hell. Everywhere we went, we had memories of being there with Shana and the kids. We couldn't go to certain restaurants, and we definitely couldn't go hunting that year even though Joe and I had both drawn tags. It was hard for Joe to be out in all the spots that he had hunted with Shana, and I felt guilty whenever I had a good time doing anything. Our hearts weren't in it.

Then came the fallout drama. All that is a long story of finger pointing and accusations. A lot of it swirling around what Joe and I did or didn't do that I don't want to get into the details of. Most of which is not true, but it doesn't help the healing process. We were passengers like everyone else, trying to navigate through sadness and grief the best we knew how.

My heart was broken, and I was stuck. I felt responsible for not doing more and guilty for not knowing. Mostly, I missed her. Stupid shit would cross my mind and a second later would come the wave of sadness when I realized she wasn't around to share it with. Then there is the never-to-be-answered question of why. Why? Round and round. Did she really mean to?

Someone very special finally told me that I needed to wake up every morning and say to myself, "Today will be better than yesterday." So I did, every day. Some days it didn't work, but some days it did, slowly. I didn't know how badly I had checked out until Jae got her report card and it wasn't good. She was always a straight A student until that semester. I was so checked out that I didn't realize she was hurting too. I think even if I did know, I couldn't have helped her. I couldn't even help myself.

Things did get better. I think of her and talk to her often, and I still miss her tremendously. But life goes on, and I want to spend mine being happy.

We decided to raise a steer. I didn't know anything about raising a steer, but I guess I was going to learn. Joe picked out the biggest, meanest steer in the coral. He wanted to make sure I didn't make friends with it since it was going to be headed off to freezer camp. We went in with some friends to split all the costs and then eventually the meat. A good-sized steer can give you a good 300 to 350 pounds of meat. That's a lot. I named him Stewie. Stewie was an asshole from day 1.

One of our neighbors came down the day he was delivered to check him out. She went in the pen with him to get a closer look. He didn't want to make any new friends and immediately charged at her. He tucked his head and rammed her so hard she flew up in the air and did a full flip. Stewie was cranky! Now I was scared to have to get in there to feed him. How was that going to go? I'm shitty at gymnastics. I can't do flips.

At first, Stewie stayed clear of me as long as I stayed clear of him. Not a problem. Even when they are babies, they are pretty big and strong. But it didn't take him long to associate me with food. He started pushing me around, not to be mean, more to speed things along with the food. I don't think he knew how hard he was pushing, but I was starting to get scared. I don't know if cows can sense fear like other animals, but I did know I didn't want to find out. Joe and Keith built me a special barricade around the door to the feed barn so the asshole would leave me alone.

Now that there was a barricade, I wanted to make friends. I bet Joe ten dollars that at some point, I would be able to kiss Stewie on the head. I won that bet, but it took a while, and it cost me three broken fingers along the way. Every time I fed him, I would hang out while he ate and do quick little touches here and there just to get him used to me. During one of those visits, I had my hand around the rail of the barricade, and Stewie bucked his enormous head up, squishing my fingers between the rail and his skull. Technically, they weren't broken, just seriously bruised, swollen, and unusable for three weeks. I probably should have had them X-rayed but didn't see the point. I already had them wrapped.

Then I heard about a woman not too far away who had three goats she wanted to get rid of. Sugar, Sprite, and Snickers got delivered to our house that weekend. These guys are cute! And friendly, unlike their asshole corral mate. My plan was to collar them and stake them out on a good twenty-foot run every once in a while to help knock down the weeds. It only took one time having the triplets staked out to learn that goats don't just eat weeds. They eat everything! I mean everything—clotheslines, clothes on the clothesline, tree bark, siding off of sheds, plastic buckets—it didn't matter. I also learned how they can climb and jump with ease when I found Sugar in the bed of the pickup truck. No clue how she got in there. This newfound knowledge limited where I could stake them out. We had limited areas with a forty-foot radius with nothing but weeds to eat. They turned into pets without a purpose.

Since we already had about forty chickens, a steer, three goats, and two dogs, I might as well get some ducks. I put them in Bacon Bits's old pen because it had the pond. Might as well get some turkeys too. I loved hearing the Tom turkey gobble when I called his name, which was Goober, by the way.

My dad thought I have lost my mind! When I told him about getting all the chickens, he wanted to know why. I told him we were raising them for the fresh eggs. He's so funny! He asked if we were going to eat the eggs right out of the chicken's butt. Yes. Here is a fun-filled fact for everyone: all chicken eggs come out of their butt. Even the nice, cleaned ones you buy from the grocery store. In fact, all birds only have one hole. They pee, poop, have sex, and lay eggs from the same hole.

I love all my animals. But it is a lot of work, and the problem is trying to go anywhere. It's hard to find someone who is willing to stay out here, do all the animal chores, and can drive in case of an emergency with one of my dogs. We paid a friend to come stay for a weekend so Joe and I could get away to Laughlin for a few days. Things started a little sketchy when she started snacking on the dog treats. We watched her eat about five cookies before I asked her if they were any good. She's like yeah, why? They're dog treats. That's why there's a big picture of a dog on the front. After we all got done laughing, we walked around and showed her the ropes, wrote some info down for her, and we took off. Maybe eating the dog treats should have been a sign that she wasn't paying attention or even really interested in the job. We got a text late Saturday night that she was bored and leaving to go hang out with some friends in Phoenix. Ahhh, okay? Joe and I had already been drinking, thinking we had things covered at home and that we could sleep in. We couldn't drive home. I told her to make sure to lock up the chickens and leave the dogs outside and we would leave first thing in the morning. I was already not happy about the whole situation when we got home that morning, but when I found out she left the dogs inside, I was pissed. They peed and pooped everywhere. I can't be mad at them. They had no choice. At least the chickens were locked up, but Stewie was more of an asshole than usual because he was hungry and didn't give a shit about the drama.

About a week before the butcher was scheduled to take Stewie to freezer camp, he died. What the hell? He was fine at seven the night before when I fed him and dead by 7:00 a.m.? At first, I thought he was taking a nap. Do steers take naps on their side? I don't know. But he was not waking up for breakfast. I walked down there, and he was dead dead. Like two legs in the air dead. What happened? I called Joe to come home from work to see if we could salvage any of the meat, but he had been gone too long.

All that time and money to raise him up—gone. All those nights we didn't stay at a BBQ so we could get home to feed and the mornings we didn't sleep in. Not to mention my three fingers. All that and not a single pound of burger? I'm pissed. I hated having to call our friends and tell them he died. Oh! And what do you do with a big dead cow body? That's a hole I don't want to dig. Thankfully, Joe got hold of a local rancher who came over with a backhoe. He loaded him up and took him out to his property somewhere and left him for the wildlife. What a waste.

Then, Jae gave me my Indian name. A lot of things had happened before that. JP graduated eighth grade as valedictorian, mainly because he was the only eighth-grade graduate, but valedictorian sounds really good to the grandparents. Our free dog, Bow, got bitten by a rattlesnake, costing us another $1,800 in vet bills, I shot my first rattlesnake, and one of Joe's sisters unfortunately passed away from breast cancer. We've had our ups and downs like all families, but we keep trudging along.

The day I got my Indian name started off like every other day. I got up, got the kids' lunch packed and got them down to the end of the dirt road for JP to catch the van to high school and Jae to get the bus to her school. I went home, did all my animal chores and my household chores, and figured out what was for dinner. I hate the "What's for dinner?" game, but I have to play it every day.

I wasn't feeling very well when I had to head back down the dirt road to pick up Jae. JP was staying at his dad's for school the next morning. On my way down the road, I noticed our neighbor was having a Dumpster he rented picked up and being loaded on a truck. No big deal. I just wanted to keep it in mind because sometimes I let Jae drive the truck back home. When I was sitting at the end of the road waiting for the bus, I started feeling like I was going to throw up. That soon changed from feeling like I was going to throw up to the feeling that I had to go poop. *I'll just wait until I get home. Hopefully, the bus isn't running late.* Things quickly turned into an ECS. I began to consider my options. Of all days, I was wearing a hot pink shirt, so hiding behind a bush at the bus stop was no go. The bus, filled with kids, was going to pass me and turn around any second, which didn't leave me enough time to make it home, go poop, and make it back. Dumpster guy was going to be driving down the road any second, so I couldn't go halfway down and squat behind a bush in my stupid hot pink shirt. I was running out of options and time. This was an ECS on steroids! Things were going to happen no matter how tightly I squeezed my cheeks together. Pure panic set in. I was actually going to poop my pants. I spotted a Walmart bag in the back seat. That was my savior. I flipped up the back seat, got in, and shit in a Walmart bag. Yes. I did. I tied off the bag and got back in the driver's seat right as Dumpster guy pulled up next to me and the bus pulled in. Jae got in the truck, and I headed home. I wasn't planning on saying anything to her, but she made a comment about how the truck smelled. I told her the story. She nodded, turned to me, and said, "Your Indian name is Shits in a Bag." In my defense, that was the start of a three-day stomach flu. The name still stuck.

Jae giving me that name didn't surprise me. There's that whole nature versus nurture thing. I can tell you that even though my kids were born from my heart and not my body, they are exactly like me. My son is kind and thoughtful. He has a dark sense of humor and gets distracted easily. My daughter is quick witted and opinionated. She thinks of others and is loyal. They have turned into some pretty great young adults. It was sketchy there for a few years, especially the dreaded puberty years. People who say the terrible twos are bad haven't had to live with teenagers yet. The worst was when they were fighting and I got caught in the crossfire.

They would constantly tell on each other even if they had to make shit up. It's like they entertained themselves by picking on each other. Some days, it would be a quick quibble and then they would be best friends all over again. Other days, it went on all day. Those were the days I would ask myself, *What was I thinking?* I had a good life. I could sleep in on the weekends, watch a whole show uninterrupted, clean a room, and have it stay that way. No one rolled their eyes at me if I asked them to take out the trash. No one acted like I asked them to chop off their own arm when in reality they were told to clean their room. And especially, no one looked at me like I was the stupidest human on earth because they obviously knew better than whatever I was saying.

Jae and I had to run to town one day to do some quick grocery shopping and planned on stopping at Burger King for some Whoppers on the ride home. When we got there, the grill was broken. Jae was pissed. She acted like I broke the grill just to make her mad and that I could fix it. There was nothing I could do, and there wasn't another Burger King within a thirty-mile radius. She could get something else. I got something else. She refused. It was the Whopper that we had talked about or nothing. Nothing it was then. Jae spent the entire drive home shooting me the daggers of death. So not getting her Whopper had ruined the entire day. Not only was I not enjoying my chicken sandwich but I was also almost afraid to take a bite. She chose not to get something else, and now I was in the crossfire. How would that work? But Shits in a Bag lived to see another day.

LIFE LESSON #4231

If you never have a shitty day, how do you
know when you're having a good one?

When you have adopted children, they don't always look like you
or like their siblings. JP could pass as a biological child, Jae not so
much. Maybe when she was younger, but the older and taller she got,
the less we looked alike. This never crossed my mind until we get
"the look." Jae and I are used to it; Joe has some catching up to do.
The first time he saw it, he couldn't figure out what was happening.
Jae and I knew. We were heading to Florida, and she needed some
shorts. The three of us decided to divide and conquer the clothes area
in Walmart. A saleswoman eventually came up to me and asked me
if I needed any help. I explained that I was looking for some shorts
for my daughter, and as she was walking me to the right area, Joe and
Jae came up. Here came "the look." Three rounds of the saleswoman
looking at me, then Joe, then Jae and back again. Yup, that's our
daughter. Shorts? When she walked away, Joe had asked what that
was all about, and we had to fill him in on "the look." He needed to
get used to it.

We got it again that same day when we went to get Jae's nails
done. She saved her money and wanted some white-tip acrylic nails
for vacation. Again with "the look." "Yes, she's my daughter. Yes, she
has my permission." After all the awkwardness was over, Jae sat down
to get her nails done. During the chit chat, it came up that we were
heading to Florida to see Grandma and Grandpa. Of course they
started asking if I was getting my nails done too. No. Now there was
two of them in on the action about how I should get my nails done
too. My daily life does not require pretty nails. But they wouldn't

quit. I explained that I did not have the time or patience to get them filled. They said I could just let them grow out. Fine! I got my nails done. While I was sitting there, getting my unwanted nails, the salon lady said I should get my eyebrows waxed. No. She says if I get my eyebrows waxed, I would look way younger. Fine. I got my eyebrows waxed. While I was getting my eyebrows waxed, the salon lady said I should get a pedicure. We should both get a pedicure. No. The salon lady said our feet would look so much better in flip flops on the beach. A person can't go all the way to Florida and not wear flip flops on the beach. We both got pedicures. *Holy. Shit.* I totally caved under the peer pressure. Thank God they weren't pushing heroin because I'm not sure where I would be right now. It took me a week to figure out how to button my jeans with those long fake nails! And as far as just letting them grow out? That took forever. I had one that was hanging on for dear life. It was all gnarly and gross looking but still hanging on. I called it my crackhead nail.

We were off to Florida, and yes, my toes did look pretty in flip flops. So did Jae's, but she got her period the day we got there. She was only using pads back then and was super mad that she couldn't swim on vacation. We had a talk to see if she wanted to try tampons, and she said she did. Joe, Jae, and Grandma were already planning to go to the store for some groceries, so I asked him to pick up some tampons while they were there. He's already raised a daughter, so that kind of stuff didn't bother him. But it turned out that he was a little out of practice. He spent far too long standing in the tampon section looking for the "waterproof tampons," thinking she wanted them so she could swim. Grandma saved him. We still joke about that around the house. It's just so fun to pick on Joe.

But then I had to pick some up. Holy shit! I had a hysterectomy at least fourteen years ago at that point. I hadn't had to walk down that aisle in a very long time. When I needed tampons, there were basically two choices. Cardboard applicators in regular and super. Now? It's a whole aisle, both sides! What the hell? There are plastic applicators, biodegradable applicators, organic applicators, no applicators. There's some for women who do sports, some for women walk, women who don't walk. There are big ones, little ones, ones you use at night, ones you use on Tuesday's. What is going on here? Then there are the pads that go with the tampons. Big ones, thin ones, some with wings, some for thongs, some for when you sleep, some for when you don't. I was lost in a vortex of feminine hygiene products, and my head was spinning. Why do women need soooo many choices? Do any of them come with a free dinner coupon? I waited until a young twenty-something gal with the same body type as Jae came down the aisle and watched what she bought. Playtex Sport regular. Jae was not playing sports at the moment. I didn't care.

I think Grandma and Grandpa are a little taken back by how openly we discuss things like tampons as a family. I want my kids to feel free and comfortable to talk about anything that's on their mind with Joe and me. I want them to love themselves as much as I love them. I don't want them to *ever* feel as though they aren't special, like I have for so long. I'm doing my best to try to adjust my way of thinking about myself, and I really think things are starting to shift. I mean, I'm not that bad. My dad and I are getting closer than we've ever been—that's progress. I know that I'm not a horrible person. I think it's okay to just be me. But that's not good enough for my kids. I want more for my kids. I want them to know, without a shadow of doubt, that they are great and loved and special.

We decided to take a family vacation out to Kansas to see Joe's son, Joey, and his family. Since I hate to fly, I had a brilliant idea to turn it into an extended vacation and drive. But not just drive the truck. I thought we should rent an RV! Have potty, will travel. No Shits in a Bag on this trip.

Turns out, renting an RV is kind of expensive. Joe needed some convincing. Let the campaign begin! I said we could see a bunch of stuff along the way. I explained there was a potty so we didn't need to take breaks for that. He's still not going for it. The kids would have more space, so there wouldn't be any arguing in the backseat. No need to find hotels. Eat while driving down the road. That's the one that hooked him. He's a foodie. Well, that and the fact that I nagged the shit out of him. I'm pretty sure he agreed just to shut me up. I'm okay with that.

The RV was perfect! About thirty feet with a queen bed, small shower, and a pooper in the back. A kitchen with a good-sized fridge, a couch that folded out to a bed on one side and a banquet across from it that also turned into a bed, driver and passenger seats in front. When parked, it had a slide out that really opened up the space in the bedroom and kitchen area. Even the color scheme was what I would pick. I've always said that an RV just like this is on my lottery list.

We picked it up a few days before we left so I could get all our stuff packed. Then I spent an entire day in the kitchen making breakfast burritos, sandwiches, lunch burritos, and snacks that we could heat and eat driving down the road. We hired someone to stay at the house to care for all the animals and keep an eye on the place. Our first day on the road was going to be the longest, so Joe wanted to leave around 3:00 a.m. The kids and I just went back to sleep. I learned that the kids could argue just as easily from the couch to the banquet as they could have in the backseat of the truck. I also learned that when the RV was all closed up while driving, we couldn't get to the microwave, so half the shit I premade was useless. That didn't matter anyway because every time we had to stop for gas, the kids needed snacks. Apparently, the things I brought and made weren't what they were in the mood for. Go figure. I also learned that when we were parked at night, the ground wasn't always level. The RV had automatic stabilizers, but when one or two of the tires weren't even touching the ground anymore, it freaked me out. What really sucked was when we were parked at night, we couldn't go anywhere or do anything. So much for sightseeing.

We got to Kansas sooner than we thought since we didn't do any sightseeing along the way. It was so nice to see Joey and the family. His wife is an amazing cook. Everything is so green in Kansas. But the humidity is killer. We weren't used to that at all. We got to go to Joe's grandson's Eagle Scout ceremony, and Joe got to go to his other grandson's baseball game. My favorite thing we did was spend a day fishing. The four of us bought a day license, and Joey took us to one of his favorite spots. We all caught fish. I didn't know Jae was such a fishing fool. The rest of us petered out and went to sit in the

RV with the air conditioner running on full blast. Not Jae and Joe. She just kept yanking out fish, one after another. We came home with a freezer full.

After several days, Joey's subdivision wouldn't let us keep the RV parked in his driveway any longer, so we had to move it to a friend's house in a different subdivision. The problem was that all our clothes were packed in there, and now we didn't have any transportation. It was what it was; we were leaving in a few days anyway. We were all heading to Branson, Missouri. Unfortunately, when we went to pick up the RV, all that food I made had gone bad. We blew the guy's circuit breaker for his garage where we had it plugged in. That was a total waste of time and money. Live and learn. After Joe plugged in the destination into the GPS, we were off to Missouri. I'd never been there, so I was kind of excited. The kids were too busy arguing to give a shit where we were headed.

The GPS lady was getting on my nerves, and I had started referring to her as "the bitch." Why is it a woman? I'm a woman, and I don't know shit about directions. When I ask my husband where something is, he's always like "It's 3.2 miles North Northwest. Longitude .30 degrees N, latitude 15 degrees NW, 4321 miles above sea level." What the fuck is that? He can't even find the mustard in the fridge, and that's how he gives me directions? Is there a Big Lots nearby that I can look for? Maybe a big yellow *M* for a McDonalds? It should be a male voice on the GPS, and he should tell me how good my boobs look. Just saying. At one point, we pulled off the road to buy some fresh peaches and "the bitch" went crazy! She keeps saying "Make a U turn," "U turn now," and "Turn around at next exit." My God! She was acting as if we had driven smack dab in the middle of an active nuclear test site! I just wanted some fresh peaches! GPS Gina finally shut up when we got back on the road to Bronson, but she is not in my friend group.

When we got to Bronson, we realized that our sightseeing was limited to wherever the RV could fit into the parking areas. Buying an RV was off my lottery list of purchases. I was ready to go home. I missed my dogs. I missed the solitude of our home, and I needed some personal space. Joe needed to have a date with "the bitch" GPS Gina and find us the quickest route home.

The first night on the way home, we camped at a really shady campground. Not shady like nice trees, shady like Jae can't use the restroom by herself. The next night was better. GPS Gina had my back on that one. We got a spot near some really nice older folks with a dog. I, of course, asked if I could pet their dog, and they said yes. We got to talking about this and that, and the subject of RVs came up. I told them ours was rented and how I'm super glad we rented one before buying one. Their RV looks no bigger than a handicap van. They even gave me a tour. It's called a conversion van. Perfect for two and a dog. It has everything a person would need and it fits in a regular parking spot. I want one! That is now on my lottery list.

When we finally got home, things were amiss. Since we live so far out and it's cheaper, we buy a lot of things in bulk. We did some of that shopping before we left on vacation, so we didn't have to worry about anything when we got home. Big mistake. Six bottles of whiskey, two bottles of vodka, all the beer we keep for when friends drop by, the hot tub was green and the filters dried up. A few other things we found over the next few weeks, but the house was still standing and my dogs were okay. That's all that really matters. Spending time with Joey and his family was great. The rest of the trip, not so much. And we need a new house sitter.

The kids are getting older; so are we. JP is driving. I won't be the one to teach Jae. It's someone else's turn. I have anxiety issues when someone who has had a driver's license for forty years is driving. When someone has only been driving for forty days, I can't take it. I tried. I had been letting the kids drive my truck down the dirt road for years, but that's a two-mile stretch at fifteen miles an hour and no traffic. The real road with real speed and real traffic is terrifying! The road to the mining town is even worse. Twists and turns, one lane, no shoulder with cliffs that drop off. Right after JP got his permit, I let him drive that road, and I thought I was going to die! Not because he was a bad driver but because I was holding my breath for so long. I had to have him pull over at the first turnout so I could get out of the car for a minute to breathe. I thought I was going to pass out. So yeah, someone else can drive with Jae.

Most likely that would be Will since the kids were staying at his house during the week for school. They didn't like having to get up an hour earlier to catch the van to school, and Jae wanted to try out for some sports. She's a social creature; she likes being involved. There's not much to get involved with at our house. It was hard to adjust to them not being around every day. I missed them. And I kept cooking way too much food for dinner. That took some time to get used to during the week.

So I did what everyone else would have done. I got a puppy! He came to live with us at the perfect time because right after I got him, Shana stole Rocky. She always said she wanted to, and she finally did. Rocky followed in Dinky's footsteps and started getting out when I had to go to town. He must have gotten into it with a herd of javelina just like Dinky did. He came home, and his front leg was shredded. So was his jaw. His injuries were severe enough for him to go live with Shana in heaven. If he couldn't be with us, I can't think of a better person for him to spend his days with.

Shortly before Rocky moved to heaven, Joe's sister, Sohnja, called us and told us that a friend of hers had gone out to the desert to do some target shooting and found a bag with two puppies in it. They had been thrown out like trash. She sent a picture of the puppies and asked if we wanted one. Yes! I picked the brown boy with the ice-blue eyes. I named him Odie. Of course that's not what I call him most of the time. He's usually referred to as Pookey Bear or Hoagie Roll. In the picture, he looked like some kind of German Shepherd mix but in real life, he's a pit mix, and he didn't have a very good start in life. He was afraid of everything, especially things that you hold in your hand. Not your hand itself, but things like a hairbrush, a swiffer duster, the broom terrifies him. I'm pretty sure he was hit with things. And I could pet him, but I could not hug him. If I tried, he would get all snarly and run to hide under the bed. I learned to show him things I held in my hand and let him sniff and get comfortable before I used it. He was young enough to turn around and learn to trust. It took some time, but he has turned into a pretty good dog. He's still a special needs dog, but Bow is his right-hand man. When something scares him, he'll run to me and look to Bow. If we're okay, he's okay. He's great with people, a little sketchy with other dogs, and he loves his Auntie Sohnja. Seeing a dog smile is heartwarming.

As for Joe, he had to get his yearly physical for work, and the doctor told him he was "of the age" to get a colonoscopy. I was so excited I could barely contain my evil joy. I can't wait for him to have his legs up in the air and have to scooch down further on the table. I tried to give him some of the rules he was going to have to follow beforehand. Poop as early as possible, shave his nads, wash with soap and water as close to his appointment as possible, the sex rule doesn't apply, and I'm not sure about having Imodium AD and Xanax on board. I know it's cruel, but I hope he farts in the doctor's face. At the time, I didn't know all the ins and outs of the colonoscopy procedure. I'm not going to lie; I was a little disappointed when I found out he would be put under. After reading all the paperwork, I realized what was involved. The prep sucks. And the power poop juice he had to drink really does its job! I tried to be supportive during his prep and not eat, but as soon as he went to the back for the procedure, I went to Subway. When everything was over and they brought Joe back to the recovery room, I was allowed to go back. He was so out of it that he was laughing really loud and showing everyone his wenis! It was hilarious! Then the doctor came in with the reports and pictures. I kept the pictures, so when I call him an asshole, I have pictures to prove it.

Unfortunately, not long after Joe's poop shoot party, I got to be "of the age" and needed to have a colonoscopy too. Getting older sucks. Fortunately for Joe, he didn't have a single snarky remark. I think he still knows I am totally capable of putting Nair in his shampoo. Unlike Joe, I asked for extra drugs and did not run around after showing off my vag.

By now, JP is driving and has turned into a pretty good kid, so we can actually go to real parties and BBQs without having to leave early to get home to all the animals. We can have him either stay at the house or be our designated driver, whatever the situation needs.

Which is actually kind of funny because after a few adult beverages, I don't mind his driving. We met some new people at one of the youth camps we went to and ended up spending a lot of time with them. He had two kids; the wife had one, all girls and all hunters. I really like the wife. She's my kind of people. Same sense of humor. No real filter so we can talk about anything. I'm not super fond of the husband, but it's a package deal. What else I really like about them is that they didn't know Shana, so our conversations never turn toward her. She knows what happened, but we don't do the "remember when" stuff. The wife's name is Tamara, but I call her, T and I call her daughter Mickey even though that's not her name. Joe took them out for Mickey and T to get their first deer. They were both so excited and proud. That makes me happy.

On a side note, T and her husband got a divorce, oh darn. T wanted to get out of the city, and I can't blame her. She got a job and a little house in the mining town, which is great because we can get together often and BBQ or just hang out and shoot the shit about life. I don't know if other people do this, but I told Joe if I die, I would approve of her to be a new wife. I'm sure she will be taken by then, but just in case he needed to know that I would not haunt and torture him for that choice. No guarantees on someone else. T is also one of those kinds of people you can depend on in a pinch, which we had to take advantage of. Another trip to Florida to see the grandparents. We hired a new gal to stay at the house, but after two days, she bailed. Granted, she had a legitimate emergency, but I couldn't leave the dogs and animals outside and alone for a week! T drove back and forth from the mining town to care for the animals while she was working twelve-hour shifts. We owe her big.

We got another cow to raise for freezer camp, but Joe wouldn't let me bring this one to our house. This one was a baby baby. It had to be bottle fed for a while first, and Joe was afraid that if I got to bottle feed a cow, it would never make it to freezer camp. He's right. Joe's daughter, Jenny, and her husband got one too, so Joe made a deal with them to keep ours and raise it with theirs. I was allowed to visit only. I named her Phylis because she was going to fill us a freezer. I hate saying Joe was right, but he was. She was way too cute. She would never have made it to camp if she was at my house. I do not need a pet cow. She did eventually make it to freezer camp, and we did get a freezer full of organic, healthy beef because I only went to visit her a few times, and she wouldn't let me pet her.

It's weird how things just fall into place sometimes without even knowing the why of it all until you can look back. Besides our trips to Florida to see my folks, Joe and I did not live extravagantly. When we bought our house, we took out a fifteen-year mortgage, but the goal was always to try to pay it off as soon as possible. We saved whatever we could. If I wanted a $120 pair of jeans, I would ask myself if I wanted the jeans or if I wanted the $120 to go toward the house. The house always won. We got the things we needed, and some of the things we wanted if we could find them on sale or used. Sometimes we traded for things on the barter system. Joe would find things cheap, buy them, and resell them for a profit. Every dollar counts.

Then I decided our feed bill was too high, so I got rid of everything that didn't have a purpose. Except the dogs of course. They are useless, but I love them too much. I gave away the goats, the ducks, and the turkeys, but I kept the chicken for their eggs. Sadly, a bobcat got in the hen house and not in a good way. It decimated our flock. It got all but six hens. Six hens aren't worth all the work, so I gave them to Jenny. I thought if I really missed them, I could start over again the following spring, but since the kids were busy in school and not here on a daily basis, most of the work fell to me. Taking a break was okey dokey for now. Plus, our feed bill dropped dramatically. More for the savings account.

Not long after that, Joe and I walked into the bank and paid off our mortgage. It took us a little over eight years. I can't tell you how exciting and satisfying that was. That was a very proud day for us. Our house is free and clear, baby! We took pictures and went out to lunch to celebrate our freedom from the loan.

It wasn't even a month later when Joe got sick. He came home from work one day with a rash of tiny red dots all over his back and sides. We thought it was really dry skin, and I slathered him up with a natural coconut oil-based moisturizing lotion. It didn't help, and the rash got worse over the next few days. The red bumps were spreading and getting larger. We thought that maybe he was having an allergic reaction to the coconut oil, so we switched to slathering him up with calamine lotion. That didn't help either, and the red bumps were turning into little blisters, still spreading and now burning.

On our first trip to the ER, they looked at him, didn't do a skin scrape or any other testing, and told him he had scabies. When I asked what that was, the nurse told me I needed to google it and that I was going to need medication as well. I did google it. Scabies are a skin mite that you can only get from prolonged skin to skin contact. I was pissed for a minute until I realized Joe didn't have time for any secret kind of "prolonged skin to skin contact." I always know where he is, and I know he wouldn't do that. Plus, we've had some "prolonged skin to skin contact," and I don't have any blisters on my body. He used the medicated shampoo anyway; he needed any kind of relief he could get. I didn't.

Another week went by. More blisters everywhere; now some were the size of a dime. He couldn't wear regular clothes anymore because they rubbed on his skin, which meant he couldn't go to work. Back to the R. This time, we were quarantined for possible measles. Even I knew it's not measles. I'd been sleeping next to him the whole time, and I was not sick. No skin scrape, no biopsy, no tests of any kind. Just a shrug of the shoulders, a shot of steroids, and a "See ya later." They said we should go to a dermatologist. Ahhh…thanks?

It took a couple of days to get into the dermatologist; Joe's skin issues had been going on for more than a month. The blisters were covering his entire body except his face, bottoms of his feet, and his palms. The rest of his body had blisters in different stages. Some the size of quarters, some dimes, some tiny ones starting to grow, and some that had popped, leaving open wounds. Dr. K came into the room, and within minutes, she said she was pretty sure she knew what was going on but wanted to take a biopsy and skin scrape to be sure. Finally! We had been dismissed and sent home without help for far too long. Joe was suffering and there was nothing I could do. It's a helpless feeling. She sent us home with some medicines and creams to get started with while we waited for the results to come in.

Dr. K was right. Joe had an extremely rare autoimmune disease called bullous pemphigoid. Basically, he had developed an allergy to his own skin. It will never go away, but it can get under control. How? How does someone wake up one day allergic to their own skin? No one knows why. She already had Joe on the right medications; we just needed to find the right dose. The problem was that we were already over a month behind the blisters, and we needed to catch up and surpass the race.

That weekend, we ended up back in the ER. Some of Joe's blisters were the size of half dollars; they were forming in his mouth and his toes were turning black. But this time, we had a diagnosis, so surely, they would help us. The doctor came in for about three minutes, looked at Joe, and said that he needed to be admitted. Thank God. I was scared to death that his blisters would grow in his mouth and block his airway and we live an hour from any ER. And he was suffering. That's when the doctor told us that he wasn't getting admitted there. He said they couldn't care for him there. What? The doctor wanted to transfer him to a burn center in Phoenix. What? I wasn't prepared for that. I didn't have our medications, mine included, and my dogs were outside. Sohnja's husband, Rodger, came to sit with us in the ER. I was so happy he was there. He asked the questions I was too tired to even think about. The burn center didn't want him. It took another three hours to find a hospital that had room and a doctor to care for him. And another hour to get the transport ambulance to pick him up to get him there. Thankfully, Rodger waited for the transport and followed it to Phoenix and waited for him to get settled in his room. I went home. Worry and stress is exhausting.

He spent five days in the hospital. That drive all the way to Phoenix sucks. I don't understand why everyone is in such a hurry on the highway. I went a little above the speed limit, and people were passing me, flipping me off. Why don't they leave five minutes earlier so they don't have to be assholes on the road? Anyway, the doctors loaded Joe up with huge amounts of steroids and some anti-rejection medications. But after five days, they had slowed the growth of new blisters. Well, most of the blisters, but it's a huge start. On the downside, the huge doses of steroids had left Joe extremely bloated, hungry all the time, and now had to take an insulin shot three times a day.

Remember how I said it's weird when things fall into place without knowing why and I got rid of all our animals? I figured out why when Joe got home from the hospital. I was going to be way too busy taking care of him to be taking care of them.

Joe could no longer dress himself. The hardest thing about dressing someone is putting on their socks. And Joe wears the old-fashioned tube socks. At least they're all white, no 1970s red stripes. He also couldn't dry himself off after a shower because he couldn't rub at his skin, I had to pat him dry. I also had to strip and wash the sheets every day because his blisters would pop as he slept. Then there were all the medications, checking his blood sugar, and giving him his insulin shots. The worst was having to rub him down from head to toe with the medicated cream.

I started calling him Drippy Rippey to lighten things up and mainly because I'm a smart ass. Trust me, things needed to be lightened up because the huge doses of steroids turned him into a dick. He'd snap at me for everything, and I was not used to being talked to like that from him. And he was hungry all the time. And not hungry for healthy food, always for crap food. He also couldn't drive anymore, so I was stuck with a backseat driver sitting next to me every time we had to go to a doctor's appointment. We were on our way to see Dr. K. I figured he would want a snack even though he just ate breakfast, so I made a left to head to Burger King. We always get their chicken nuggets as a snack because they're good and cheap. Joe snapped at me and asked where I was going. Burger King, where we always go. He freaked out and started screaming at me, "God dammit, Mel! God dammit! I want a fucking McGriddle!" First of all, he never talks to me like that. Second, how was I supposed to know that? And third, he was acting like an eight-year-old brat! I swear, if we weren't in the truck, he would have been jumping up and down, stomping his feet. What is going on? Then he was all apologetic, saying how sorry he was for talking like that, but he just wanted his McGriddle. I was torn; on one hand, I knew it was the medication making him act like that. On the other hand, I thought I was going to have to kill him. On another trip to a different doctor, I stopped to get him a snack of about twenty mini tacos. He was shoving them in his pie hole like his very life depends on them. It's annoying. The car in front of me jammed on its brakes, making me have to jam on mine. Joe's bag of mini tacos went flying off his lap and landed on the floor by his feet. Que the tantrum. He was seatbelted in, swollen from the medication, hangry, and desperately trying to reach for his tacos. He's reaching with his right arm, his left arm, back and forth over and over unsuccessfully. Screaming for his tacos, screaming at me for jamming on the brakes, grunting with each attempt to reach the bag. It's not just food that makes him cranky, it's everything. He chipped a tooth and, it left a sharp edge that he kept messing with his tongue, so his tongue was getting sore. It was a weekend and the dentist wasn't open, so I asked if he wanted a nail file to try to sand it down a bit to not be so sharp. He snapped at me and asked if I have one that I hadn't shoved up my ass. I'm like, *What?* I told him, "That's a very good question. Let me think about that. I mean, it's standard operating procedure for girls. It's in the handbook. SOP #51: When purchasing nail files—immediately go home and shove them up your ass!"

Joe starts screaming that that wasn't what he meant and I should have known that. Screw the medication; I was going to kill him. Simple as that. I called Sohnja and told her if I called her and told her to come out here and bring a shovel, don't ask any questions, just come. She said she had my back, and I trusted her.

I have decided that I am not a good long-term care provider. I'll do all the things he needs me to do for him, but I'll make him try first. I didn't want him to get stuck in a Catch 22 kind of thing. He didn't feel good, so he wasn't doing anything, but because he wasn't doing anything, he didn't feel good. It was a vicious circle of misery that only he could break by trying to do something. Things were getting better. We realized his toes were turning black because they were covered in blisters that he walked on, popped, and then they reformed on top of that. The same thing was happening with his hands. All those blisters finally popped and didn't reform but left him with dry, flaky skin. I started calling him Crusty Rusty at that point. Dr. K was a godsend; she had no problem cutting away at the dead flappy skin. It grossed me out. We kept trying to drop his steroid dose, but then he would have another breakout and it would start all over.

After about four months of Joe not being able to work and being home with me all day, cranky, I started to get stressed out. Money was getting tight, the medical bills kept coming, and even the sound of him chomping on potato chips was getting on my nerves. My hair started to fall out. I started taking mental health days and going to town by myself here and there just for a break. It helped, but I missed my happy-go-lucky husband. Every time he got to drop the dose of the steroids, his attitude improved a tiny bit. Each improvement kept more hair on my head and less dirt covering his cold, dead body. Unfortunately, it didn't help the cat. We had a feral barn cat on the property to help keep the mouse population at bay. I called him Tom because he was a tomcat, not fixed, not nice, and definitely not allowed in the house. I put food out by the barn for him and made him a fort to sleep in when it was cold or wet, but he mostly stuck to himself. Sometimes I wouldn't see him for a week or so, and I would think he got eaten by a bobcat or coyote, but then he would show back up. For some reason, he started spraying everywhere. He would come up on the porch at night and spray on the arcadia door, he sprayed on the air conditioner unit, which made the whole house smell awful. Paul came up for a visit, and Tom got in his car and sprayed; he even climbed a tree and sprayed on a friend who walked underneath the tree. Got him right on the head. I made an appointment to get him fixed, but that was one of those times he disappeared for a week, so I missed the appointment. Again, I thought he was dead. In the meantime, Joe ordered some new tractor tires and had them leaning up against the barn until they could get put on. Tom came home and sprayed on Joe's tires. I was in the house doing dishes when Joe came shuffling in bitching about how the cat pissed all over his new tires. Sorry? Joe. Was. Mad. Let's just say, Joe sent Tom to go live at the zoo. I was mad! It just so happened that one of T's friends' cat had a litter of kittens. I got two, and these guys were allowed in the house. It amazes me how two tiny kittens running through the house at 2:00 a.m. can sound like a herd of stampeding elephants. This pissed Joe off. Too bad, so sad—that's what you got for sending Tom to the zoo. He also got to pay for them to get fixed so they could stay in the house whenever they wanted. What's really funny is watching my big, badass pit bull run from the kittens in sheer terror. In his defense, one of them launched themselves off the couch and stuck himself onto Odie's ass. Poor Odie was spinning in circles, yelping and trying to get it to let go. I came to the rescue.

Then I made a crucial mistake. I trusted Joe. I went outside to have a ciggy on the porch and thought I felt something on my back. When I came in, I stood in front of Joe, who was watching TV, and asked him if there was something on my back. He leaned around me so he could still see the tv, brushed my back a couple of times and declared, "Nope, nothing there." Okey dokey. I had to use the restroom. I was sitting on the toilet, peacefully playing Candy Crush, and going poop when something ran down the crack of my ass. I screamed and jumped up at the exact moment my purpose was being completed. It was a fucking lizard. A four-inch lizard *was* on my back and was now running around on the bathroom floor. Joe comes running in to see if I was ok. Ahhh...*no*! I was asking him how he could have possibly missed a 4-inch lizard on my back when he saw the poop on the toilet seat. He started gagging because men can't handle poop; it's in their DNA. And now I was really pissed. My pants are down around my ankles, there's poop on the toilet seat, I can't sit down to wipe, there's a lizard freaking out, running around my feet that now has a piece of toilet paper stuck to its foot. *And you think you're going to puke?* I yelled at him that if he pukes, he's cleaning up the puke and the poop. I never saw him turn on his heels and run so fast. Fan. Fucking, Tastic. Now what? This was a new level of ECS. I needed a second to access the order of what tasks need to come first. I went selfish; I took care of myself first, lizard second. I left the toilet paper stuck to his foot when I caught it and put it outside, toilet seat last.

LIFE LESSON #5018

Men are stupid. Enough said.

Even though I made that bold statement, I have had my moments too. Joe and I were coming home one evening, I was driving which is getting more and more difficult for me at night because I can't see as well anymore. Especially at dusk. We live in an open range area, so sometimes there are cows on the road. At night, it's hard for me to tell if it's a bush or a cow. My go-go-gadget night vision has gone to shit. Joe was snoozing in the passenger seat when I saw something walking along the side of the road. It was a puppy! Poor thing. There's no traffic, so I stopped the truck on the road, opened the door, and started calling the puppy. It was all black, super fluffy, and very apprehensive. But it started slowly waddling to my calls. "Here puppy, puppy!" Joe woke up. "Here puppy, puppy!" What the? Joe started yelling at me to stop. Why? I tell him it's a puppy. In my head, I was thinking he needed to shut up. He was going to scare it; it was almost to the truck! Shut up!

Joe screamed, "Mel! That's a skunk!"

"No, it isn't, it's a puppy." He demanded I shut the door right before it got to the truck, and I was thinking he was being a total ass. Huh, I smell burnt tires, that's not right. Well…shit. That was a skunk! Good thing he woke up. In my defense, a friend of ours found a puppy on the side of the road a few days prior. Guess it was still on my mind. Oopsy, poopsy!

Since the kids were adopted and getting older, I thought it would be cool for all of us to do the DNA testing. I ordered four kits; of course, five showed up. We gave the extra to Joey just for fun.

We all sat around the table and spit in our tubes as a team. Apparently, I don't hold a lot of spit in my mouth at any given moment. I felt like it took me forever to fill my tube. We packed them up and sent them off that day. I was teasing Joe that our Christmas table was getting ready to get a lot bigger from his teenage slut days. Kids were going to be coming out of the woodwork!

Joe's came in first. He had six different regions in his pie chart. Mostly Eastern Europe, Russia, England, and Wales. Pretty much what he was expecting, and so far, no extra kids. My fingers were still crossed that that remains the same. I would accept any kid he had; I just didn't want another college tuition bill.

JP's came in next. Strangely, his was a lot like Joe's. He had six regions in his pie chart too. Mostly from England, Wales, and Northwestern Europe. The smaller stuff matched too. They could be related.

Jae's was next in. Hers was completely unexpected and amazing. She had twelve regions in her pie chart. We found out she's only 6 percent Spanish. She's 40 percent Native American. She even has 3 percent Congo and the Bantu peoples. How cool is that? Right after her pie chart came in, we were at Walmart, and I was checking out. I had all kinds of stuff to make some good old Mexican food, which is Joe's favorite, and Jae asked me if I thought that if I ate enough Mexican food, did I think I'd turn brown like her? I said no; we just liked it. The poor cashier was staring at us in shock. Then Jae said really loud, "Oh...white people!" We started cracking up; the cashier was mortified. What am I going to do? She's a smartass just like her mama. That white people line was her thing for a while though. Meanwhile, my chart hadn't come in yet, and I could not wait to see it.

When my chart finally came in, I was super disappointed. Two things. I only had two things on my pie chart. I am white and whiter. Nothing cool or interesting. Nothing with any color whatsoever. I couldn't even have 2 percent Congo? Something? I am officially Chalk-casian. How boring.

I don't feel boring. I feel pretty good actually. I'm creative and entertain myself by repurposing furniture and building new stuff. I've made a one of a kind dining room table for us; I've made a kitchen island and side tables. I've painted some and cooked a lot. I always have some kind of project either happening or in the plans.

Out of the blue, through the wonders of modern technology, I reconnected with Christina. It was so beautiful to be able to talk to her again. I felt that my life was coming around full circle. I'm where I'm supposed to be. We even got to get together when her family took a vacation to Arizona. We met them on the road and got to catch up and tell stories of days gone by. She's remarried now. I like her hubby; he seems to genuinely care for her, which she deserves. And her daughter was absolutely beautiful. She looked exactly the same except for curly hair. Her laugh was the same, and so was her happy heart. I've missed her. Seeing her made me think of fireflies and easier days. Of singing off key around a campfire, and nobody cared. The day ended too soon, but I know she's only a phone call away.

Then I reconnected with Cuz. Out of the blue, he got in touch with me. My side of the family has gotten smaller and smaller. He's doing good. Driving a truck. We chat on the phone every once in a while and need to do a better job at staying in touch.

The most important person I reconnected with is my dad. This is going to sound horrible, but it took my brothers passing for us to get close. I'm not sure why that is. For my dad, I get it. Losing a child makes a parent value the ones they have left that much more. I meant, I'm not sure why I didn't feel close to him. I know I've spent years of my life not feeling good enough for anyone. What a waste of time. My father is an amazing man, and I'm sorry it took me so long to figure that out.

After seven months of Joe being home with me, chomping his chips, bobbing for tacos, and literally doing a shitty job of having my back, Joe was well enough to go back to work. He's not cured, never will be, nor is he in total remission, but he can wear real clothes and attempt to get back to normal even though our normal is different. But that's okay.

Life is really just a never-ending series of adjustments. They may be physical adjustments or adjusting who we are with or what we are doing or even adjusting the things we tell ourselves. Sometimes, that's the most important adjustment of all.

Here's the thing—I titled this book before I wrote a single word because that's how I felt about myself for a very long time. Too long. I told myself I wasn't special every day because of someone else's actions that I could not control. I told myself that until I believed it.

If it works that way, why can't I make an adjustment and turn it around?

This I Know for Sure

I am special. We are all special. Each and every
one of us has been put here for a purpose.

Whether you do a simple act of kindness to a stranger or a huge act
of devotion to a loved one, we are all special for our own reasons.
Maybe you make the best chocolate chip cookies or make someone
laugh when they're having a bad day. Maybe you spend your free
time volunteering or donate your hard-earned money. You don't have
to be a hero to be special. You don't have to be loud and proud to
make a difference in someone's life. You just have to be kind and
thoughtful. You have to show compassion, acceptance, and love to
the people who come into your life. Those are the things that make
someone special. Those are the things that make me special.

My hope is that everyone realizes they are special. And they
remember those reasons every day.

About the Author

Melanie Rippey grew up in the suburbs of Philadelphia, Pennsylvania. She moved to Phoenix, Arizona, in her late twenties and resides in a tiny country town in northwestern Arizona today. She lives a quiet, happy life with her husband, two children, and her two best friends: a yellow lab named Bow and a pit bull named Odie.

9 781649 524546